Typography is what language looks like.

Dedicated to GEORGE SADEK (1928–2007) *and all my teachers.*

ELLEN LUPTON

thinking
with
type

A CRITICAL GUIDE

FOR DESIGNERS,

WRITERS, EDITORS,

& STUDENTS

SECOND, REVISED AND
EXPANDED EDITION

 PRINCETON ARCHITECTURAL PRESS · NEW YORK

Published by
Princeton Architectural Press
37 East Seventh Street
New York, New York 10003

For a free catalog of books, call 1.800.722.6657.
Visit our web site at www.papress.com.

Library of Congress Cataloging-in-Publication Data

Lupton, Ellen.
  Thinking with type : a critical guide for designers,
writers, editors, & students / Ellen Lupton. — 2nd
rev. and expanded ed.
     p. cm.
  Includes bibliographical references and index.
  ISBN 978-1-56898-969-3 (alk. paper)
  1. Graphic design (Typography) 2. Type and
type-founding. I. Title.
    Z246.L87 2010
    686.2'2—dc22

                              2010005389

BOOK DESIGNER
Ellen Lupton

EDITOR
First edition: Mark Lamster
Second edition: Nicola Bednarek

COVER DESIGNERS
Jennifer Tobias and Ellen Lupton

DIVIDER PAGES
Paintings by Ellen Lupton

PHOTOGRAPHER
Dan Meyers

PRIMARY TYPEFACES
Scala Pro, designed by Martin Majoor
Thesis, designed by Luc(as) de Groot

SPECIAL THANKS TO
Nettie Aljian, Bree Anne Apperley, Sara Bader, Janet Behning,
Becca Casbon, Carina Cha, Tom Cho, Penny (Yuen Pik) Chu,
Carolyn Deuschle, Russell Fernandez, Pete Fitzpatrick,
Wendy Fuller, Jan Haux, Linda Lee, Laurie Manfra, John Myers,
Katharine Myers, Steve Royal, Dan Simon, Andrew Stepanian,
Jennifer Thompson, Paul Wagner, Joe Weston, and Deb Wood
of Princeton Architectural Press
—Kevin C. Lippert, publisher

This project was produced with editorial support from the
Center for Design Thinking, Maryland Institute College of Art.

DESIGN BRIEFS—essential texts on design.
Also available in this series:

D.I.Y. Design It Yourself, Ellen Lupton, 978-1-56898-552-7
Elements of Design, Gail Greet Hannah, 978-1-56898-329-5
Geometry of Design, Kimberly Elam, 978-1-56898-249-6
Graphic Design Theory, Helen Armstrong, 978-1-56898-772-9
Grid Systems, Kimberly Elam, 978-1-56898-465-0
Lettering & Type, Bruce Willen, Nolen Strals, 978-1-56898-765-1
Indie Publishing, Ellen Lupton, 978-1-56898-760-6
Typographic Systems, Kimberly Elam, 978-1-56898-687-6
Visual Grammar, Christian Leborg, 978-1-56898-581-7
The Wayfinding Handbook, David Gibson, 978-1-56898-769-9

CONTENTS

HOOD'S SARSAPARILLA Advertisement, lithograph, 1884.
Reproduced at actual size. *A woman's healthy face bursts through a
sheet of text, her bright complexion proving the product's efficacy better
than any written claim. Both text and image were drawn by hand,
reproduced via color lithography.*

INTRODUCTION

Since the first edition of *Thinking with Type* appeared in 2004, this book has been widely adopted in design programs around the world. Whenever a young designer hands me a battered copy of *Thinking with Type* to sign at a lecture or event, I am warmed with joy from serif to stem. Those scuffed covers and dinged corners are evidence that typography is thriving in the hands and minds of the next generation.

I've put on some weight since 2004, and so has this book. For the new edition, I decided to let out the seams and give the content more room to breathe. If you—like most graphic designers—like to sweat the little stuff, you'll find a lot to love, honor, and worry about in the pages that follow. Finicky matters such as kerning, small capitals, non-lining numerals, punctuation, alignment, and baseline grids that were touched on briefly in the first edition are developed here in more detail, along with new topics that were previously omitted, such as how to style a drop capital, what you need to know about optical sizes, and when to say "typeface" instead of "font" at your next AIGA wine-and-carrot-stick party. This new book has more of everything: more fonts, more exercises, more examples, a more bodacious index, and best of all, more type crimes—more disgraceful "don'ts" to complement the dignified "do's."

Worried? See page 81

I was inspired to write the first edition of this book while searching for a textbook for my own type classes, which I have been teaching at Maryland Institute College of Art (MICA) since 1997. Some books on typography focus on the classical page; others are vast and encyclopedic, overflowing with facts and details. Some rely heavily on illustrations of their authors' own work, providing narrow views of a diverse practice, while others are chatty and dumbed down, presented in a condescending tone.

I sought a book that is serene and intelligible, a volume where design and text gently collaborate to enhance understanding. I sought a work that is small and compact, economical yet well constructed—a handbook designed for the hands. I sought a book that reflects the diversity of typographic life, past and present, exposing my students to history, theory, and ideas. Finally, I sought a book that would be relevant across the media of visual design, from the printed page to the glowing screen.

I found no alternative but to write the book myself.

Thinking with Type is assembled in three sections: LETTER, TEXT, and GRID, building from the basic atom of the letterform to the organization of words into coherent bodies and flexible systems. Each section opens with a narrative essay about the cultural and theoretical issues that fuel typographic design across a range of media. The demonstration pages that follow each essay show not just *how* typography is structured, but *why*, asserting the functional and cultural basis for design habits and conventions. Throughout the book, examples of design practice demonstrate the elasticity of the typographic system, whose rules can (nearly) all be broken.

The first section, LETTER, reveals how early typefaces referred to the body, emulating the work of the hand. The abstractions of neoclassicism bred the strange progeny of nineteenth-century commercial typography. In the twentieth century, avant-garde artists and designers explored the alphabet as a theoretical system. With the rise of digital design tools, typography revived its connections with the body.

The second section, TEXT, considers the massing of letters into larger bodies. Text is a field or texture whose grain, color, density, and silhouette can be endlessly adjusted. Technology has shaped the design of typographic space, from the concrete physicality of metal type to the flexibility—and constraints—offered by digital media. Text has evolved from a closed, stable body to a fluid and open ecology.

The third section, GRID, looks at spatial organization. In the early twentieth century, Dada and Futurist artists attacked the rectilinear constraints of metal type and exposed the mechanical grid of letterpress. Swiss designers in the 1940s and 1950s created design's first total methodology by rationalizing the grid. Their work, which introduced programmatic thinking to a field governed by taste and convention, remains profoundly relevant to the systematic thinking required when designing for multimedia.

This book is about thinking *with* typography—in the end, the emphasis falls on *with*. Typography is a tool for doing things *with*: shaping content, giving language a physical body, enabling the social flow of messages. Typography is an ongoing tradition that connects you *with* other designers, past and future. Type is *with* you everywhere you go—the street, the mall, the web, your apartment. This book aims to speak to, and *with*, all the readers and writers, designers and producers, teachers and students, whose work engages the ordered yet unpredictable life of the visible word.

ACKNOWLEDGMENTS

As a designer, writer, and visual thinker, I am indebted to my teachers at the Cooper Union, where I studied art and design from 1981 to 1985. Back then, the design world was neatly divided between a Swiss-inflected modernism and an idea-based approach rooted in American advertising and illustration. My teachers, including George Sadek, William Bevington, and James Craig, staked out a place between those worlds, allowing the modernist fascination with abstract systems to collide with the strange, the poetic, and the popular.

The title of this book, *Thinking with Type*, is an homage to James Craig's primer *Designing with Type*, the utilitarian classic that was our textbook at the Cooper Union. If that book was a handyman's manual to basic typography, this one is a naturalist's field guide, approaching type as a phenomenon that is more evolutionary than mechanical. What I really learned from my teachers was not rules and facts but how to think: how to use visual and verbal language to develop ideas. For me, discovering typography was like finding the bridge that connects art and language.

To write my own book for the twenty-first century, I decided to educate myself again. In 2003 I enrolled in the Doctorate in Communications Design program at the University of Baltimore and completed my degree in 2008. There I worked with Stuart Moulthrop and Nancy Kaplan, world-class scholars, critics, and designers of networked media and digital interfaces. Their influence is seen throughout this book.

My colleagues at MICA have built a distinctive design culture at the school; special thanks go to Ray Allen, Fred Lazarus, Guna Nadarajan, Brockett Horne, Jennifer Cole Phillips, and all my students.

The editor of *Thinking with Type*'s first edition, Mark Lamster, remains one of my most respected colleagues. The editor of the second edition, Nicola Bednarek, helped me balance and refine the expanded content. I thank Kevin Lippert, publisher at Princeton Architectural Press, for many, many years of support. Numerous designers and scholars helped me along the way, including Peter Bilak, Matteo Bologna, Vivian Folkenflik, Jonathan Hoefler, Eric Karnes, Elke Gasselseder, Hans Lijklema, William Noel, and Jeffrey Zeldman, as well as all the other designers who shared their work.

I learn something every day from my children, Jay and Ruby, and from my parents, my twin sister, and the amazing Miller family. My friends—Jennifer Tobias, Edward Bottone, Claudia Matzko, and Joy Hayes—sustain my life. My husband, Abbott Miller, is the greatest designer I know, and I am proud to include his work in this volume.

{LETTER}

Upper Case.

Lower Case.
A PAIR OF CASES.

California Job Case.
FIG. 2.—Showing Lay of Cases.

TYPE, SPACES, AND LEADS
Diagram, 1917. Author:
Frank S. Henry. *In a
letterpress printing shop,
gridded cases hold fonts of type
and spacing material. Capital
letters are stored in a drawer
above the minuscule letters.
Hence the terms "uppercase"
and "lowercase" are derived
from the physical space of the
print shop.*

LETTER

THIS IS NOT A BOOK ABOUT FONTS. It is a book about how to use them. Typefaces are an essential resource employed by graphic designers, just as glass, stone, steel, and other materials are employed by architects. Graphic designers sometimes create their own typefaces and custom lettering. More commonly, however, they tap the vast library of existing typefaces, choosing and combining them in response to a particular audience or situation. To do this with wit and wisdom requires knowledge of how—and why—letterforms have evolved.

Words originated as gestures of the body. The first typefaces were directly modeled on the forms of calligraphy. Typefaces, however, are not bodily gestures—they are manufactured images designed for infinite repetition. The history of typography reflects a continual tension between the hand and the machine, the organic and the geometric, the human body and the abstract system. These tensions, which marked the birth of printed letters over five hundred year ago, continue to energize typography today.

Movable type, invented by Johannes Gutenberg in Germany in the early fifteenth century, revolutionized writing in the West. Whereas scribes had previously manufactured books and documents by hand, printing with type allowed for mass production: large quantities of letters could be cast from a mold and assembled into "forms." After the pages were proofed, corrected, and printed, the letters were put away in gridded cases for reuse.

Movable type had been employed earlier in China but had proven less useful there. Whereas the Chinese writing system contains tens of thousands of distinct characters, the Latin alphabet translates the sounds of speech into a small set of marks, making it well-suited to mechanization. Gutenberg's famous Bible took the handmade manuscript as its model. Emulating the dense, dark handwriting known as "blackletter," he reproduced its erratic texture by creating variations of each letter as well as numerous ligatures (characters that combine two or more letters into a single form).

JOHANNES GUTENBERG Printed text, 1456.

This chapter extends and revises "Laws of the Letter," Ellen Lupton and J. Abbott Miller, *Design Writing Research: Writing on Graphic Design* (New York: Kiosk, 1996; London: Phaidon, 1999), 53–61.

NICOLAS JENSON *learned to print in Mainz, the German birthplace of typography, before establishing his own printing press in Venice around 1465. His letters have strong vertical stems, and the transition from thick to thin emulates the path of a broad-nibbed pen.*

ílos appellatur mariti
euir dicitur frater mar
ratriæ appellantur qua
mitini fratrum & mat
atrueles matrum fratr
ōſobrini ex duabus ed
ta ſunt in antiquis au

the iiii wekis, and how l
lord, yet the chirche mal
that is to wete, of that he
and of that he cometh t
in thoffyce of the chircl
tynges that ben in this
one partie, & that othe
cause of the comynge of
ben of joye and gladne:

GOLDEN TYPE *was created by the English design reformer William Morris in 1890. He sought to recapture the dark and solemn density of Jenson's pages.*

CENTAUR, *designed from 1912 to 1914 by Bruce Rogers, is a revival of Jenson's type that emphasizes its ribbonlike stroke.*

Lorem ipsum dolor si
consectetuer adipiscing el
Integer pharetra, nisl u
luctus ullamcorper, au
tortor egestas ante, vel
pede urna ac neque. N
ac mi eu purus tincidu

Lorem ipsum dolor si
consectetuer adipiscin
Integer pharetra, nisl
luctus ullamcorper, au
tortor *egestas* ante, vel
pharetra pede urna ac
neque. Mauris ac mi e

ADOBE JENSON *was designed in 1995 by Robert Slimbach, who reconceives historical type-faces for digital use. Adobe Jenson is less mannered and decorative than Centaur.*

RUIT *was designed in the 1990s by the Dutch typographer, teacher, and theorist Gerrit Noordzij. This digitally constructed font captures the dynamic, three-dimensional quality of fifteenth-century roman*

vanum laboraverunt
si Dominus custodie
ustra vigilavit qui cos
num est vobis ante l
gere postquam sede
i manducatis panem
m dederit dilectis sui
ALMI IVXTA LXX

Lorem ipsum dolor s
consectetuer adipisci
Integer pharetra, nis
ullamcorper, augue t
ante, vel *pharetra* pec
neque. Mauris ac mi
tincidunt faucibus. P
dignissim lectus. Nun

typefaces as well as their gothic (rather than humanist) origins. As Noordzij explains, Jenson "adapted the German letters to Italian fashion (somewhat rounder, somewhat lighter), and thus created roman type."

SCALA *was introduced in 1991 by the Dutch typographer Martin Majoor. Although this thoroughly contemporary typeface has geometric serifs and rational, almost modular forms, it reflects the calligraphic origins of type, as seen in letters such as a.*

HUMANISM AND THE BODY

In fifteenth-century Italy, humanist writers and scholars rejected gothic scripts in favor of the *lettera antica*, a classical mode of handwriting with wider, more open forms. The preference for *lettera antica* was part of the Renaissance (rebirth) of classical art and literature. Nicolas Jenson, a Frenchman who had learned to print in Germany, established an influential printing firm in Venice around 1469. His typefaces merged the gothic traditions he had known in France and Germany with the Italian taste for rounder, lighter forms. They are considered among the first—and finest—roman typefaces.

Many typefaces we use today, including Garamond, Bembo, Palatino, and Jenson, are named for printers who worked in the fifteenth and sixteenth centuries. These typefaces are generally known as "humanist." Contemporary revivals of historical typefaces are designed to conform with modern technologies and current demands for sharpness and uniformity. Each revival responds to—or reacts against—the production methods, printing styles, and artistic habits of its own time. Some revivals are based on metal types, punches (steel prototypes), or drawings that still exist; most rely solely on printed specimens.

Italic letters, also introduced in fifteenth-century Italy, were modeled on a more casual style of handwriting. While the upright humanist scripts appeared in expensively produced books, the cursive form thrived in the cheaper writing shops, where it could be written more rapidly than the carefully formed *lettera antica*. Aldus Manutius, a Venetian printer, publisher, and scholar, used italic typefaces in his internationally distributed series of small, inexpensive printed books. For calligraphers, the italic form was economical because it saved time, while in printing, the cursive form saved space. Aldus Manutius often paired cursive letters with roman capitals; the two styles still were considered fundamentally distinct.

In the sixteenth century, printers began integrating roman and italic forms into type families with matching weights and x-heights (the height of the main body of the lowercase letter). Today, the italic style in most fonts is not simply a slanted version of the roman; it incorporates the curves, angles, and narrower proportions associated with cursive forms.

FRANCESCO GRIFFO designed roman and italic types for Aldus Manutius. The roman and italic were conceived as separate typefaces.

S ed ne forte tuo care a
Hic timor eft ipfis
N on adeo leuiter noft
Vt meus oblito pulu
I llic phylacides iucui
Non potuit cæcis im
S ed cupidus falfis atti
Theffalis antiquam
I llic quicquid ero fer
Traicit & fati litto
I llic formofæ ueniau
Quas dedit argui
Quarum nulla tua fu
Gratior, & tellus h
Quamuis te longæ rei
Cara tamen lachry

JEAN JANNON created roman and italic types for the Imprimerie Royale, Paris, 1642, that are coordinated into a larger type family.

comme i'ay des-ia remarqué, ª S. Augu-
ftin demande aux Donatiftes en vne fem-
blable occurrence : *Quoy donc ? lors que*
nous lifons , oublions nous comment nous auons
accouftumé de parler? l'efcriture du grand Dieu

ª *Aug. lib.33. contra Fauft.c. 7.* Quid er- go? cum legi- mus , obliui- fcimur quem- admodum lo- qui foleamus? An fcriptura Dei aliter no-

On the complex origins of roman type, see Gerrit Noordzij, *Letterletter* (Vancouver: Hartley and Marks, 2000).

GEOFROY TORY *argued that letters should reflect the ideal human body. Regarding the letter A, he wrote: "the cross-stroke covers the man's organ of generation, to signify that Modesty and Chastity are required, before all else, in those who seek acquaintance with well-shaped letters."*

LOUIS SIMONNEAU *designed model letterforms for the printing press of Louis XIV. Instructed by a royal committee, Simonneau designed his letters on a finely meshed grid. A royal typeface (romain du roi) was then created by Philippe Grandjean, based on Simonneau's engravings.*

WILLIAM CASLON *produced typefaces in eighteenth-century England with crisp, upright characters that appear, as Robert Bringhurst has written, "more modelled and less written than Renaissance forms."*

By WILLIAM CASLON, Letter-Founder, in Chifwell

ABCD
ABCDE
ABCDEFG

DOUBLE PICA ROMAN.
Quoufque tandem abutere, Catilina, patientia noftra? quamdiu nos etiam furor ifte tuus eludet? quem ad finem fefe effrenata jac-
ABCDEFGHJIKLMNOP

GREAT PRIMER ROMAN.
Quoufque tandem abutere, Catilina, pa-

Double Pica Italick.
Quoufque tandem abutere, Catilina, patientia noftra? quamdi na, patientia noftra? quamdi nos etiam furor ifte tuus eludet quem ad finem fefe effrenata jac
ABCDEFGHJIKLMNO

Great Primer Italick.
Quoufque tandem abutére, Catilina, pa-

SPECIMEN

By *JOHN BASKERVILLE of Birmingham.*

I·Am indebted to you for two Letters dated from Corcyra.

if to mean well to the Interest of my Country and to approve that meaning

JOHN BASKERVILLE *was a printer working in England in the 1750s and 1760s. He aimed to surpass Caslon by creating sharply detailed letters with more vivid contrast between thick and thin elements. Whereas Caslon's letters were widely used during his own time, Baskerville's work was denounced by many of his contemporaries as amateur and extremist.*

GIAMBATTISTA BODONI *created letters at the close of the eighteenth century that exhibit abrupt, unmodulated contrast between thick and thin elements, and razor-thin serifs unsupported by curved brackets. Similar typefaces were designed in the same period by François-Ambroise Didot (1784) in France and Justus Erich Walbaum (1800) in Germany.*

AUSTERLITI.

RELATAM A GALL

DUCE

ENLIGHTENMENT AND ABSTRACTION

Aabcdef

A B C D

aabbccddee,

A B C D

N O P Q

Renaissance artists sought standards of proportion in the idealized human body. The French designer and typographer Geofroy Tory published a series of diagrams in 1529 that linked the anatomy of letters to the anatomy of man. A new approach—distanced from the body—would unfold in the age of scientific and philosophical Enlightenment.

A committee appointed by Louis XIV in France in 1693 set out to construct roman letters against a finely meshed grid. Whereas Tory's diagrams were produced as woodcuts, the gridded depictions of the *romain du roi* (king's alphabet) were engraved, made by incising a copper plate with a tool called a graver. The lead typefaces derived from these large-scale diagrams reflect the linear character of engraving as well as the scientific attitude of the king's committee.

Engraved letters—whose fluid lines are unconstrained by the letterpress's mechanical grid—offered an apt medium for formal lettering. Engraved reproductions of penmanship disseminated the work of the great eighteenth-century writing masters. Books such as George Bickham's *The Universal Penman* (1743) featured roman letters—each engraved as a unique character—as well as lavishly curved scripts.

Eighteenth-century typography was influenced by new styles of handwriting and their engraved reproductions. Printers such as William Caslon in the 1720s and John Baskerville in the 1750s abandoned the rigid nib of humanism for the flexible steel pen and the pointed quill, writing instruments that rendered a fluid, swelling path. Baskerville, himself a master calligrapher, would have admired the thinly sculpted lines that appeared in the engraved writing books. He created typefaces of such sharpness and contrast that contemporaries accused him of "blinding all the Readers in the Nation; for the strokes of your letters, being too thin and narrow, hurt the Eye." To heighten the startling precision of his pages, Baskerville made his own inks and hot-pressed his pages after printing.

At the turn of the nineteenth century, Giambattista Bodoni in Italy and Firmin Didot in France carried Baskerville's severe vocabulary to new extremes. Their typefaces—which have a wholly vertical axis, sharp contrast between thick and thin, and crisp, waferlike serifs—were the gateway to an explosive vision of typography unhinged from calligraphy.

This accusation was reported to Baskerville in a letter from his admirer Benjamin Franklin. For the full letter, see F. E. Pardoe, *John Baskerville of Birmingham: Letter-Founder and Printer* (London: Frederick Muller Limited, 1975), 68. See also Robert Bringhurst, *The Elements of Typographic Style* (Vancouver: Hartley and Marks, 1992, 1997).

The *romain du roi* was designed not by a typographer but by a government committee consisting of two priests, an accountant, and an engineer. —ROBERT BRINGHURST, 1992

P. VIRGILII MARONIS

BUCOLICA

ECLOGA I. cui nomen *TITYRUS*.

MELIBOEUS, TITYRUS.

Tityre, tu patulæ recubans fub tegmine fagi
Silveſtrem tenui Muſam meditaris avena:
Nos patriæ fines, et dulcia linquimus arva;
Nos patriam fugimus: tu, Tityre, lentus in umbra
5 Formoſam reſonare doces Amaryllida ſilvas.
T. O Melibœe, Deus nobis hæc otia fecit:
Namque erit ille mihi ſemper Deus: illius aram
Sæpe tener noſtris ab ovilibus imbuet agnus.
Ille meas errare boves, ut cernis, et ipſum
10 Ludere, quæ vellem, calamo permiſit agreſti.
M. Non equidem invideo; miror magis: undique totis
Uſque adeo turbatur agris. en ipſe capellas
Protenus æger ago: hanc etiam vix, Tityre, duco:
Hic inter denſas corylos modo namque gemellos,
15 Spem gregis, ah! filice in nuda connixa reliquit.
Sæpe malum hoc nobis, ſi mens non læva fuiſſet,
De cœlo taĉtas memini prædicere quercus:
Sæpe ſiniſtra cava prædixit ab ilice cornix.
Sed tamen, iſte Deus qui fit, da, Tityre, nobis.
20 *T.* Urbem, quam dicunt Romam, Melibœe, putavi
Stultus ego huic noſtræ ſimilem, quo ſæpe ſolemus
Paſtores ovium teneros depellere fœtus.
Sic canibus catulos ſimiles, ſic matribus hœdos
A   Noram;

VIRGIL (LEFT) Book page, 1757. Printed by John Baskerville. *The typefaces created by Baskerville in the eighteenth century were remarkable—even shocking— in their day for their sharp, upright forms and stark contrast between thick and thin elements. In addition to a roman text face, this page utilizes italic capitals, large-scale capitals (generously letterspaced), small capitals (scaled to coordinate with lowercase text), and non-lining or old-style numerals (designed with ascenders, descenders, and a small body height to work with lowercase characters).*

RACINE (RIGHT) Book page, 1801. Printed by Firmin Didot. *The typefaces cut by the Didot family in France were even more abstract and severe than those of Baskerville, with slablike, unbracketed serifs and a stark contrast from thick to thin. Nineteenth-century printers and typographers called these glittering typefaces "modern."*

Both pages reproduced from William Dana Orcutt, In Quest of the Perfect Book *(New York: Little, Brown and Company, 1926); margins are not accurate.*

LA THÉBAÏDE,

OU

LES FRERES ENNEMIS,

TRAGÉDIE.

~~~~~~~~~~~~~~~~~~~~~~~~~~~~~~

ACTE PREMIER.

———

SCENE I.

JOCASTE, OLYMPE.

JOCASTE.

Ils sont sortis, Olympe? Ah! mortelles douleurs!
Qu'un moment de repos me va coûter de pleurs!
Mes yeux depuis six mois étoient ouverts aux larmes,
Et le sommeil les ferme en de telles alarmes!
Puisse plutôt la mort les fermer pour jamaïs,
Et m'empêcher de voir le plus noir des forfaits!
Mais en sont-ils aux mains?

440 *Plan for the Improvement of the Art of Paper War.*

whilst a passionate man, engaged in a warm controversy, would thunder vengeance in

French Canon

It follows of course, that writers of great irascibility should be charged higher for a work of the same length, than meek authors; on account of the extraordinary space their performances must necessarily occupy; for these gigantic, wrathful types, like ranters on the stage, must have sufficient elbow-room.

For example: Suppose a newspaper quarrel to happen between * M and L.   M begins the attack pretty smartly in

Long Primer.

L replies in

Pica Roman.

M advances to

Great Primer.

L retorts in

Double Pica.

And so the contest swells to

Rascal, Villain

* Lest some ill-disposed person should misapply these initials, I think proper to declare, that M signifies Merchant, and L Lawyer.

Coward.

Cow-
ard,

In five line Pica ; which, indeed, is as far as the art of printing, or a modern quarrel can well go.

A philofophical reafon might be given to prove that large
types will more forcibly affect the optic nerve than thofe of a
fmaller fize, and are therefore naturally expreffive of energy
and vigour. But I leave this difcuffion for the amufement of
the gentlemen lately elected into our philofophical fociety.
It is fufficient for me, if my fyftem fhould be found to be juf-
tified by experience and fact, to which I appeal.

I recollect a cafe in point. Some few years before the war,
the people of a weftern county, known by the name of Paxton
Boys, affembled, on account of fome difcontent, in great
numbers, and came down with hoftile intentions againft the
peace of government, and with a particular view to fome leading men in the city. Sir John St. Clair, who affumed military
command for defence of the city, met one of the obnoxious
perfons in the ftreet, and told him that he had feen the manifefto of the infurgents, and that his name was particularifed
in letters as long as his fingers. The gentleman immediately
packed up his moft valuable effects, and fent them with his
family into Jerfey for fecurity. Had fir John only faid that he
had feen his name in the manifefto, it is probable that he would
not have been fo ferioufly alarmed : but the unufual fize of
the letters was to him a plain indication, that the infurgents
were determined to carry their revenge to a proportionable
extremity.

I could confirm my fyftem by innumerable inftances in
fact and practice. The title-page of every book is a proof in
point. It announces the fubject treated of, in confpicuous
characters ; as if the author ftood at the door of his edifice,

H   calling

5

PLAN FOR THE IMPROVEMENT OF
THE ART OF PAPER WAR Satirical
essay by Francis Hopkinson, *The
American Museum*, Volume 1 (1787).
Courtesy of the Boston Public
Library. *This eighteenth-century essay
is an early example of expressive
typography. The author, poking fun at
the emerging news media, suggests a
"paper war" between a lawyer and a
merchant. As the two men toss attacks
at each other, the type gets progressively
bigger. The terms Long Primer, Pica
Roman, Great Primer, Double Pica,
and Five Line Pica were used at the
time to identify type sizes. The ſ symbol
is an s. Hopkinson was no stranger to
design. He created the stars and stripes
motif of the American flag.*

1825;

At 10 o'Clock in the Morning:

A QUANTITY OF OL

ORDAG

Sails &c

ing the rema
ek of the Sch

[J. Soulb

FAT FACE *is the name given to the inflated, hyperbold type style introduced in the early nineteenth century. These faces exaggerated the polarization of letters into thick and thin components seen in the typographic forms of Bodoni and Didot.*

EXTRA CONDENSED *typefaces are designed to fit in narrow spaces. Nineteenth-century advertisements often combined fonts of varying style and proportion on a single page. These bombastic mixtures were typically aligned, however, in static, centered compositions.*

EGYPTIAN, *or slab, typefaces transformed the serif from a refined detail to a load-bearing slab. As an independent architectural component, the slab serif asserts its own weight and mass. Introduced in 1806, this style was quickly denounced by purists as "a typographical monstrosity."*

GOTHIC *is the nineteenth-century term for letters with no serifs. Gothic letters command attention with their massive frontality. Although sans-serif letters were later associated with rationality and neutrality, they lent emotional impact to early advertising.*

My person was hideous, my stature gigantic. What did this mean? Who was I? What was I?...
Accursed creator! Why did you create a monster so hideous that even you turned away from
me in disgust? —MARY SHELLEY, *Frankenstein,* **1831**

MONSTER FONTS

Although Bodoni and Didot fueled their designs with the calligraphic practices of their time, they created forms that collided with typographic tradition and unleashed a strange new world, where the structural attributes of the letter—serif and stem, thick and thin strokes, vertical and horizontal stress—would be subject to bizarre experiments. In search of a beauty both rational and sublime, Bodoni and Didot had created a monster: an abstract and dehumanized approach to the design of letters.

With the rise of industrialization and mass consumption in the nineteenth century came the explosion of advertising, a new form of communication demanding new kinds of typography. Type designers created big, bold faces by embellishing and engorging the body parts of classical letters. Fonts of astonishing height, width, and depth appeared—expanded, contracted, shadowed, inlined, fattened, faceted, and floriated. Serifs abandoned their role as finishing details to become independent architectural structures, and the vertical stress of traditional letters canted in new directions.

| ANTIQUE | CLARENDON | LATIN/ANTIQUE TUSCAN | TUSCAN |

Type historian Rob Roy Kelly studied the mechanized design strategies that served to generate a spectacular variety of display letters in the nineteenth century. This diagram shows how the basic square serif form—called Egyptian or slab—was cut, pinched, pulled, and curled to spawn new species of ornament. Serifs were transformed from calligraphic end-strokes into independent geometric elements that could be freely adjusted.

Lead, the material for casting metal type, is too soft to hold its shape at large sizes under the pressure of the printing press. In contrast, type cut from wood can be printed at gigantic scales. The introduction of the combined pantograph and router in 1834 revolutionized wood-type manufacture. The pantograph is a tracing device that, when linked to a router for carving, allows a parent drawing to spawn variants with different proportions, weights, and decorative excrescences.

This mechanized design approach treated the alphabet as a flexible system divorced from calligraphy. The search for archetypal, perfectly proportioned letterforms gave way to a new view of typography as an elastic system of formal features (weight, stress, stem, crossbars, serifs, angles, curves, ascenders, descenders). The relationships among letters in a typeface became more important than the identity of individual characters.

For extensive analysis and examples of decorated types, see Rob Roy Kelly, *American Wood Type: 1828–1900, Notes on the Evolution of Decorated and Large Letters* (New York: Da Capo Press, 1969). See also Ruari McLean, "An Examination of Egyptians," in *Texts on Type: Critical Writings on Typography*, ed. Steven Heller and Philip B. Meggs (New York: Allworth Press, 2001), 70–76.

DURYEAS' IMPORTED CORNSTARCH (LEFT)
Lithographic trade card, 1878. *The rise of advertising in the nineteenth century stimulated demand for large-scale letters that could command attention in urban space. Here, a man is shown posting a bill in flagrant disregard for the law, while a police officer approaches from around the corner.*

FULL MOON (RIGHT)
Letterpress poster, 1875. *A dozen different fonts are used in this poster for a steamship cruise. A size and style of typeface has been chosen for each line to maximize the scale of the letters in the space allotted. Although the typefaces are exotic, the centered layout is as static and conventional as a tombstone.*

Printing, having found in the book a refuge in which to lead an autonomous existence, is pitilessly dragged out into the street by advertisements....Locust swarms of print, which already eclipse the sun of what is taken for intellect in city dwellers, will grow thicker with each succeeding year. —WALTER BENJAMIN, 1925

FULL MOON.

ST. MICHAEL'S
TEMPERANCE BAND !

Prof. V. Yeager, Leader, will give a

GRAND
MOONLIGHT
EXCURSION

On the Steamer

BELLE !

To Osbrook and Watch Hill,
On Saturday Evening, July 17th,

Leaving Wharf at 7½ o'clock.   Returning to Westerly
at 10½ o'clock.   Kenneth will be at Osbrook.

TICKETS, - FORTY CENTS.

G. B. & J. H. Utter, Steam Printers, Westerly, R. I.

THEO VAN DOESBURG, *founder and chief promoter of the Dutch De Stijl movement, designed this alphabet with perpendicular elements in 1919. Applied here to the letterhead of the Union of Revolutionary Socialists, the hand-drawn characters vary in width, allowing them to fill out the overall rectangle. The De Stijl movement called for the reduction of painting, architecture, objects, and letters to elemental units.*

BOND VAN REVOLUTIONNAIR-SOCIALISTISCHE INTELLECTUEELEN

DE STIJL

VILMOS HUSZÁR *designed this logo for the magazine De Stijl in 1917. Whereas van Doesburg's characters are unbroken, Huszár's letters consist of pixel-like modules.*

abcdefghi jklmnopqr stuvwxyz a   dd

HERBERT BAYER *created this typeface design, called universal, at the Bauhaus in 1925. Consisting only of lowercase letters, it is built from straight lines and circles.*

FETTE FUTURA

GOETH STOFF

PAUL RENNER *designed Futura in Germany in 1927. Although it is strongly geometric, with perfectly round Os, Futura is a practical, subtly designed typeface that remains widely used today.*

EDWARD JOHNSTON *based this 1906 diagram of "essential" characters on ancient Roman inscriptions. While deriding commercial lettering, Johnston accepted the embellishment of medieval-inspired forms.*

On Futura, see Christopher Burke, *Paul Renner: The Art of Typography* (New York: Princeton Architectural Press, 1998). On the experimental typefaces of the 1920s and 1930s, see Robin Kinross, *Unjustified Texts: Perspectives on Typography* (London: Hyphen Press, 2002), 233–45.

Some designers viewed the distortion of the alphabet as gross and immoral, tied to a destructive and inhumane industrial system. Writing in 1906, Edward Johnston revived the search for an essential, standard alphabet and warned against the "dangers" of exaggeration. Johnston, inspired by the nineteenth-century Arts and Crafts movement, looked back to the Renaissance and Middle Ages for pure, uncorrupted letterforms.

Although reformers like Johnston remained romantically attached to history, they redefined the designer as an intellectual distanced from the commercial mainstream. The modern design reformer was a critic of society, striving to create objects and images that would challenge and revise dominant habits and practices.

The avant-garde artists of the early twentieth century rejected historical forms but adopted the model of the critical outsider. Members of the De Stijl group in the Netherlands reduced the alphabet to perpendicular elements. At the Bauhaus, Herbert Bayer and Josef Albers constructed letters from basic geometric forms—the circle, square, and triangle—which they viewed as elements of a universal language of vision.

Such experiments approached the alphabet as a system of abstract relationships. Like the popular printers of the nineteenth century, avant-garde designers rejected the quest for essential letters grounded in the human hand and body, but they offered austere, theoretical alternatives in place of the solicitous novelty of mainstream advertising.

Assembled like machines from modular components, these experimental designs emulated factory production. Yet most were produced by hand rather than as mechanical typefaces (although many are now available digitally). Futura, completed by Paul Renner in 1927, embodied the obsessions of the avant garde in a multipurpose, commercially available typeface. Although Renner disdained the active movement of calligraphy in favor of forms that are "calming" and abstract, he tempered the geometry of Futura with subtle variations in stroke, curve, and proportion. Renner designed Futura in numerous weights, viewing his type family as a painterly tool for constructing a page in shades of gray.

The calming, abstract forms of those new typefaces that dispense with handwritten movement offer the typographer new shapes of tonal value that are very purely attuned. These types can be used in light, semi-bold, or in saturated black forms. —PAUL RENNER, 1931

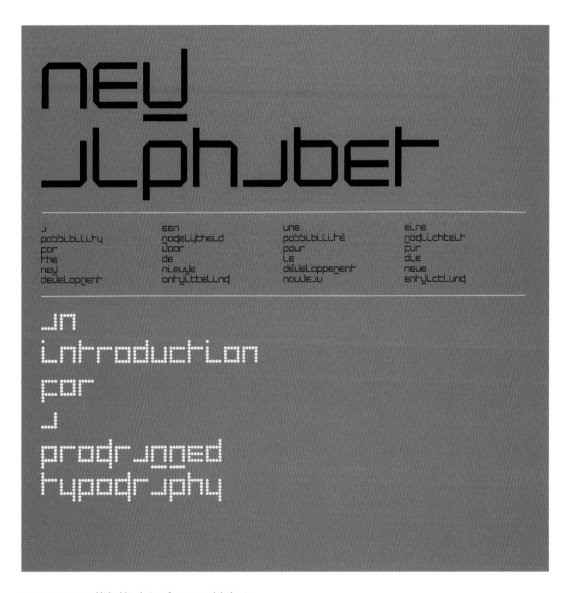

WIM CROUWEL *published his designs for a "new alphabet,"*
consisting of no diagonals or curves, in 1967. The Foundry (London)
began releasing digital editions of Crouwel's typefaces in 1997.

TYPE AS PROGRAM

Responding in 1967 to the rise of electronic communication, the Dutch designer Wim Crouwel published designs for a "new alphabet" constructed from straight lines. Rejecting centuries of typographic convention, he designed his letters for optimal display on a video screen (CRT), where curves and angles are rendered with horizontal scan lines. In a brochure promoting his new alphabet, subtitled "An Introduction for a Programmed Typography," he proposed a design methodology in which decisions are rule-based and systematic.

WIM CROUWEL *presented this "scanned" version of a Garamond* a *in contrast with his own new alphabet, whose forms accept the gridded structure of the screen. See* Wim Crouwel, New Alphabet *(Amsterdam: Total Design, 1967).*

ZUZANA LICKO *created coarse-resolution fonts for desktop screens and printers in 1985. These fonts have since been integrated into Emigre's extensive Lo-Res font family, designed for print and digital media.*

See Rudy VanderLans and Zuzana Licko, *Emigre: Graphic Design into the Digital Realm* (New York: Van Nostrand Reinhold, 1993) and *Emigre No. 70: The Look Back Issue, Selections from Emigre Magazine, 1984–2009* (Berkeley: Gingko Press, 2009).

In the mid-1980s, personal computers and low-resolution printers put the tools of typography in the hands of a broader public. In 1985 Zuzana Licko began designing typefaces that exploited the rough grain of early desktop systems. While other digital fonts imposed the coarse grid of screen displays and dot-matrix printers onto traditional typographic forms, Licko embraced the language of digital equipment. She and her husband, Rudy VanderLans, cofounders of Emigre Fonts and *Emigre* magazine, called themselves the "new primitives," pioneers of a technological dawn.

By the early 1990s, with the introduction of high-resolution laser printers and outline font technologies such as PostScript, type designers were less constrained by low-resolution outputs. While various signage systems and digital output devices still rely on bitmap fonts today, it is the fascination with programmed, geometric structures that has enabled bitmap forms to continue evolving as a visual ethos in print and digital media.

Living with computers gives funny ideas. —WIM CROUWEL, 1967

CURATOR : JOSEPH WESNEF
Linda Ferguson

Steve Handschu
James Hay

Matthew Holl and **SCULPTURI**
Gary Laatsch
Brian Liljeblad
Dora Natella
Matthew Schellenberg
Richard String
Michell Thomas

Robert Wilhelm

Opening Recep tion : Friday Jun e 8 ,5:30 8:30 pm

SCULPTURE

June 8 — July 7, 1990

Detroit Focus Gallery (313)96 2 -90 2 5
743 Beaubien, Third Floor
DETROIT, MICHIGAN 48 2 26
WEDNESDAY - SATURDAY
Hours : Noon to 6 pm

ALSO IN THE AREA: THE MARKET PRESENTS Peter Gilleran · Gordon Orear   Op ening 5 - 7:30 pm. Friday, June 8.

ED FELLA *produced a body of experimental typography that strongly influenced typeface design in the 1990s. His posters for the Detroit Focus Gallery feature damaged and defective forms, drawn by hand or culled from third-generation photocopies or from sheets of transfer lettering. Collection of the Cooper-Hewitt, National Design Museum.*

In the early 1990s, as digital design tools began supporting the seamless reproduction and integration of media, many designers grew dissatisfied with clean, unsullied surfaces, seeking instead to plunge the letter into the harsh and caustic world of physical processes. Letters, which for centuries had sought perfection in ever more exact technologies, became scratched, bent, bruised, and polluted.

Template Gothic: flawed technology

Barry Deck's typeface Template Gothic, designed in 1990, is based on letters drawn with a plastic stencil. The typeface thus refers to a process that is at once mechanical and manual. Deck designed Template Gothic while he was a student of Ed Fella, whose experimental posters inspired a generation of digital typographers. After Template Gothic was released commercially by Emigre Fonts, its use spread worldwide, making it an emblem of digital typography for the 1990s.

Dead History: feeding on the past

P. Scott Makela's typeface Dead History, also designed in 1990, is a pastiche of two existing typefaces: the traditional serif font Centennial and the Pop classic VAG Rounded. By manipulating the vectors of readymade fonts, Makela adopted the sampling strategy employed in contemporary art and music. He also embraced the burden of history and precedent, which play a role in nearly every typographic innovation.

CcDdEeFfGgHhIiJjKk

The Dutch typographers Erik van Blokland and Just van Rossum have combined the roles of designer and programmer, creating typefaces that embrace chance, change, and uncertainty. Their 1990 typeface Beowulf was the first in a series of typefaces with randomized outlines and programmed behaviors.

The industrial methods of producing typography meant that all letters had to be identical....Typography is now produced with sophisticated equipment that doesn't impose such rules. The only limitations are in our expectations. — ERIK VAN BLOKLAND AND JUST VAN ROSSUM, 2000

BACK TO WORK

Although the 1990s are best remembered for images of chaos and decay, serious type designers continued to build general purpose typefaces designed to comfortably accommodate broad bodies of text. Such workhorse type families provide graphic designers with flexible palettes of letterforms.

Mrs Eaves: WORKING *woman* **seeks** *reliable* **mate**

Licko produced historical revivals during the 1990s alongside her experimental display faces. Her 1996 typeface Mrs Eaves, inspired by the eighteenth-century types of Baskerville, became one of the most popular typefaces of its time. In 2009, Mrs Eaves was joined by Mr Eaves, a sans-serif version of the feminine favorite.

Quadraat: *all-purpose* hard**core** BAROQUE

Fred Smeijers's Quadraat (above) and Martin Majoor's Scala (used for the text of this book) offer crisp interpretations of typographic tradition. These typefaces look back to sixteenth-century printing from a contemporary point of view, as seen in their simply drawn, decisively geometric serifs. Introduced in 1992, the Quadraat family soon expanded to include sans-serif forms in numerous weights and styles.

Gotham: Blue-Collar **Curves**

In 2000 Tobias Frere-Jones introduced Gotham, derived from letters found at the Port Authority Bus Terminal in New York City. With its distinctive yet utilitarian style, Gotham became the signature typeface of Barack Obama's 2008 presidential campaign. By 2009, typography's First Family had over fifty weights and styles.

When choosing a typeface, graphic designers consider the history of typefaces, their current connotations, as well as their formal qualities. The goal is to find an appropriate match between a style of letters and the specific social situation and body of content that define the project at hand. There is no playbook that assigns a fixed meaning or function to every typeface; each designer must confront the library of possibilities in light of a project's unique circumstances.

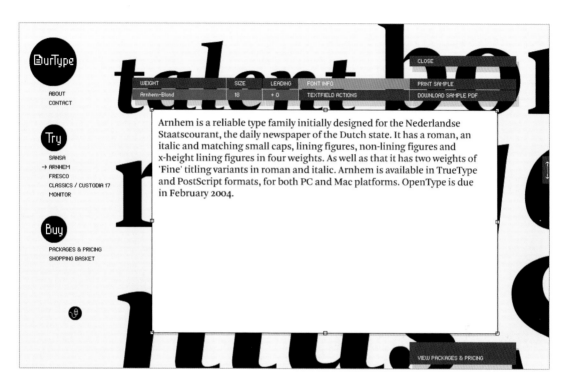

OURTYPE.COM Website, 2004. Design: Fred Smeijers and Rudy Geeraerts. *This Flash-based website for a digital type foundry allows users to test fonts on the fly. The designers launched their own "label" after creating typefaces such as Quadraat for FontShop International. Shown here is Arnhem.*

Can we envision

1. a font that asks more questions than it an...

2. a font that has projective memory that reminds you to reme...

3. a font with a limited life...

4. a font with an expiry...

5. a font that's gon...

6. a font without temporal inflection, without the imprint of its...

7. an apolitical font, a font that doesn't...

8. a font unaffected by the force of gravity and the weight of human h...

9. a font without family, without anc...

10. a Marshall McLuhan font that stubbornly persists in bidding farewell to...

11. a font that takes advantage of all that promised "processing po...

12. a font that does something other than sit on its ass in a digital mus...

310

13. a font with the capacity to breed with other...

14. a recombinant font — every letterform the unruly child of a predictable but random pro...

15. a font that sounds as good as it...

16. a font that writes its own s...

17. a font that thickens the...

18. a font that responds and reacts to the meaning it carries and co...

19. a font that assumes the intelligence of its re...

20. a font that might sense your level of agitation, fear, or aggre...

21. a font prone to sudden outbursts and tant...

22. a font that exceeds the typographic ge...

23. a font whose parents are Father Time and the Mother of Inve...

24. an ambient font, a font without qua...

25. an everyday font, a font of common s...

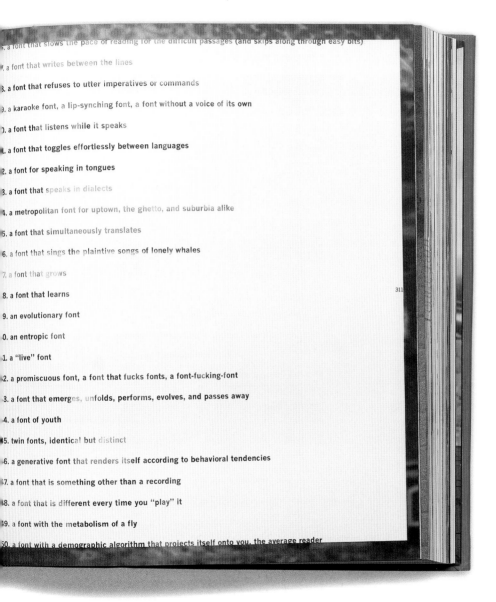

. a font that slows the pace of reading for the difficult passages (and skips along through easy bits)

. a font that writes between the lines

. a font that refuses to utter imperatives or commands

. a karaoke font, a lip-synching font, a font without a voice of its own

. a font that listens while it speaks

. a font that toggles effortlessly between languages

. a font for speaking in tongues

. a font that speaks in dialects

. a metropolitan font for uptown, the ghetto, and suburbia alike

. a font that simultaneously translates

. a font that sings the plaintive songs of lonely whales

. a font that grows

. a font that learns

. an evolutionary font

. an entropic font

. a "live" font

. a promiscuous font, a font that fucks fonts, a font-fucking-font

. a font that emerges, unfolds, performs, evolves, and passes away

. a font of youth

. twin fonts, identical but distinct

. a generative font that renders itself according to behavioral tendencies

. a font that is something other than a recording

. a font that is different every time you "play" it

. a font with the metabolism of a fly

. a font with a demographic algorithm that projects itself onto you, the average reader

311

LIFE STYLE Book, 2000. Design: Bruce Mau. Publisher:
Phaidon. Photograph: Dan Meyers. *In this postindustrial
manifesto, graphic designer Bruce Mau imagines a typeface that
comes alive with simulated intelligence.*

CAP HEIGHT
X-HEIGHT
BASELINE
STEM · BOWL · SERIF · DESCENDER

LIGATURE · ASCENDER
FINIAL

TERMINAL · ASCENDER
SPINE

UPPERCASE · SMALL CAPITAL
CROSS BAR · COUNTER · LOWERCASE

ASCENDER HEIGHT
Some elements may extend slightly above the cap height.

CAP HEIGHT
The distance from the baseline to the top of the capital letter determines the letter's point size.

DESCENDER HEIGHT
The length of a letter's descenders contributes to its overall style and attitude.

skin, Body

X-HEIGHT *is the height of the main body of the lowercase letter (or the height of a lowercase x), excluding its ascenders and descenders.*

THE BASELINE *is where all the letters sit. This is the most stable axis along a line of text, and it is a crucial edge for aligning text with images or with other text.*

OVERHANG *The curves at the bottom of letters hang slightly below the baseline. Commas and semicolons also cross the baseline. If a typeface were not positioned this way, it would appear to teeter precariously. Without overhang, rounded letters would look smaller than their flat-footed compatriots.*

Bone

Although kids learn to write using ruled paper that divides letters exactly in half, most typefaces are not designed that way. The x-height usually occupies more than half of the cap height. The larger the x-height is in relation to the cap height, the bigger the letters appear to be. In a field of text, the greatest density occurs between the baseline and the x-height.

Hey, look! They supersized my x-height.

Two blocks of text are often aligned along a shared baseline. Here, 14/18 Scala Pro (14-pt type with 18 pts of line spacing) is paired with 7/9 Scala Pro.

*12 points
equal 1 pica*

*6 picas
(72 points)
equal 1 inch*

60-POINT SCALA
*A typeface is measured
from the top of the
capital letter to the
bottom of the lowest
descender, plus a small
buffer space.*

*In metal type,
the point size
is the height of
the type slug.*

HEIGHT Attempts to standardize the measurement of type began in the eighteenth century. The *point system* is the standard used today. One *point* equals 1/72 inch or .35 millimeters. Twelve points equal one *pica*, the unit commonly used to measure column widths. Typography can also be measured in inches, millimeters, or pixels. Most software applications let the designer choose a preferred unit of measure; picas and points are standard defaults.

NERD ALERT:
ABBREVIATING PICAS AND POINTS
8 picas = 8p
8 points = p8, 8 pts
8 picas, 4 points = 8p4
8-point Helvetica with 9 points of line spacing = 8/9 Helvetica

WIDE LOAD

INTERSTATE BLACK
*The set width is the body of the letter
plus the space beside it.*

TIGHT WAD

INTERSTATE BLACK COMPRESSED
*The letters in the compressed version of the typeface
have a narrower set width.*

WIDE LOAD
TIGHT WAD

TYPE CRIME
HORIZONTAL & VERTICAL SCALING
*The proportions of the letters have been
digitally distorted in order to create wider
or narrower letters.*

WIDTH A letter also has a horizontal measure, called its *set width*. The set width is the body of the letter plus a sliver of space that protects it from other letters. The width of a letter is intrinsic to the proportions and visual impression of the typeface. Some typefaces have a narrow set width, and some have a wide one.

You can change the set width of a typeface by fiddling with its horizontal or vertical scale. This distorts the line weight of the letters, however, forcing heavy elements to become thin, and thin elements to become thick. Instead of torturing a letterform, choose a typeface that has the proportions you are looking for, such as condensed, compressed, wide, or extended.

32-PT SCALA PRO   32-PT INTERSTATE REGULAR   32-PT BODONI   32-PT MRS EAVES

Do I **look fat** in this paragraph?

When two typefaces are set in the same point size, one often looks bigger than the other. Differences in x-height, line weight, and set width affect the letters' apparent scale.

Mrs Eaves rejects the twentieth-century appetite for supersized x-heights. This typeface, inspired by the eighteenth-century designs of Baskerville, is named after Sarah Eaves, Baskerville's mistress, housekeeper, and collaborator. The couple lived together for sixteen years before marrying in 1764.

Mr. Big versus *Mrs.* & Mr. Little

32-PT HELVETICA   32-PT MRS EAVES   32-PT MR EAVES

The x-height of a typeface affects its apparent size, its space efficiency, and its overall visual impact. Like hemlines and hair styles, x-heights go in and out of fashion. Bigger type bodies became popular in the mid-twentieth century, making letterforms look larger by maximizing the area within the overall point size.

12/14 HELVETICA

Because of its huge x-height, Helvetica can remain legible at small sizes. Set in 8 pts for a magazine caption, Helvetica can look quite elegant. The same typeface could look bulky and bland, however, standing 12 pts tall on a business card.

8/10 HELVETICA

The default type size in many software applications is 12 pts. Although this generally creates readable type on screen displays, 12-pt text type usually looks big and horsey in print. Sizes between 9 and 11 pts are common for printed text. This caption is 7.5 pts.

Typefaces with small x-heights, such as MRS EAVES, use space less efficiently than those with big lower bodies. However, their delicate proportions have lyrical charm.

12/14 MRS EAVES

Like his lovely wife, **MR EAVES** has a low waist and a small body. His loose letterspacing also makes him work well with his mate.

12/14 MR EAVES

The size of a typeface is a matter of context. A line of text that looks tiny on a television screen may appear appropriately scaled in a page of printed text. Smaller proportions affect legibility as well as space consumption. A diminutive x-height is a luxury that requires sacrifice.

8/10 MRS AND MR EAVES

All the typefaces shown below were inspired by the sixteenth-century printing types of Claude Garamond, yet each one reflects its own era. The lean forms of Garamond 3 appeared during the Great Depression, while the inflated x-height of ITC Garamond became an icon of the flamboyant 1970s.

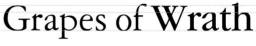

Grapes of Wrath

30-PT GARAMOND 3   30-PT ITC GARAMOND

GARAMOND IN THE TWENTIETH CENTURY: VARIATIONS ON A THEME

1930s: Franklin D. Roosevelt, SALVADOR DALÍ, Duke

18-PT GARAMOND 3, *designed by Morris Fuller Benton and Thomas Maitland Cleland for ATF, 1936*

Ellington, *Scarface*, chicken and waffles, shoulder pads, radio.

1970s: Richard Nixon, Claes Oldenburg, Van Halen,

18-PT ITC GARAMOND, *designed by Tony Stan, 1976*

The Godfather, bell bottoms, guacamole, sitcoms.

1980s: Margaret Thatcher, BARBARA KRUGER, Madonna,

18-PT ADOBE GARAMOND, *designed by Robert Slimbach, 1989*

Blue Velvet, shoulder pads, pasta salad, desktop publishing.

2000s: Osama Bin Laden, MATTHEW BARNEY, the White

18-PT ADOBE GARAMOND PREMIERE PRO MEDIUM SUBHEAD, *designed by Robert Slimbach, 2005*

Stripes, *The Sopranos*, mom jeans, heirloom tomatoes, Twitter.

A type family with *optical sizes* has different styles for different sizes of output. The graphic designer selects a style based on context. Optical sizes designed for headlines or display tend to have delicate, lyrical forms, while styles created for text and captions are built with heavier strokes.

No Job *Too Small*

48-PT BODONI   8-PT BODONI

TYPE CRIME

Some typefaces that work well at large sizes look too fragile when reduced.

OPTICAL SIZES

HEADLINES are slim, *high-strung* prima donnas.

27-PT ADOBE GARAMOND PREMIERE PRO DISPLAY

SUBHEADS are *frisky* supporting characters.

27-PT ADOBE GARAMOND PREMIERE PRO SUBHEAD

TEXT is the *everyman* of the printed stage.

27-PT ADOBE GARAMOND PREMIERE PRO REGULAR

CAPTIONS get *heavy* to play small roles.

27-PT ADOBE GARAMOND PREMIERE PRO CAPTION

10 PT

In the era of METAL TYPE, type designers created a different *punch* for each size of type, adjusting its weight, spacing, and other features. Each size required a unique typeface design.

ADOBE GARAMOND PREMIERE PRO DISPLAY

When the type design process became automated in the NINETEENTH CENTURY, many typefounders economized by simply *enlarging or reducing* a base design to generate different sizes.

ADOBE GARAMOND PREMIERE PRO REGULAR

This MECHANIZED APPROACH to type sizes became the norm for photo and digital type production. When a text-sized letterform is enlarged to poster-sized proportions, its thin features become too heavy (and vice versa).

ADOBE GARAMOND PREMIERE PRO CAPTION

8 PT

A DISPLAY or *headline* style looks spindly and weak when set at small sizes. Display styles are intended for use at 24 pts. and larger.

Basic TEXT styles are designed for sizes ranging from 9 to 14 pts. Their features are strong and *meaty* but not too assertive.

CAPTION styles are built with the heaviest stroke weight. They are *designed* for sizes ranging from 6 to 8 pts.

80 PT

Scale is the size of design elements in comparison to other elements in a layout as well as to the physical context of the work. Scale is relative. 12-pt type displayed on a 32-inch monitor can look very small, while 12-pt type printed on a book page can look flabby and overweight. Designers create hierarchy and contrast by playing with the scale of letterforms. Changes in scale help create visual contrast, movement, and depth as well as express hierarchies of importance. Scale is physical. People intuitively judge the size of objects in relation to their own bodies and environments.

THE
WORLD
IS FLAT

TYPE CRIME
Minimal differences in type size make this design look tentative and arbitrary.

THE
WORLD
IS FLAT

SCALE CONTRAST
The strong contrast between type sizes gives this design dynamism, decisiveness, and depth.

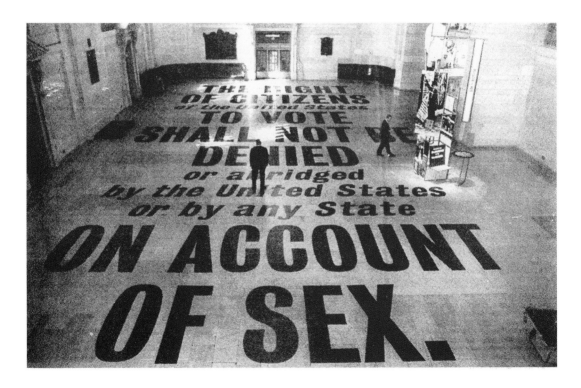

THE XIX AMENDMENT Typographic installation at Grand Central Station, New York City, 1995. Designer: Stephen Doyle. Sponsors: The New York State Division of Women, the Metropolitan Transportation Authority, Revlon, and Merrill Lynch. *Large-scale text creates impact in this public installation.*

BLOW-UP: (WARREN NIEDICH) PHOTOGRAPHY, CINEMA AND THE BRAIN

BLOW-UP: PHOTOGRAPHY, CINEMA, AND THE BRAIN
Book cover, 2003. Designers: Paul Carlos and Urshula
Barbour/Pure + Applied. Author: Warren Niedich. *Cropping the
letters increases their sense of scale. The overlapping colors suggest
an extreme detail of a printed or photographic process.*

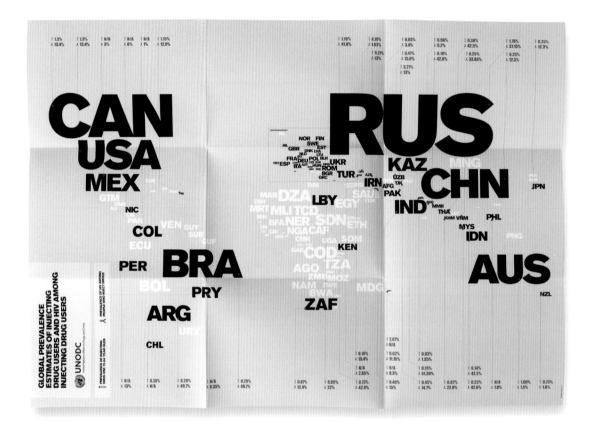

Maps, 2009. Design: Harry Pearce and Jason Ching/
Pentagram. *This series of posters for the United Nations' Office on
Drugs and Crime uses typographic scale to compare drug treatment
programs, HIV incidence, and other data worldwide. The designers
built simple world maps from country abbreviation codes (GBR,
USA, RUS, etc.). The posters are aimed specifically at the Russian
police, whose country has a poor track record in drug treatment.
Note Russia's high incidence of HIV and low availability of
addiction rehabilitation programs.*

REVOLVER: ZEITSCHRIFT FÜR FILM (MAGAZINE FOR FILM) Magazine, 1998–2003.
Designer: Gerwin Schmidt.
This magazine is created by and for film directors. The contrast between the big type and the small pages creates drama and surprise.

SABON

Aa

HUMANIST OR OLD STYLE
The roman typefaces of the fifteenth and sixteenth centuries emulated classical calligraphy. Sabon was designed by Jan Tschichold in 1966, based on the sixteenth-century typefaces of Claude Garamond.

BASKERVILLE

Aa

TRANSITIONAL
These typefaces have sharper serifs and a more vertical axis than humanist letters. When the typefaces of John Baskerville were introduced in the mid-eighteenth century, their sharp forms and high contrast were considered shocking.

BODONI

Aa

MODERN
The typefaces designed by Giambattista Bodoni in the late eighteenth and early nineteenth centuries are radically abstract. Note the thin, straight serifs; vertical axis; and sharp contrast from thick to thin strokes.

A basic system for classifying typefaces was devised in the nineteenth century, when printers sought to identify a heritage for their own craft analogous to that of art history. *Humanist* letterforms are closely connected to calligraphy and the movement of the hand. *Transitional* and *modern* typefaces are more abstract and less organic. These three main groups correspond roughly to the Renaissance, Baroque, and Enlightenment periods in art and literature. Historians and critics of typography have since proposed more finely grained schemes that attempt to better capture the diversity of letterforms. Designers in the twentieth and twenty-first centuries have continued to create new typefaces based on historic characteristics.

CLARENDON

EGYPTIAN OR SLAB SERIF
Numerous bold and decorative typefaces were introduced in the nineteenth century for use in advertising. Egyptian typefaces have heavy, slablike serifs.

GILL SANS

Aa

HUMANIST SANS SERIF
Sans-serif typefaces became common in the twentieth century. Gill Sans, designed by Eric Gill in 1928, has humanist characteristics. Note the small, lilting counter in the letter a, and the calligraphic variations in line weight.

HELVETICA

Aa

TRANSITIONAL SANS SERIF
Helvetica, designed by Max Miedinger in 1957, is one of the world's most widely used typefaces. Its uniform, upright character makes it similar to transitional serif letters. These fonts are also referred to as "anonymous sans serif."

FUTURA

Aa

GEOMETRIC SANS SERIF
Some sans-serif types are built around geometric forms. In Futura, designed by Paul Renner in 1927, the Os are perfect circles, and the peaks of the A and M are sharp triangles.

CLASSIC TYPEFACES

Sabon
14 PT

This is not a book about fonts. It is a book about how to use them. Typefaces are essential resources for the graphic designer, just as glass, stone, steel, and other materials are employed by the architect.

SABON 9/12

Selecting type with wit and wisdom requires knowledge of how and why letterforms evolved.

7/9

Baskerville
14 PT

This is not a book about fonts. It is a book about how to use them. Typefaces are essential resources for the graphic designer, just as glass, stone, steel, and other materials are employed by the architect.

BASKERVILLE 9/12

Selecting type with wit and wisdom requires knowledge of how and why letterforms evolved.

7/9

Bodoni
14 PT

This is not a book about fonts. It is a book about how to use them. Typefaces are essential resources for the graphic designer, just as glass, stone, steel, and other materials are employed by the architect.

BODONI BOOK 9.5/12

Selecting type with wit and wisdom requires knowledge of how and why letterforms evolved.

7.5/9

Clarendon
14 PT

This is not a book about fonts. It is a book about how to use them. Typefaces are essential resources for the graphic designer, just as glass, stone, steel, and other materials are employed by the architect.

CLARENDON LIGHT 8/12

Selecting type with wit and wisdom requires knowledge of how and why letterforms evolved.

6/9

Gill Sans
14 PT

This is not a book about fonts. It is a book about how to use them. Typefaces are essential resources for the graphic designer, just as glass, stone, steel, and other materials are employed by the architect.

GILL SANS REGULAR 9/12

Selecting type with wit and wisdom requires knowledge of how and why letterforms evolved.

7/9

Helvetica
14 PT

This is not a book about fonts. It is a book about how to use them. Typefaces are essential resources for the graphic designer, just as glass, stone, steel, and other materials are employed by the architect.

HELVETICA REGULAR 8/12

Selecting type with wit and wisdom requires knowledge of how and why letterforms evolved.

6/9

Futura
14 PT

This is not a book about fonts. It is a book about how to use them. Typefaces are essential resources for the graphic designer, just as glass, stone, steel, and other materials are employed by the architect.

FUTURA BOOK 8.5/12

Selecting type with wit and wisdom requires knowledge of how and why letterforms evolved.

6.5/9

In the sixteeenth century, printers began organizing roman and italic typefaces into matched families. The concept was formalized in the early twentieth century.

ANATOMY OF A TYPE FAMILY   ADOBE GARAMOND PRO, *designed by Robert Slimbach, 1988*

The roman form is the core or spine from which a family of typefaces derives.

ADOBE GARAMOND PRO REGULAR

The roman form, also called plain *or* regular, *is the standard, upright version of a typeface. It is typically conceived as the parent of a larger family.*

Italic letters, which are based on cursive writing, have forms distinct from roman.

ADOBE GARAMOND PRO ITALIC

The italic form is used to create emphasis. Especially among serif faces, it often employs shapes and strokes distinct from its roman counterpart. Note the differences between the roman and italic a.

SMALL CAPS HAVE A HEIGHT THAT IS SIMILAR TO the lowercase x-HEIGHT.

ADOBE GARAMOND PRO REGULAR (ALL SMALL CAPS)

Small caps (capitals) are designed to integrate with a line of text, where full-size capitals would stand out awkwardly. Small capitals are slightly taller than the x-height of lowercase letters.

Bold (and semibold) typefaces are used for emphasis within a hierarchy.

ADOBE GARAMOND PRO BOLD AND SEMIBOLD

Bold versions of traditional text fonts were added in the twentieth century to meet the need for emphatic forms. Sans-serif families often include a broad range of weights (thin, bold, black, etc.).

Bold (and semibold) typefaces each need to include an italic version, too.

ADOBE GARAMOND PRO BOLD AND SEMIBOLD ITALIC

The typeface designer tries to make the two bold versions feel similar in comparison to the roman, without making the overall form too heavy. The counters need to stay clear and open at small sizes. Many designers prefer not to use bold and semi-bold versions of traditional typefaces such as Garamond, because these weights are alien to the historic families.

Italics are not *slanted* letters.

TRUE	**TYPE CRIME:**
ITALIC	PSEUDO ITALICS
	The wide, ungainly forms of these mechanically skewed letters look forced and unnatural.

Some italics aren't slanted at all. In the type family Quadraat, the italic form is upright.

QUADRAAT, *designed by Fred Smeijers, 1992.*

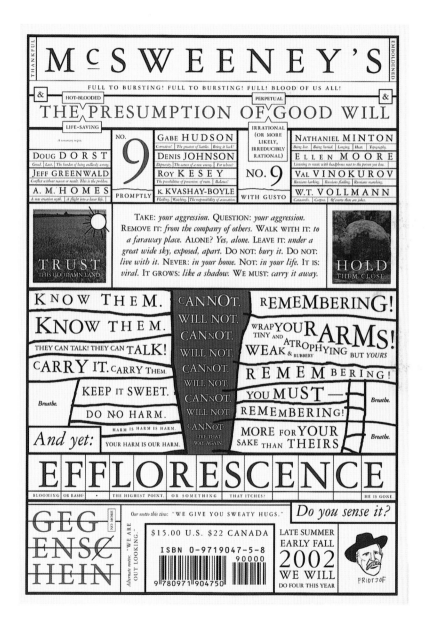

MCSWEENEY'S Magazine cover, 2002. Design: Dave Eggers.
This magazine cover uses the Garamond 3 typeface family in
various sizes. Although the typeface is classical and conservative,
the obsessive, slightly deranged layout is distinctly contemporary.

A traditional roman book face typically has a small family—an intimate group consisting of roman, italic, small caps, and possibly bold and semibold (each with an italic variant) styles. Sans-serif families often come in many more weights and sizes, such as thin, light, black, compressed, and condensed. A *superfamily* consists of dozens of related fonts in multiple weights and/or widths, often with both sans-serif and serif versions. Small capitals and non-lining numerals (once found only in serif fonts) are included in the sans-serif versions of Thesis, Scala Pro, and many other contemporary superfamilies.

ANATOMY OF A SUPERFAMILY

Scala

Scala Italic

SCALA CAPS

Scala Bold

SCALA PRO, *designed by Martin Majoor, includes Scala (1991) and Scala Sans (1993). The serif and sans-serif forms have a common spine. Scala Pro (OpenType format) was released in 2005.*

Scala Sans Light

Scala Sans

Scala Sans Condensed

Scala Sans Cond Bold

Scala Sans Bold

Scala Sans Black

SCALA JEWEL CRYSTAL

SCALA JEWEL DIAMOND

SCALA JEWEL PEARL

SCALA JEWEL SAPHYR

UNIVERS *was designed by the Swiss typographer Adrian Frutiger in 1957. He designed twenty-one versions of Univers, in five weights and five widths. Whereas some type families grow over time, Univers was conceived as a total system from its inception.*

TRILOGY, *a superfamily designed by Jeremy Tankard in 2009, is inspired by three nineteenth-century type styles: sans serif, Egyptian, and fat face. The inclusion of the fat face style, with its wafer-thin serifs and ultrawide verticals, gives this family an unusual twist.*

ANATOMY OF A SUPERFAMILY

This is not a book about fonts. It is a book about how to use them. Typefaces

THE SERIF MEDIUM ROMAN

are essential resources for the graphic designer, just as glass, stone, steel, and

THE SERIF MEDIUM ITALIC

OTHER MATERIALS ARE EMPLOYED BY THE ARCHITECT. SOME DESIGNERS CREATE

THE SERIF MEDIUM SMALL CAPS

their own custom fonts. But most

THE SERIF BLACK ROMAN

graphic designers will tap the vast

THE SERIF EXTRA BOLD ROMAN

store of already existing typefaces,

THE SERIF BOLD ROMAN

choosing and combining each with

THE SERIF SEMI BOLD ROMAN

regard to the audience or situation.

THE SERIF MEDIUM ROMAN

Selecting type with wit and wisdom

THE SERIF SEMI LIGHT

requires knowledge of how and why

THE SERIF LIGHT ROMAN

letterforms have evolved. The history

THE SERIF EXTRA LIGHT ROMAN

of typography reflects a continual tension between the hand and machine, the

THE SANS MEDIUM ROMAN

organic and geometric, the human body and the abstract system. These tensions

THE SANS MEDIUM ITALIC

MARKED THE BIRTH OF PRINTED LETTERS FIVE CENTURIES AGO, AND THEY CONTINUE TO

THE SANS MEDIUM SMALL CAPS

energize typography today. Writing

THE SANS BLACK ROMAN

in the West was revolutionized early

THE SANS EXTRA BOLD ROMAN

in the Renaissance, when Johannes

THE SANS BOLD ROMAN

Gutenberg introduced moveable type

THE SANS SEMI BOLD ROMAN

in Germany. Whereas documents and

THE SANS MEDIUM ROMAN

books had previously been written by

THE SANS SEMI LIGHT ROMAN

hand, printing with type mobilized all

THE SANS LIGHT ROMAN

of the techniques of mass production.

THE SANS EXTRA LIGHT ROMAN

THESIS, *designed by Lu(cas) de Groot, 1994*

A word set in ALL CAPS within running text can look big and bulky, and A LONG PASSAGE SET ENTIRELY IN CAPITALS CAN LOOK UTTERLY INSANE. SMALL CAPITALS are designed to match the x-height of lowercase letters. Designers, enamored with the squarish proportions of true SMALL CAPS, employ them not only within bodies of text but for subheads, bylines, invitations, and more. Rather than MIXING SMALL CAPS WITH CAPITALS, many designers prefer to use ALL SMALL CAPS, creating a clean line with no ascending elements. InDesign and other programs allow users to create FALSE SMALL CAPS at the press of a button; these SCRAWNY LETTERS look out of place.

+ CAPITAL
  investment
− CAPITAL
  punishment
  CAPITAL
  crime

TYPE CRIME
In this stack of lowercase and capital letters, the spaces between lines appear uneven because caps are tall but have no descenders.

CAPITAL
investment
CAPITAL
punishment
CAPITAL
crime

ADJUSTED LEADING
The leading has been fine-tuned by selectively shifting the baselines of the small capitals to make the space between lines look even.

PSEUDO SMALL CAPS are shrunken versions of FULL-SIZE CAPS.

TYPE CRIME
PSEUDO SMALL CAPS
Helvetica was never meant to include small caps. These automatically generated characters look puny and starved; they are an abomination against nature.

TRUE SMALL CAPS integrate PEACEFULLY with lowercase letters.

SMALL CAPS, SCALA PRO
Only use small caps when they are officially included with the type family. When working with OpenType fonts (labeled Pro), access small caps in InDesign via the Character Options>OpenType menu. Older formats list small caps as a separate file in the Type>Font menu.

Tasty Vagabonds
The two camps of the burgeoning food-truck phenomenon: stable and nomadic.
BY AILEEN GALLAGHER

TRUCKS THAT ROVE

CUPCAKE STOP
The inevitable cupcakes-only truck rolled out in May. *twitter. com/cupcakestop.*

TREATS TRUCK
Cookies, crispy treats,

NEW YORK MAGAZINE
Design: Chris Dixon, 2009. *This page detail mixes serif types from the Miller family (including true Small Caps) with the sans-serif family Verlag.*

AMUSEMENT × SIMS 3

« JE FINIRAI PAR METTRE LE BAZAR *UN PEU* PARTOUT ! » SARA FORESTIER *CASSE LA BARAQUE* DANS LES SIMS 3

Jean **Apc**
Veste blazer **Louis Vuitton**
Bague et collier **Jean Tize**
quartz formul/Oxements **Pasquale Bruni**
Chaussures **Louis Vuitton**

Bague Extrait Pastel Rose Chaivenrs
Organdi Chair rouge
'Tara Vier Rouge,
Fauteuil Chair Orologio
Wire Chair OES rouge
Vitra

Simuler avec une grande finesse ses traits psychologiques, personnaliser son avatar avec tant de possibilités qu'elles le rendent unique, proposer une expérience interactive qui va au-delà du simple jeu, et vous propulse dans les subtilités de nos modes de vie ? Voici un petit aperçu de ce que propose *Les Sims 3*, dernier épisode de la saga culte lancée il y a tout juste dix ans.

Jeune actrice pleine d'énergie et aux réactions imprévisibles, Sara Forestier montre dans chacun de ses rôles une grande créativité qu'elle exprime également depuis plusieurs années dans la réalisation de courts-métrages. A l'affiche à la rentrée dans *Victor*, une comédie de Thomas Gilou sur les relations familiales, Sara était toute trouvée pour casser la baraque dans *Les Sims 3* ! Et elle ne s'est pas gênée !

Photographie François Rousseau

AMUSEMENT NUMÉRO 5 JUIN 2009

FREE PLAYERS

FREE PLAYERS

« MA PHILOSOPHIE *PASSE PAR LE GAMEPLAY »* KEITA TAKAHASHI

En cette fin du mois de mars, Keita Takahashi fait escale en France. Quelques jours plus tôt, le game designer japonais était à San Francisco pour la Game Developers Conference, grand raout annuel de la profession où, comme à son habitude, il a abreuvé ses confrères de réflexions rafraîchissantes sur le jeu vidéo. Mais, avant toute chose, il leur a montré sa nouvelle écharpe, qu'il porte encore sur lui pour ce mini-séjour parisien. Confectionnée par Madame Takahashi mère, celle-ci a notamment pour avantage de permettre au fiston d'y glisser ses mains afin de les protéger en cas de grand froid. Ce précieux tricot est aussi le premier « produit dérivé » de *Noby Noby Boy*, le dernier jeu en date de Keita Takahashi, disponible depuis le mois de février sur le service de téléchargement de la PS3 pour la somme quasi-ridicule de 3,99 euros. Cette écharpe à l'effigie du souriant Boy se révèle même remarquablement en phase avec le jeu qui l'a inspirée : tranquillement singulière, résolument artisanale et conçue pour qu'on se sente bien quand on y met les mains.

Clin Figénn Erwan Higuinen
Photographie Sébastien Agnetti

AMUSEMENT MAGAZINE
Design: Alice Litscher, 2009.
This French culture magazine employs a startling mix of tightly leaded Didot capitals in roman and italic. Running text is set in Glypha.

Combining typefaces is like making a salad. Start with a small number of elements representing different colors, tastes, and textures. Strive for contrast rather than harmony, looking for emphatic differences rather than mushy transitions. Give each ingredient a role to play: sweet tomatoes, crunchy cucumbers, and the pungent shock of an occasional anchovy. When mixing typefaces on the same line, designers usually adjust the point size so that the x-heights align. When placing typefaces on separate lines, it often makes sense to create contrast in scale as well as style or weight. Try mixing big, light type with small, dark type for a criss-cross of contrasting flavors and textures.

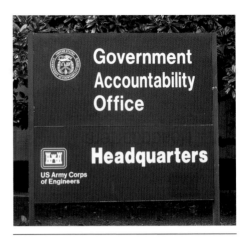

TYPE CRIME: WHO'S ACCOUNTABLE FOR THIS? *A slightly squeezed variant of the primary font has been used to make the second line fit better (as if we wouldn't notice). Yet another weight appears on the bottom line.*

SINGLE-FAMILY MIXES

Creamy and **Extra Crunchy** | *Differences within a **single family***

UNIVERS 47 LIGHT CONDENSED AND UNIVERS 67 BOLD CONDENSED

Sweet Child of **MINE** | *Differences within a* **SUPERFAMILY**

QUADRAAT REGULAR AND ITALIC; QUADRAAT SANS BOLD

Noodles with **Potato Sauce** | *Bland and blander*

HELVETICA NEUE 56 MEDIUM AND HELVETICA NEUE 75 BOLD

TYPE CRIME
These typefaces are from the same family, but they are too close in weight to mix well.

MULTIPLE-FAMILY MIXES

Jack Sprat and his **voluptuous wife** | *Two-way* **contrast**

THESIS SERIF EXTRA LIGHT AND VAG ROUNDED BOLD

Sweet, SOUR, and **hot** | *THREE-way* **contrast**

BODONI ROMAN, THESIS SERIF EXTRA LIGHT SMALL CAPS, AND FUTURA BOLD

Mr. Potatohead and Mrs. Pearbutt | *Too close for comfort*

ADOBE GARAMOND PRO BOLD AND ADOBE JENSON PRO BOLD

TYPE CRIME
These two type styles are too similar to provide a counterpoint to each other.

The Word

EDITED BY EMMA PEARSE

GLYPHA THIN, *designed by Adrian Frutiger, 1979. The large scale of the letters is counterbalanced by the fine line of the stroke.*

MILLER SMALL CAPS, *designed by Matthew Carter with Jonathan Hoefler and Tobias Frere-Jones, 1997–2000. Known as a Scotch Roman typeface, it has crisp serifs and strong contrast between thick and thin.*

EGYPTIAN BOLD CONDENSED, *a Linotype font based on a typeface from 1820. This quirky, chunky face has been used intermittently at New York Magazine since the publication was first designed by Milton Glaser in the 1970s. Here, the ultra-black type set at a relatively small size makes an incisive bite in the page.*

VERLAG, *designed by Jonathan Hoefler, 1996. Originally commissioned by Abbott Miller for exclusive use by the Guggenheim Museum, Verlag has become a widely used general-purpose typeface. Its approachable geometric forms are based on Frank Lloyd Wright's lettering for the facade of the Guggenheim.*

EVENTS

BENOIT DENIZET-LEWIS
The Powerhouse Arena, 37 Main St., nr. Water St., Dumbo (718-666-3049)
The writer from *The New York Times Magazine* reads from *American Voyeur: Dispatches From the Far Reaches of Modern Life*, a collection of his analytical reportage on everything from pro-life summer camps to the clothing company Abercrombie & Fitch; 1/13 at 7.

SOUTHERN WRITERS READING SERIES
Happy Ending Lounge, 302 Broome St., nr. Forsyth St. (212-334-9676)
An open mike for writers from below the Mason-Dixon line, where they'll read and discuss (and drink) all things southern; 1/13 at 8.

SUZE ORMAN
Barnes & Noble, 33 E. 17th St., nr. Broadway (212-253-0810)
The high priestess of financial invincibility presents her latest, *Women and Money: Owning the Power to Control Your Destiny*; 1/14 at 7.

MARY JO BANG
McNally Jackson, 52 Prince St., nr. Mulberry St. (212-274-1160)
Two poets in one room: Susan Wheeler hosts a discussion with the spectacularly named National Book Critics Circle Award winner, whose latest collection is titled *The Bride of E*; 1/14 at 7.

JOYCE CAROL OATES AND ELAINE SHOWALTER
92nd St. Y, 1395 Lexington Ave. (212-415-5500)
What two better authorities to discuss women and writing on the occasion of the publication of Showalter's *A Jury of Her Peers*, a history of American women writers from 1650 to 2000; 1/17 at 11 a.m.

PATTI SMITH
Barnes & Noble, 33 E. 17th St., nr. Broadway (212-253-0810)
The poet queen of punk reads from her book *Just Kids: From Brooklyn to the Chelsea Hotel, a Life of Art and Friendship*, about the fabulous, rocky friendship with Robert Mapplethorpe; 1/19 at 7. *Smith will also appear with the playwright Sam Shepard on January 21 at 8 p.m. at 92nd St. Y, 1395 Lexington Ave. (212-415-5500).*

COUNTESS LUANN DE LESSEPS
Borders, 10 Columbus Circle, nr. Eighth Ave. (212-823-9775)
The Real Housewife of New York, who says that "class is a state of mind," appears in the glamorous flesh to share her intimate knowledge of sophisticated living; 1/21 at 7.

IN THE FLESH
Happy Ending Lounge, 302 Broome St., nr. Forsyth St. (212-334-9676)
Former sex columnist, editor of *Best Sex Writing 2010*, and blogge Rachel Kramer Bussel hosts her monthly series of erotic re this time with the theme of sex and food (and rumo cupcakes all around); 1/21 at 8.

NICK FLYNN
BookCourt, 163 Court St., nr. Pacific
The cult hit memoirist (an Taylor) reads from his lates hitting work about child obsession with torture, of the Iraqi men depic 1/22 at 7.

OZZY OSBOU
Borders, 10 C
The filt
cr

THE WORD: NEW YORK MAGAZINE Design: Chris Dixon, 2010. *This content-intensive page detail mixes four different type families from various points in history, ranging from the early advertising face Egyptian Bold Condensed to the functional contemporary sans Verlag. These diverse ingredients are mixed here at different scales to create typographic tension and contrast.*

Lining numerals take up uniform widths of space, enabling the numbers to line up when tabulated in columns. They were introduced around the turn of the twentieth century to meet the needs of modern business. Lining numerals are the same height as capital letters, so they sometimes look big and bulky when appearing in running text.

Non-lining numerals, also called *text* or *old style* numerals, have ascenders and descenders, like lowercase letters. Non-lining numerals returned to favor in the 1990s, valued for their idiosyncratic appearance and their traditional typographic attitude. Like letterforms, old style numerals are proportional; each one has its own set width.

LINING NUMERALS

FUTURA BOLD   HELEVETICA NEUE BOLD

NON-LINING NUMERALS

ADOBE GARAMOND PRO   SCALA SANS PRO BOLD

TEXT SET WITH LINING NUMERALS

What is the cost of *War and Peace*? The cover price of the Modern Library Classics paperback edition is $15.00, discounted 32% by Amazon to $10.50. But what about the human cost in terms of hours squandered reading a super-sized work of literary fiction? If you can read 400 words per minute, double the average, it will take you 1,476 minutes (24.6 hours) to read *War and Peace*. Devoting just four hours per day to the task, you could finish the work in a little over six days. If you earn $7.25 per hour (minimum wage in the U.S.), the cost of reading *War and Peace* will be $184.50 (€130.4716, £11.9391, or ¥17676.299).

ADOBE GARAMOND PRO *includes both lining and non-lining numerals, allowing designers to choose a style in response to the circumstances of the project. The lining numerals appear large, because they have the height of capital letters.*

TEXT SET WITH NON-LINING NUMERALS

What is the cost of *War and Peace*? The cover price of the Modern Library Classics paperback edition is $15.00, discounted 32% by Amazon to $10.50. But what about the human cost in terms of hours squandered reading a super-sized work of literary fiction? If you can read 400 words per minute, double the average, it will take you 1,476 minutes (24.6 hours) to read *War and Peace*. Devoting just four hours per day to the task, you could finish the work in a little over six days. If you earn $7.25 per hour (minimum wage in the U.S.), the cost of reading *War and Peace* will be $184.50 (€130.4716, £11.9391, or ¥17676.299).

Non-lining numerals integrate visually with the text. Different math and currency symbols are designed to match the different numeral styles. Smaller currency symbols look better with non-lining numerals.

99.8	32.3	**DOM** DomCasual	...	26	7451	57.0	-
73.8	16.1	**EGIZ** Egiziano	...	dd	2789	61.6	+
32.7	18.5	**EURO** Eurostile	...	9	1449	99.5	-
69.6	59.4	**FKTR** FetteFraktur	...	dd	3944	87.0	+
66.8	2.8	**FRNK** FrnklinGthc	...	dd	11712	48.8	+
17	7	**FRUT** Frutiger55	...		1814	34.5	-
35.8	15	**FUTU** FuturaBook	...	18	11325	20.5	+
52.3	10.1	**GDY** GoudyOldStyl	...	dd	2685	46.5	-
95.3	26.8	**GILL** GillSans	...	dd	10748	72.3	+
96.2	35.4	**GLRD** Galliard	...	26	1566	1.1	-
72.7	9.6	**GMND** Garamond	...	27	2376	62.3	-
102.3	20.7	**GROT** Grotesque9	...	47	6147	8.0	-
87.8	19.1	**HLV** Helvetica	...	dd	3009	63.3	+
79.3	35.6	**HOBO** Hobo	...	dd	5981	25.2	-
97.3	56.9	**HTXT** HoeflerText	.5e 1.3 dd	4548	93.7	+
85.1	11.4	**INTR** Interstate	.32 2.1 dd	10127	19.3	+
72.7	59.1	**JNSN** Janson	...	17	8065	63.2	+
84.8	68.7	**KIS** KisJanson	...	dd	4641	80.9	+
65	7.9	**KSMK** FFKosmik	...	20	510	26.3	+
35.9	8.9	**LTHS** LithosBlack	...		1669	39.8	+
104.7	1.5	**LtrG** LetterGothic	...	dd	8091	20.6	+

HLV Helvetica			...	dd	3009	63.3	+0.35
HOBO Hobo			...	dd	5981	25.2	+0.79
HTXT HoeflerText	.5e	1.3	dd	4548	93.7	+0.99
INTR Interstate	.32	2.1	dd	10127	19.3	+1.86
JNSN Janson			...	17	8065	63.2	+1.11
KIS KisJanson			...	dd	4641	80.9	-0.29
KSMK FFKosmik			...	20	510	26.3	+0.92

123

RETINA, *designed by Tobias Frere-Jones, 2000, was created for the extreme typographic conditions of the Wall Street Journal's financial pages. The numerals are designed to line up into columns. The different weights of Retina have matching set widths, allowing the newspaper to mix weights while maintaining perfectly aligned columns. The notched forms (called ink traps) prevent ink from filling in the letterforms when printed at tiny sizes.*

MONTHLY CALENDAR, 1892
The charming numerals in this calendar don't line up into neat columns, because they have varied set widths. They would not be suitable for setting modern financial data.

{["'',.;:"']}

{[""",.;:""]}

COMMONLY ABUSED PUNCTUATION MARKS

5'2" eyes of blue

PRIME OR HATCH MARKS INDICATE INCHES AND FEET

It's a dog's life.

APOSTROPHES SIGNAL CONTRACTION
OR POSSESSION

He said, "That's what she said."

QUOTATION MARKS SET OFF DIALOGUE

A well-designed comma carries the essence of the typeface down to its delicious details. Helvetica's comma is a chunky square mounted to a jaunty curve, while Bodoni's is a voluptuous, thin-stemmed orb. Designers and editors need to learn various typographic conventions in addition to mastering the grammatical rules of punctuation. A pandemic error is the use of straight prime or hatch marks (often called *dumb quotes*) in place of apostrophes and quotation marks (also known as *curly quotes, typographer's quotes,* or *smart quotes*). Double and single quotation marks are represented with four distinct characters, each accessed with a different keystroke combination. Know thy keystrokes! It usually falls to the designer to purge the client's manuscript of spurious punctuation.

"The thoughtless overuse" of quotation marks is a disgrace upon literary style—and on typographic style as well.

TYPE CRIME
Quotation marks carve out chunks of white space from the edge of the text.

"Hanging punctuation" prevents quotations and other marks from taking a bite out of the crisp left edge of a text block.

HANGING QUOTATION MARKS
Make a clean edge by pushing the quotation marks into the margin.

NERD ALERT: To create hanging punctuation in InDesign, insert a word space before the quotation mark. Pressing the option key, use the left arrow key to back the quotation mark into the margin. You can also use the Optical Margin Alignment or Indent to Here tools.

See APPENDIX for more punctuation blunders.

TYPE CRIMES

NEW YORK CITY TOUR

City streets have become a dangerous place. Millions of dollars a year are spent producing commercial signs that are fraught with typographic misdoings. While some of these signs are cheaply made over-the-counter products, others were designed for prominent businesses and institutions. There is no excuse for such gross negligence.

GETTIN' IT RIGHT

Apostrophes and quotation marks are sometimes called curly quotes. Here, you can enjoy them in a meat-free environment.

GETTIN' IT WRONG

The correct use of hatch marks is to indicate inches and feet. Alas, this pizza is the hapless victim of a misplaced keystroke. In InDesign or Illustrator, use the Glyphs palette to find hatch marks when you need them.

Not all typographic elements represent language. For centuries, ornaments have been designed to integrate directly with text. In the letterpress era, printers assembled decorative elements one by one to build larger forms and patterns on the page. Decorative rules served to frame and divide content. In the nineteenth century, printers provided their customers with vast collections of readymade illustrations that could easily be mixed with text. Today, numerous forms of ornament are available as digital fonts, which can be typed on a keyboard, scaled, and output like any typeface. Some contemporary ornaments are modular systems designed to combine into larger patterns and configurations, allowing the graphic designer to invent new arrangements out of given pieces. Themed collections of icons and illustrations are also available as digital fonts.

TYPOGRAPHIC ORNAMENTS Fry and Steele, London, 1794. Collection of Jan Tholenaar, Reinoud Tholenaar, and Saskia Ottenhoff-Tholenaar.

SPEAKUP, *designed by Supisa Wattanasansanee/Cadson Demak, 2008. Distributed by T26.*

RESTRAINT Ornaments, 2007. Design: Marian Bantjes.

DANCE INK MAGAZINE Design: Abbott Miller, 1996. *The designer repeated a single ornament from the font Whirligigs, designed by Zuzana Licko in 1994, to create an ethereal veil of ink. Whirligigs are modular units that fit together to create an infinite variety of patterns.*

WHIRLIGIGS, *designed by Zuzana Licko, Emigre, 1994.*

GESCHAD. FANTAISIE KAPITALEN

UIT DE

LETTERGIETERIJ VAN JOH. ENSCHEDÉ EN ZONEN TE HAARLEM

Nº 5170. Op 11 Augustijn.

HAARLEM

Nº 5168. Op 11 Augustijn.

ITALIE

Nº 5081. Op 102 Punten.

GRAFT

Nº 5040. Op 10½ Augustijn.

MARS

Dl. V. Bl. 123.

FANTAISIE KAPITALEN Type specimen, 1897. Design: Joh.
Enchedé & Zohnen. Collection of Jan Tholenaar, Reinoud
Tholenaar, and Saskia Ottenhoff-Tholenaar.

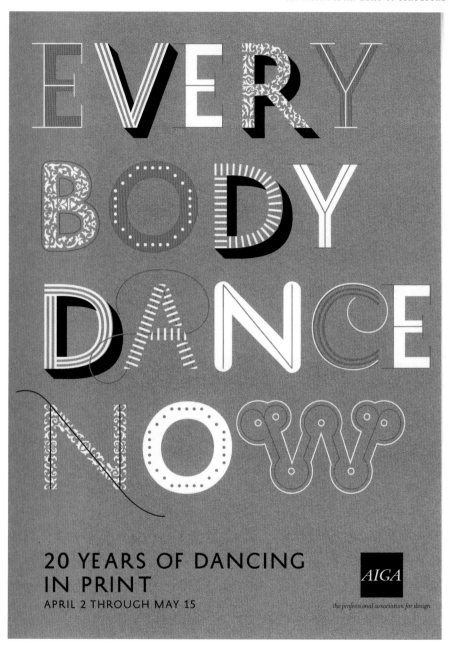

EVERYBODY DANCE NOW Postcard, 2009. Design: Abbott
Miller, Kristen Spilman, Jeremy Hoffman/Pentagram. *Peter
Bilak's typeface History, designed in 2008, consists of numerous
decorative and structural elements that can be layered into
distinctive combinations.*

Creating letters by hand allows graphic artists to integrate imagery and text, making design and illustration into fluidly integrated practices. Lettering can emulate existing typefaces or derive from the artist's own drawing or writing style. Designers create lettering by hand and with software, often combining diverse techniques.

TOKION MAGAZINE: KINGS
Designer: Deanne Cheuk,
2002–2003. *These magazine
headlines combine drawing and
painting with digital techniques.*

THE LOCUST (LEFT) and MELT BANANA (RIGHT) Screenprint posters, 2002. Designer: Nolen Strals. *Hand lettering is a vibrant force in graphic design, as seen in these music posters. Lettering is the basis of many digital typefaces, but nothing is quite as potent as the real thing.*

A *logotype* uses typography or lettering to depict the name or initials of an organization in a memorable way. Whereas some trademarks consist of an abstract symbol or a pictorial icon, a logotype uses words and letters to create a distinctive visual image. Logotypes can be built with existing typefaces or with custom-drawn letterforms. A logotype is part of an overall visual brand, which the designer conceives as a "language" that lives (and changes) in various circumstances. A complete visual identity can consist of colors, patterns, icons, signage components, and a selection of typefaces. Sometimes a logotype becomes the basis for the design of a complete typeface. Many type designers collaborate with graphic designers to create typefaces that are unique to a given client.

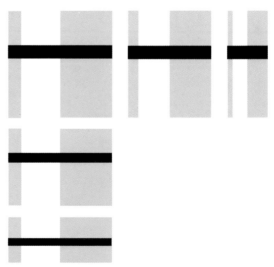

HÜBNER Identity program, 1998. Design: Jochen Stankowski. *This identity for an engineering firm is built around the H, whose proportions change in different contexts.*

STADSSCHOUWBURG UTRECHT

UTRECHT CITY THEATER
Identity, 2009. Design: Edenspiekermann.
This ambitious visual identity program uses custom letterforms based on the typeface Agenda. The letters in the custom typeface are designed to split apart into elements that can be mirrored, layered, flipped, and animated for a variety of applications, including signage, posters, printed matter, and web communications.

el banco de uno Visual branding, 2007. Agency: Saffron.
Identity design: Joshua Distler, Mike Abbink, Gabor Schreier,
Virginia Sardón. Custom typeface design: Mike Abbink, Paul van
der Laan. *This elaborate identity program for a Mexican bank uses
a custom typeface whose blocky forms are inspired by Mayan glyphs.*

ABCDEFGHIJKLMNOPQRSTUVWXYZ
abcdefghijklmnopqrstuvwxyz
0123456789

ABCDEFGHIJKLMNOPQRSTUVWXYZ
abcdefghijklmnopqrstuvwxyz
0123456789

NEW FRENCH BAKERY Visual branding, 2009. Design: Duffy & Partners. *A logotype is part of a larger graphic language. Duffy & Partners develop logotypes in concert with a rich range of elements, including colors, patterns, and typefaces. The designers use techniques such as outlining, layering, and framing to create depth, detail, and the sense of a human touch. These elements work together to express the personality of the brand.*

During the early years of the World Wide Web, designers were forced to work within the narrow range of typefaces commonly installed on the computers of their end users. Since then, several techniques have emerged for embedding fonts within web content or for delivering fonts to end users when they visit a site. In one approach, specially formatted fonts are hosted on a third-party server and then downloaded by users; designers pay a fee for the service. Another approach implements the `@font-face` rule in CSS, which can download any kind of digital font hosted on a server; only typefaces licensed for this use can be accessed legally via `@font-face`.

WEB FONTS 1.0

Verdana was designed by the legendary typographer *Matthew Carter* in 1996 for digital display. Verdana has a large x-height, simple curves, open forms, and loose spacing.

Georgia is a serif screen face built with sturdy strokes, simple curves, open counters, and generous spacing. Designed by Matthew Carter in 1996 for Microsoft, Georgia is widely used on the web.

VERDANA AND GEORGIA, *released in 1996 by Microsoft, were designed specifically for the web. Prior to the rise of font embedding, these were among a handful of typefaces that could be relilably used online.*

FONT EMBEDDING Screen shot, detail, 2009. Typefaces: Greta and Fedra, designed by Peter Bilak/Typotheque. *In 2009, the digital type foundry Typotheque launched a pioneering service that allows designers to display Typotheque fonts on any website in exchange for a one-time license fee. Typotheque's Open Type fonts, which support global languages including Arabic and Hindi, are hosted by Typotheque and accessed using the CSS* `@font-face` *rule.*

BOBULATE Website, 2009. Designed by Jason Santa Maria for Liz Danzico. Typeface: Skolar, designed by David Brezina/Typetogether. *This site design uses Typekit, a third-party service that delivers fonts to end users when they visit a site. Typekit deters piracy by obscuring the origins of the font. Designers or site owners pay a subscription fee to the service.*

Anti-aliasing creates the appearance of smooth curves on screen by changing the brightness of the pixels or sub-pixels along the edges of each letterform. Photoshop and other software packages allow designers to select strong or weak anti-aliasing. When displayed at very small sizes, strongly anti-aliased type can look blurry. It also increases the number of colors in an image file.

ANTI-ALIASED LETTER   BITMAPPED LETTER

smooth <small>smooth</small>

ANTI-ALIASED TYPE: SMOOTH SETTING *(simulated screen capture)*

none <small>none</small>

ANTI-ALIASING DISABLED: NONE SETTING *(simulated screen capture)*

LETTERSCAPES Website, 2002. Design: Peter Cho. *Simple bitmapped letters are animated in three-dimensional space.*

Bitmap typefaces are built out of the *pixels* (picture elements) that structure a screen display or other output device. While a PostScript letter consists of a vector outline, a true bitmap character contains a fixed number of rectilinear units that are displayed either on or off. True bitmap characters are used on devices such as cash registers, signboard displays, and various small-scale screens.

Most contemporary bitmap typefaces are not true bitmaps. They are drawn as outlines on a grid and then output as PostScript, TrueType, or OpenType fonts. Thus they can be easily used with any standard layout software. Many designers like to exploit the visible geometry of pixelated characters.

LoResNine | LoResNine

LoResTwelve | LoResTwelve

LoResFifteen | LoResFifteen

LoResTwentyEight | LoResTwentyEight

Set at size of root resolution (9, 12, 15, and 28 pts) | *All set at 28 pts*

LO-RES NARROW, *designed by Zuzana Licko, Emigre. Released in 2001, the Lo-Res type family is a collection of outline (PostScript) fonts based on bitmap designs created by Licko in 1985. Lo-Res Narrow consists of a series of different sizes, each one constructed with a one-pixel stroke weight. Thus Lo-ResTwentyEight Narrow has dramatically lighter and tighter forms than Lo-ResNine Narrow, which gets blockier as it is enlarged. Designed for display on screen at low resolutions, a bitmap font should be used at its root size or at integer multiples of that size. (Enlarge 9-pixel type to 18, 27, 36, and so on).*

```
   B:OEKHANDEL NIJHOF & LEE
       STAALSTRAAT 13-A
     1011 JK AMSTERDAM


  22/05/03 13:12          01
  000000 #0094     BED.1

  VERZENDKOST.         42.50
  TYPOGRAFIE            6.00
  TYPOGRAFIE           16.50
  TYPOGRAFIE           19.50
  TYPOGRAFIE           33.95
  TYPOGRAFIE           55.35
  TYPOGRAFIE           32.00
  TYPOGRAFIE           59.00
  TYPOGRAFIE           40.00
  TYPOGRAFIE           50.40
  TYPOGRAFIE           47.25
  TYPOGRAFIE           80.00
  TYPOGRAFIE           37.70
  SUBTOTAL            520.15
  BTW LAAG             29.44

  STUKS                  13Q
  CREDIT          520.15

     ODK ANTIQUARIAAT
     TEL:020-6203980
     FAX:020-6393294
```

NIJHOF & LEE Receipt, 2003. *This cash register receipt, printed with a bitmap font, is from a design and typography bookstore in Amsterdam.*

ELEMENTAR, *designed by Gustavo Ferreira in 2009 and distributed by Typotheque. Elementar is a bitmap type family consisting of dozens of weights and styles made by manipulating common parameters such as height, width, and the degree of contrast between horizontal and vertical elements. Elementar is suitable for print, screen, and interfaces. It is inspired by Adrian Frutiger's Univers type family.*

Fontlab and other applications allow designers to create functional fonts that work seamlessly with standard software programs such as InDesign and Photoshop.

The first step in designing a typeface is to define a basic concept. Will the letters be serif or sans serif? Will they be modular or organic? Will you construct them geometrically or base them on handwriting? Will you use them for display or for text? Will you work with historic source material or invent the characters more or less from scratch?

The next step is to create drawings. Some designers start with pencil before working digitally, while others build their letterforms directly with font design software. Begin by drawing a few core letters, such as *o*, *u*, *h*, and *n*, building curves, lines, and shapes that will reappear throughout the font. All the letters in a typeface are distinct from each other, yet they share many attributes, such as x-height, line weight, stress, and a common vocabulary of forms and proportions.

You can control the spacing of the typeface by adding blank areas next to each character as well as creating kerning pairs that determine the distance between particular characters. Producing a complete typeface is an enormous task. However, for people with a knack for drawing letterforms, the process is hugely rewarding.

Castaways

CASTAWAYS Drawing and finished type, 2001. Art and type direction: Andy Cruz. Typeface design: Ken Barber/House Industries. Font engineering: Rich Roat. *House Industries is a digital type foundry that creates original typefaces inspired by popular culture and design history. Designer Ken Barber makes pencil drawings by hand and then digitizes the outlines. Castaways is from a series of typefaces based on commercial signs from Las Vegas. The shapes of the letters recall the handpainted strokes made by traditional sign painters and lettering artists.*

MERCURY BOLD Page proof and screen shot, 2003. Design: Jonathan Hoefler/Hoefler & Frere-Jones. *Mercury is a typeface designed for modern newspapers, whose production demands fast, high-volume printing on cheap paper. The typeface's bullet-proof letterforms feature chunky serifs and sturdy upright strokes. The notes marked on the proof below comment on everything from the width or weight of a letter to the size and shape of a serif. Many such proofs are made during the design process. In a digital typeface, each letterform consists of a series of curves and lines controlled by points. In a large type family, different weights and widths can be made automatically by interpolating between extremes such as light and heavy or narrow and wide. The designer then adjusts each variant to ensure legibility and visual consistency.*

Create a prototype for a bitmap typeface by designing letters on a grid of squares or a grid of dots. Substitute the curves and diagonals of traditional letterforms with gridded and rectilinear elements. Avoid making detailed "staircases," which are just curves and diagonals in disguise. This exercise looks back to the 1910s and 1920s, when avant-garde designers made experimental typefaces out of simple geometric parts. The project also speaks to the structure of digital technologies, from cash register receipts and LED signs to on-screen font display, showing that a typeface is a system of elements.

Wendy Neese

Brendon McClean

Bruce Willen

James Alvarez

Examples of student work from Maryland Institute College of Art

Joey Potts

READ
Becky Slogeris

PUSH
Bryan Connor

Look
Virginia Sasser

SPAM
Julia Kim

copy
Michelle Ghiotti

Where do fonts come from, and why are there so many different formats? Some come loaded with your computer's operating system, while others are bundled with software packages. A few of these widely distributed typefaces are of the highest quality, such as Adobe Garamond Pro and **Hoefler Text**, while others (including **Comic Sans**, *Apple Chancery*, and Papyrus) are reviled by design snobs everywhere.

If you want to expand your vocabulary beyond this familiar fare, you will need to purchase fonts from digital type foundries. These range from large establishments like Adobe and FontShop, which license thousands of different typefaces, to independent producers that distribute just a few, such as Underware in the Netherlands or Jeremy Tankard Typography in the U.K. You can also learn to make your own fonts as well as find fonts that are distributed for free online.

The different font formats reflect technical innovations and business arrangements developed over time. Older font formats are still generally usable on modern operating systems.

POSTSCRIPT/TYPE 1 was developed for desktop computer systems in the 1980s by Adobe. Type 1 fonts are output using the PostScript programming language, created for generating high-resolution images on paper or film. A Type 1 font consists of two files: a screen font and a printer font. You must install both files in order to fully use these fonts.

TRUETYPE is a later font format, created by Apple and Microsoft for use with their operating systems. TrueType fonts are easier to install than Type 1 fonts because they consist of a single font file rather than two.

OPENTYPE, a format developed by Adobe, works on multiple platforms. Each file supports up to 65,000 characters, allowing multiple styles and character variations to be contained in a single font file. In a TrueType or Type 1 font, small capitals, alternate ligatures, and other special characters must be contained in separate font files (sometimes labelled "Expert"); in an OpenType font they are part of the main font. These expanded character sets can also include accented letters and other special glyphs needed for typesetting a variety of languages. OpenType fonts with expanded character sets are commonly labeled "Pro." OpenType fonts also automatically adjust the position of hyphens, brackets, and parentheses for letters set in all-capitals.

{[(HALF-BAKED?)]}

SCALA, *PostScript/Type 1 font format*

{[(HALF-BAKED?)]}

SCALA PRO, *OpenType font format*

£ § ¥ ¼ ½ ¾ É Ë Ì Å
Ã Â Á Ý ø å ë ð ñ ò þ
ÿ Ą ą ě ę ġ ġ dž z ž ž
ő Ġ Ġ į į ĭ † ‡ ☞ ☜

SCALA PRO, *OpenType font, designed by Martin Majoor, 2005. Scala Pro has numerous special characters for typesetting diverse European languages. You can access these characters using the Glyphs palette in InDesign.*

SMALL CAPS AND OLD-STYLE NUMERALS, WHERE ARE YOU HIDING?

NERD ALERT: Access small caps and numerals quickly through the Type>OpenType options menu or other OpenType layout tool in your design software. Small caps will not appear as a style variant in the Font menu, because OpenType treats them as part of the main font. With any font, you can view all the special characters through the Type and Tables>Glyphs menu. You will find many unexpected elements, including swashes, ligatures, ornaments, fractions, and more. Double click a glyph to insert it into to your text frame.

SAVE YOURSELF SOME EMBARRASSMENT
AND LEARN TO USE THESE COMMONLY
ABUSED TERMS CORRECTLY.

typeface or font?

A *typeface* is the design of the letterforms; a *font* is the delivery mechanism. In metal type, the design is embodied in the punches from which molds are made. A font consists of the cast metal printing types. In digital systems, the typeface is the visual design, while the font is the software that allows you to install, access, and output the design. A single typeface might be available in several font formats. In part because the design of digital typefaces and the production of fonts are so fluidly linked today, most people use the terms interchangeably. Type nerds insist, however, on using them precisely.

character or glyph?

Type designers distinguish *characters* from *glyphs* in order to comply with Unicode, an international system for identifying all of the world's recognized writing systems. Only a symbol with a unique function is considered a character and is thus assigned a code point in Unicode. A single character, such as a lowercase *a*, can be embodied by several different glyphs (a, *a*, ᴀ). Each glyph is a specific expression of a given character.

Roman or roman?

The Roman Empire is a proper noun and thus is capitalized, but we identify roman letterforms, like italic ones, in lowercase. The name of the Latin alphabet is capitalized.

Who is the user of a typeface? In the end, the user is the reader. But before a set of letters can find their way onto the cover of a book or the back of a cereal box, they must pass through the hands of another user: the graphic designer.

Digital fonts are easy to copy, alter, and distribute, but when you purchase a font, you accept an *end user license agreement* (EULA) that limits how you can use it. Intellectual property law in the United States protects the font as a piece of software (a unique set of vector points), but it does not protect the visual design of the typeface. Thus it is a violation of standard EULAs to copy a digital font and share it with other people (your friends, your clients, or your Uncle Bob). It is also illegal to open a font file in FontLab, add new glyphs or alter some of its characters, and save the font under a new name or under its trademarked name. In additon to having economic concerns, typeface designers worry about their work being corrupted as users edit their fonts and then share them with other people.

Most EULAs do allow you to alter the outlines of a font for use in a logo or headline, however, as long as you do not alter the software itself. It is also legal to create new digital versions of printed type specimens. For example, you could print out an alphabet in Helvetica, redraw the letters, digitize them with font design software, and release your own bespoke edition of Helvetica. If nothing else, this laborious exercise would teach you the value of a well-designed typeface. A broadly usable typeface includes numerous weights, styles, and special characters as well as a strong underlying design. Fonts are expensive because they are carefully crafted products.

FREE FONTS

Most of the FREE FONTS found on the Internet have poor spacing and incomplete character sets. Many are *stolen property* distributed without CONSENT. The fonts displayed here, however, are freely given by their creators. A typeface comes to life and finds a voice as people begin to use it.

FONTIN, *designed by Jos Buivenga/Ex Ljbris, 2004*

DESIGNERS have long sought to CONTROL the behavior of users, clients, manufacturers, retailers, and the press. How will a work be interpreted? Will it survive over time in its DESIRED STATE of completion? An architect succeeds when the occupants of his house behave ACCORDING TO PLAN. The rise of online tools has challenged designers' sense of CONTROL in every discipline: the user has become a designer.

AUDIMAT, *designed by Jack Usine/SMeltery.net, 2003*

Some fonts are *distributed freely* in order to preserve UNFAMILIAR traditions. Disseminating a historic revival at no cost to users encourages a broader understanding of history. Reviving typefaces is a DEEP-ROOTED practice. Why should one creator *claim ownership* of another's work? Who controls the past?

ANTYKWA POLTAWSKIEGO, *designed by Adam Półtawski, 1920s–1930s; digitized by Janusz Marian Nowacki, 1996*

SOME FREE FONTS are produced for *underserved linguistic communities* for whom few typefaces are available. Still others are created by people who want to participate in the *open source movement*. The OFL (Open Font License) permits users to alter a typeface and contribute to its ongoing evolution.

GENTIUM *Open Font License, designed by Victor Gaultney, 2001*

TO PARTICIPATE IN a viable, diverse *ecology of content* (journalism, design, art, typography, and more), *everyone has to pay*. BUT PERHAPS everyone shouldn't have to *pay for everything*. If some resources are willingly given away, the result is a RICHER WORLD.

OFL SORTS MILL GOUDY, *revival of Frederic W. Goudy's Goudy Old Style, 1916, designed by Barry Schwartz, 2010; distributed by the League of Moveable Type*

EVERY OBJECT IN THE WORLD CAN PASS FROM A

LEAGUE GOTHIC, *designed by the League of Moveable Type, 2009; revival of Morris Fuller Benton's*

CLOSED, SILENT EXISTENCE TO AN ORAL STATE,

ALTERNATE GOTHIC NO.1., *released by American Type Founders Company (ATF) in 1903.*

OPEN TO APPROPRIATION BY SOCIETY, FOR THERE

DOWNCOME, *designed by Eduardo Recife/ Misprinted Type, 2002*

IS NO LAW, WHETHER NATURAL OR NOT, WHICH

FORBIDS TALKING ABOUT THINGS. A TREE IS A

SHORTCUT, *designed by Eduardo Recife, 2003*

TREE. YES, OF COURSE. BUT A TREE AS EXPRESSED BY

Minou Drouet was a French child poet and composer widely derided by intellectuals in the 1950s.

MINOU DROUET IS NO LONGER QUITE A TREE, IT IS A

DIRTY EGO, *designed by Eduardo Recife, 2001*

TREE WHICH IS DECORATED, ADAPTED TO A CERTAIN

TYPE OF CONSUMPTION, LADEN WITH LITERARY SELF-

MISPROJECT, *designed by Eduardo Recife, 2001*

INDULGENCE, REVOLT, IMAGES, IN SHORT WITH A TYPE

OF SOCIAL USAGE WHICH IS ADDED TO PURE MATTER.

TEXT: *Roland Barthes, "Myth Today," 1957; translated by Annette Lavers.*

{TEXT}

CYBERSPACE AND CIVIL
SOCIETY Poster, 1996.
Designer: Hayes Henderson.
*Rather than represent
cyberspace as an ethereal grid,
the designer has used blotches
of overlapping text to build an
ominous, looming body.*

TEXT

LETTERS GATHER INTO WORDS, WORDS BUILD INTO SENTENCES. In typography, "text" is defined as an ongoing sequence of words, distinct from shorter headlines or captions. The main block is often called the "body," comprising the principal mass of content. Also known as "running text," it can flow from one page, column, or box to another. Text can be viewed as a thing—a sound and sturdy object—or a fluid poured into the containers of page or screen. Text can be solid or liquid, body or blood.

As body, text has more integrity and wholeness than the elements that surround it, from pictures, captions, and page numbers to banners, buttons, and menus. Designers generally treat a body of text consistently, letting it appear as a coherent substance that is distributed across the spaces of a document. In digital media, long texts are typically broken into chunks that can be accessed by search engines or hypertext links. Contemporary designers and writers produce content for various contexts, from the pages of print to an array of software environments, screen conditions, and digital devices, each posing its own limits and opportunities.

Designers provide ways into—and out of—the flood of words by breaking up text into pieces and offering shortcuts and alternate routes through masses of information. From a simple indent (signaling the entrance to a new idea) to a highlighted link (announcing a jump to another location), typography helps readers navigate the flow of content. The user could be searching for a specific piece of data or struggling to quickly process a volume of content in order to extract elements for immediate use. Although many books define the purpose of typography as enhancing the readability of the written word, one of design's most humane functions is, in actuality, to help readers *avoid* reading.

PSALTER-HOURS English
manuscript, thirteenth
century. Walters Ms. W.102,
fol. 33v. Collection of the
Walters Art Museum,
Baltimore. *The monk is
climbing up the side of the page
to replace a piece of faulty text
with the corrected line in the
bottom margin.*

ERRORS AND OWNERSHIP

Typography helped seal the literary notion of "the text" as a complete, original work, a stable body of ideas expressed in an essential form. Before the invention of printing, handwritten documents were riddled with errors. Copies were copied from copies, each with its own glitches and gaps. Scribes devised inventive ways to insert missing lines into manuscripts in order to salvage and repair these laboriously crafted objects.

Printing with movable type was the first system of mass production, replacing the hand-copied manuscript. As in other forms of mass production, the cost of manufacturing (setting type, insuring its correctness, and running a press) drops for each unit as the size of the print run increases. Labor and capital are invested in tooling and preparing the technology, rather than in making the individual unit. The printing system allows editors and authors to correct a work as it passes from handwritten manuscript to typographic galley. "Proofs" are test copies made before final production begins. The proofreader's craft ensures the faithfulness of the printed text to the author's handwritten original.

Yet even the text that has passed through the castle gates of print is inconstant. Each edition of a book represents one fossil record of a text, a record that changes every time the work is translated, quoted, revised, interpreted, or taught. Since the rise of digital tools for writing and publishing, manuscript originals have all but vanished. ~~Electronic redlining is replacing the hieroglyphics of the editor.~~ Online texts can be downloaded by users and reformatted, repurposed, and recombined.

Print helped establish the figure of the author as the owner of a text, and copyright laws were written in the early eighteenth century to protect the author's rights to this property. The digital age is riven by battles between those who argue, on the one hand, for the fundamental liberty of data and ideas, and those who hope to protect—sometimes indefinitely—the investment made in publishing and authoring content.

A classic typographic page emphasizes the completeness and closure of a work, its authority as a finished product. Alternative design strategies in the twentieth and twenty-first centuries reflect the contested nature of authorship by revealing the openness of texts to the flow of information and the corrosiveness of history.

Marshall McLuhan, *The Gutenberg Galaxy* (Toronto: University of Toronto Press, 1962).

On the future of intellectual property, see Lawrence Lessig, *Free Culture: How Big Media Uses Technology and the Law to Lock Down Culture and Control Creativity* (New York: Penguin, 2004).

Typography tended to alter language from a means of perception and exploration to a portable commodity. —MARSHALL MCLUHAN, 1962

On the Way to Language

"How indeed could I aim my argument at some singular destination, at one or another among you whose proper name I might know? And then, is knowing a proper name tantamount to knowing someone?" (MC, 2). Derrida demonstrates for his part that the most general structure of the mark participates in a speech destined in advance to addressees (destinataires) who are not easily determinable or who, as far as any possible calculation is concerned, in any case command a great reserve of indetermination. This involves a language operating as a system of marks: "Language, however, is only one among those systems of marks that claim this curious tendency as their property: they simultaneously incline towards increasing the reserves of random indetermination as well as the capacity for coding and overcoding or, in other words, for control and self-regulation" (MC, 2). We begin to discern how the simultaneity of determining, coding, and even supercoding forms a deep cooperation with the inclination in language toward anticoding, or what Derrida sees as the inflated reserves of random indeterminateness. This double-edged coding, we must remember, regards, as it were, nonschizophrenic language, if such a thing there be. "Such competition between randomness and code disrupts the very systematicity of the system while it also, however, regulates the restless, unstable interplay of the system. Whatever its singularity in this respect, the linguistic system of these traces or marks would merely be, it seems to me, just a particular example of the law of destabilization" (MC, 2). It may be useful to note that Derrida understands language in terms primarily of traces and marks, where Lainguage concerns signs in the first place, and in particular the broken rapport of that which is signifying to what ostensibly lies hidden behind it, or the disconnection between signs and signs or signs and referents. Laing is led to assume the latency of a single, unique, localizable but timid presence—rather than trace or residual mark—from where it could be securely determined who speaks, and to whom. This all too brief excursion into "My Chances," which may unwittingly reproduce the effect and trauma of a chance encounter, means to engage a dialogue between the question of address raised by Laing and the ones raised in turn by Derrida. For it now appears that Laing places his bets on the sustained systematicity of the system which Derrida shows always already to fall under a law of destabilization.[89] Moreover, Derrida does not suggest lan-

guage to be some e
seems to want to e
translation of signs
light of an audiovis
been saying as som
make contact with
stract or terrorizin
touch. In fact Derr
that I throw, eject,
come across to you
and Laing had thin
part, that, thrown
whose destination
the case with their
muteness was relate
guage were armed
release-controls the
structurally mainta
ratus. The Other in
fully retrievable or
is there to be given,
agement begins with
or alive, traversing y
fort slashing into the
as self or Other ma
telephone to raise th
the telephone speaks,
sound waves: "'she'
tem as though it was
be hallucinated" (DS,
"Anything she wanted,
one time. Reality did
or fear. Every wish
and every dread like
tom way. Thus she
203). He reads her
The case history ne
weed garden. Is the
taneity of omnipre

THE TELEPHONE BOOK:
TECHNOLOGY, SCHIZO-
PHRENIA, ELECTRIC SPEECH
Book, 1989. Designer:
Richard Eckersley. Author:
Avital Ronell. Compositor:
Michael Jensen. Publisher:
University of Nebraska Press.
Photograph: Dan Meyers.
*This book, a philosophical study
of writing as a material
technology, uses typography
to emphasize the rhetorical
argument of the text. This
spread, for example, is fractured
by typographic "rivers," spaces
that connect vertically through
the page. Rivers violate the
even, unified texture that is a
sacred goal within traditional
typographic design.*

SPACING

Design is as much an act of spacing as an act of marking. The typographer's art concerns not only the positive grain of letterforms, but the negative gaps between and around them. In letterpress printing, every space is constructed by a physical object, a blank piece of metal or wood with no raised image. The faceless slugs of lead and slivers of copper inserted as spaces between words or letters are as physical as the relief characters around them. Thin strips of lead (called "leading") divide the horizontal lines of type; wider blocks of "furniture" hold the margins of the page.

Although we take the breaks between words for granted, spoken language is perceived as a continuous flow, with no audible gaps. Spacing has become crucial, however, to alphabetic writing, which translates the sounds of speech into multiple characters. Spaces were introduced after the invention of the Greek alphabet to make words intelligible as distinct units. Tryreadingalineoftextwithoutspacingtoseehowimportantithasbecome.

With the invention of typography, spacing and punctuation ossified from gap and gesture to physical artifact. Punctuation marks, which were used differently from one scribe to another in the manuscript era, became part of the standardized, rule-bound apparatus of the printed page. The communications scholar Walter Ong has shown how printing converted the word into a visual object precisely located in space: "Alphabet letterpress printing, in which each letter was cast on a separate piece of metal, or type, marked a psychological breakthrough of the first order.…Print situates words in space more relentlessly than writing ever did. Writing moves words from the sound world to the world of visual space, but print locks words into position in this space." Typography made text into a thing, a material object with known dimensions and fixed locations.

Walter Ong, *Orality and Literacy: The Technologizing of the Word* (London and New York: Methuen, 1981). See also Jacques Derrida, *Of Grammatology*, trans. Gayatri Chakravorty Spivak (Baltimore: Johns Hopkins University Press, 1976).

The French philosopher Jacques Derrida, who devised the theory of deconstruction in the 1960s, wrote that although the alphabet represents sound, it cannot function without silent marks and spaces. Typography manipulates the silent dimensions of the alphabet, employing habits and techniques—such as spacing and punctuation—that are seen but not heard. The Latin alphabet, rather than evolve into a transparent code for recording speech, developed its own visual resources, becoming a more powerful technology as it left behind its connections to the spoken word.

That a speech supposedly alive can lend itself to spacing in its own writing is what relates to its own death. —JACQUES DERRIDA, 1976

LINEARITY

In his essay "From Work to Text," the French critic Roland Barthes presented two opposing models of writing: the closed, fixed "work" versus the open, unstable "text." In Barthes's view, the work is a tidy, neatly packaged object, proofread and copyrighted, made perfect and complete by the art of printing. The text, in contrast, is impossible to contain, operating across a dispersed web of standard plots and received ideas. Barthes pictured the text as "woven entirely with citations, references, echoes, cultural languages (what language is not?), antecedent and contemporary, which cut across and through in a vast stereophony....The metaphor of the Text is that of the *network*." Writing in the 1960s and 1970s, Barthes anticipated the Internet as a decentralized web of connections.

Roland Barthes, "From Work to Text," in *Image/Music/Text,* trans. Stephen Heath (New York: Hill and Wang, 1977), 155–64.

Barthes was describing literature, yet his ideas resonate for typography, the visual manifestation of language. The singular body of the traditional text page has long been supported by the navigational features of the book, from page numbers and headings that mark a reader's location to such tools as the index, appendix, abstract, footnote, and table of contents. These devices were able to emerge because the typographic book is a fixed sequence of pages, a body lodged in a grid of known coordinates.

All such devices are attacks on linearity, providing means of entrance and escape from the one-way stream of discourse. Whereas talking flows in a single direction, writing occupies space as well as time. Tapping that spatial dimension—and thus liberating readers from the bonds of linearity—is among typography's most urgent tasks.

Although digital media are commonly celebrated for their potential as nonlinear potential communication, linearity nonetheless thrives in the electronic realm, from the "CNN crawl" that marches along the bottom of the television screen to the ticker-style LED signs that loop through the urban environment. Film titles—the celebrated convergence of typography and cinema—serve to distract the audience from the inescapable tedium of a contractually decreed, top-down disclosure of ownership and authorship. Basic electronic book readers, such as Amazon's Kindle (2007), provide a highly sequential, predominantly linear experience; flipping back or skipping ahead is more cumbersome in some electronic books than in paper ones.

Linearity dominates many commercial software applications. Word processing programs, for example, treat documents as a linear stream.

A text...is a multi-dimensional space in which a variety of writings, none of them original, blend and clash. —ROLAND BARTHES, 1971

On the linearity of word processing, see Nancy Kaplan, "Blake's Problem and Ours: Some Reflections on the Image and the Word," *Readerly/Writerly Texts*, 3.2 (Spring/Summer 1996), 125. On PowerPoint, see Edward R. Tufte, "The Cognitive Style of PowerPoint," (Cheshire, Conn.: Graphics Press, 2003).

(In contrast, page layout programs such as Quark XPress and Adobe InDesign allow users to work spatially, breaking up text into columns and pages that can be anchored and landmarked.) PowerPoint and other presentation software programs are supposed to illuminate the spoken word by guiding the audience through the linear unfolding of an oral address. Typically, however, PowerPoint enforces the one-way flow of speech rather than alleviating it. While a single sheet of paper could provide a map or summary of an oral presentation, a PowerPoint show drags out in time across numerous screens.

Not all digital media favor linear flow over spatial arrangement, however. The database, one of the defining information structures of our time, is a nonlinear form. Providing readers and writers with a simultaneous menu of options, a database is a system of elements that can be arranged in countless sequences. Page layouts are built on the fly from chunks of information, assembled in response to user feedback. The web is pushing authors, editors, and designers to work inventively with new modes of microcontent (page titles, key words, alt tags) that allow data to be searched, indexed, tagged, or otherwise marked for recall.

On the aesthetics of the database, see Lev Manovich, *The Language of New Media* (Cambridge: MIT Press, 2002).

Databases are the structure behind electronic games, magazines, and catalogues, genres that create an information *space* rather than a linear *sequence*. Physical stores and libraries are databases of tangible objects found in the built environment. Media critic Lev Manovich has described language itself as a kind of database, an archive of elements from which people assemble the linear utterances of speech. Many design projects call for the emphasis of space over sequence, system over utterance, simultaneous structure over linear narrative. Contemporary design often combines aspects of architecture, typography, film, wayfinding, branding, and other modes of address. By dramatizing the spatial quality of a project, designers can foster understanding of complex documents or environments.

The history of typography is marked by the increasingly sophisticated use of space. In the digital age, where characters are accessed by keystroke and mouse, not gathered from heavy drawers of manufactured units, space has become more liquid than concrete, and typography has evolved from a stable body of objects to a flexible system of attributes.

Database and narrative are natural enemies. Competing for the same territory of human culture, each claims an exclusive right to make meaning of the world. —LEV MANOVICH, 2002

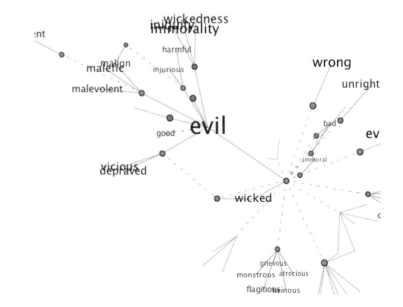

VISUAL THESAURUS 2.0. Interactive media, 2003. Designers: Plumb Design Inc. *This digital thesaurus presents words within a dynamic web of relationships. The central term is linked to nodes representing that word's different senses. The more connections each of these satellite nodes contain, the bigger and closer it appears on the screen. Clicking on a satellite word brings it to the center.*

IMAGE/MUSIC/TEXT
Concordance and text stats
for Roland Barthes's book
Image/Music/Text. Publisher:
Amazon.com, 2010. *Amazon
presents automated analyses
of a book's text in order to
give readers an idea of what is
inside. The concordance feature
lists the book's one hundred
most commonly used words
in alphabetical order and
sizes them according to their
frequency.*

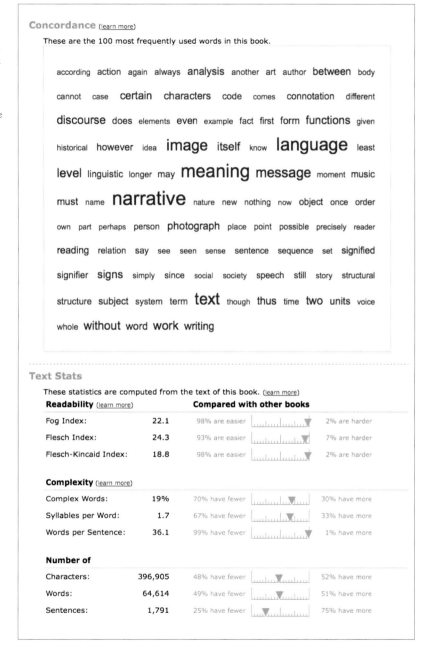

Concordance (learn more)

These are the 100 most frequently used words in this book.

according action again always **analysis** another art author **between** body cannot case **certain** **characters** code comes **connotation** different **discourse** does elements **even** example fact first **form** **functions** given historical **however** idea **image** itself know **language** least **level** linguistic longer may **meaning** **message** moment music **must** name **narrative** nature new nothing now **object** once order own part perhaps person **photograph** place point possible precisely reader **reading** relation say see seen sense **sentence** **sequence** set **signified** **signifier** **signs** simply since social society **speech** still **story** structural **structure** **subject** **system** term **text** though **thus** time **two** units voice whole **without** word **work** writing

Text Stats

These statistics are computed from the text of this book. (learn more)

Readability (learn more)

		Compared with other books	
Fog Index:	22.1	98% are easier	2% are harder
Flesch Index:	24.3	93% are easier	7% are harder
Flesch-Kincaid Index:	18.8	98% are easier	2% are harder

Complexity (learn more)

Complex Words:	19%	70% have fewer	30% have more
Syllables per Word:	1.7	67% have fewer	33% have more
Words per Sentence:	36.1	99% have fewer	1% have more

Number of

Characters:	396,905	48% have fewer	52% have more
Words:	64,614	49% have fewer	51% have more
Sentences:	1,791	25% have fewer	75% have more

Succeeding the Author, the scriptor no longer bears within him
passions, humours, feelings, impressions, but rather this immense
dictionary from which he draws a writing that can know no halt.
—ROLAND BARTHES, 1968

KATHERINE mcCoy
MICHAEL
mcCoy

ART / science

Nothing pulls you into the territory between art and science quite so quickly as design. It is the borderline where contradictions and tensions exist between the quantifiable and the poetic. It is the field between desire and necessity. Designers thrive in those conditions, moving between land and water. A typical critique at Cranbrook can easily move in a matter of minutes between

MATHEMATIC / poetic

a discussion of the object as a validation of being to the precise mechanical proposal for actuating the object. The discussion moves from Heidegger to the "strange material of the week" or from Lyotard to printing technologies without missing a beat. The free flow of ideas, and the leaps from the technical to the mythical, stem from the attempt to maintain a studio plat- form that supports each student's search to

DESIRE / necessity

find his or her own voice as a designer. The studio is a hothouse that enables students

the
new

process that is at times chaotic, and faculty to encounter their own visions of the world and act on them — a conflicting, and occasionally inspiring.

Watching the process of students absorbing new ideas and influences, and the incredible range of in- terpretations of those ideas into design, is

MYTHOLOGY / technology

an annual experience that is always amaz- ing. In recent years, for example, the de-

discourse

partment has had the experience of watching wood craftsmen metamorphose into high technologists, and graphic designers into software humanists. Yet it all seems consistent. They are bringing a very personal vision to an area that desperately needs it. The messiness of human experi-

PURIST / pluralist

ence is warming up the cold precision of technology to make it livable, and lived in.

Unlike the Bauhaus, Cranbrook never embraced a singular teaching method or philosophy, other than Saarinen's exhortation to each student to find his or her own way, in the company of other artists and designers who were engaged in the same search. The energy at Cranbrook seems to come from the fact of

INDIVIDUAL / communal

the mutual search, although not the mutual conclusion. If design is about life, why shouldn't it have all the complexity, variety, contradiction, and sublimity of life?

Much of the work done at Cranbrook has been dedicated to changing the status quo. It is polemical, calculated to ruffle designers' feathers. And

DANGEROUS / rigorous

Ferndal...
1981
Kenne...
Cranbr...
A block...
cial ma...
tograph...
collage
graphic...

BIRTH OF THE USER

Barthes's model of the text as an open web of references, rather than a closed and perfect work, asserts the importance of the reader over the writer in creating meaning. The reader "plays" the text as a musician plays an instrument. The author does not control its significance: "The text itself plays (like a door, like a machine with 'play') and the reader plays twice over, playing the Text as one plays a game, looking for a practice which reproduces it." Like an interpretation of a musical score, reading is a performance of the written word.

Graphic designers embraced the idea of the readerly text in the 1980s and early 1990s, using layers of text and interlocking grids to explore Barthes's theory of the "death of the author." In place of the classical model of typography as a crystal goblet for content, this alternative view assumes that content itself changes with each act of representation. Typography becomes a mode of interpretation.

Redefining typography as "discourse," designer Katherine McCoy imploded the traditional dichotomy between seeing and reading. Pictures can be read (analyzed, decoded, taken apart), and words can be seen (perceived as icons, forms, patterns). Valuing ambiguity and complexity, her approach challenged readers to produce their own meanings while also trying to elevate the status of designers within the process of authorship.

Another model, which undermined the designer's new claim to power, surfaced at the end of the 1990s, borrowed not from literary criticism but from human-computer interaction (HCI) studies and the fields of interface and usability design. The dominant subject of our age has become neither reader nor writer but *user*, a figure conceived as a bundle of needs and impairments—cognitive, physical, emotional. Like a patient or child, the user is a figure to be protected and cared for but also scrutinized and controlled, submitted to research and testing.

How texts are *used* becomes more important than what they mean. Someone clicked here to get over there. Someone who bought this also bought that. The interactive environment not only provides users with a degree of control and self-direction but also, more quietly and insidiously, it gathers data about its audiences. Barthes's image of the text as a game to be played still holds, as the user responds to signals from the system. We may play the text, but it is also playing us.

Design a human-machine interface in accordance with the abilities and foibles of humankind, and you will help the user not only get the job done, but be a happier, more productive person. —JEF RASKIN, 2000

CRANBROOK DESIGN: THE NEW DISCOURSE Book, 1990. Designers: Katherine McCoy, P. Scott Makela, and Mary Lou Kroh. Publisher: Rizzoli. Photograph: Dan Meyers. *Under the direction of Katherine and Michael McCoy, the graduate program in graphic and industrial design at Cranbrook Academy of Art was a leading center for experimental design from the 1970s through the early 1990s. Katherine McCoy developed a model of "typography as discourse," in which the designer and reader actively interpret a text.*

Graphic designers can use theories of user interaction to revisit some of our basic assumptions about visual communication. Why, for example, are readers on the web less patient than readers of print? It is commonly believed that digital displays are inherently more difficult to read than ink on paper. Yet HCI studies conducted in the late 1980s proved that crisp black text on a white background can be read just as efficiently from a screen as from a printed page.

The impatience of the digital reader arises from culture, not from the essential character of display technologies. Users of websites have different expectations than users of print. They expect to feel "productive," not contemplative. They expect to be in search mode, not processing mode. Users also expect to be disappointed, distracted, and delayed by false leads. The cultural habits of the screen are driving changes in design for print, while at the same time affirming print's role as a place where extended reading can still occur.

Another common assumption is that icons are a more universal mode of communication than text. Icons are central to the GUIs (graphical user interfaces) that routinely connect users with computers. Yet text can often provide a more specific and understandable cue than a picture. Icons don't actually simplify the translation of content into multiple languages, because they require explanation in multiple languages. The endless icons of the digital desktop, often rendered with gratuitous detail and depth, function more to enforce brand identity than to support usability. In the twentieth century, modern designers hailed pictures as a "universal" language, yet in the age of code, text has become a more common denom-inator than images—searchable, translatable, and capable of being reformatted and restyled for alternative or future media.

Perhaps the most persistent impulse of twentieth-century art and design was to physically integrate form and content. The Dada and Futurist poets, for example, used typography to create texts whose content was inextricable from the concrete layout of specific letterforms on a page. In the twenty-first century, form and content are being pulled back apart. Style sheets, for example, compel designers to think globally and systematically instead of focusing on the fixed construction of a particular surface. This way of

On screen readability, see John D. Gould *et al.*, "Reading from CRT Displays Can Be as Fast as Reading from Paper," *Human Factors*, 29, 5 (1987): 497–517.

On the restless user, see Jakob Nielsen, *Designing Web Usability* (Indianapolis: New Riders, 2000).

On the failure of interface icons, see Jef Raskin, *The Humane Interface: New Directions for Designing Interactive Systems* (Reading, Mass.: Addison-Wesley, 2000).

Web users don't like to read....They want to keep moving and clicking.
—JAKOB NIELSEN, 2000

thinking allows content to be reformatted for different devices or users, and it also prepares for the afterlife of data as electronic storage media begin their own cycles of decay and obsolescence.

In the twentieth century, modern artists and critics asserted that each medium is specific. They defined film, for example, as a constructive language distinct from theater, and they described painting as a physical medium that refers to its own processes. Today, however, the medium is not always the message. Design has become a "transmedia" enterprise, as authors and producers create worlds of characters, places, situations, and interactions that can appear across a variety of products. A game might live in different versions on a video screen, a desktop computer, a game console, and a cell phone, as well as on t-shirts, lunch boxes, and plastic toys.

On transmedia design thinking, see Brenda Laurel, *Utopian Entrepreneur* (Cambridge: MIT Press, 2001).

The beauty and wonder of "white space" is another modernist myth that is subject to revision in the age of the user. Modern designers discovered that open space on a page can have as much physical presence as printed areas. White space is not always a mental kindness, however. Edward Tufte, a fierce advocate of visual density, argues for maximizing the amount of data conveyed on a single page or screen. In order to help readers make connections and comparisons, as well as to find information quickly, a single surface packed with well-organized information is sometimes better than multiple pages with a lot of blank space. In typography as in urban life, density invites intimate exchange among people and ideas.

In our much-fabled era of information overload, a person can still process only one message at a time. This brute fact of cognition is the secret behind magic tricks: sleights of hand occur while the attention of the audience is drawn elsewhere. Given the fierce competition for their attention, users have a chance to shape the information economy by choosing what to look at. Designers can help them make satisfying choices.

Jef Raskin talks about the scarcity of human attention as well as the myth of white space in *The Humane Interface: New Directions for Designing Interactive Systems*, cited on p. 74.

Typography is an interface to the alphabet. User theory tends to favor normative solutions over innovative ones, pushing design into the background. Readers usually ignore the typographic interface, gliding comfortably along literacy's habitual groove. Sometimes, however, the interface should be allowed to fail. By making itself evident, typography can illuminate the construction and identity of a page, screen, place, or product.

If people weren't good at finding tiny things in long lists, the *Wall Street Journal* would have gone out of business years ago. —JEF RASKIN, 2000

Typography, invented in the Renaissance, allowed text to become a fixed and stable form. Like the body of the letter, the body of text was transformed into an industrial commodity that gradually became more open and flexible.

Critics of electronic media have noted that the rise of networked communication did not lead to the much feared destruction of typography (or even to the death of print), but rather to the burgeoning of the alphabetic empire. As Peter Lunenfeld points out, the computer has revived the power and prevalence of writing: "Alphanumeric text has risen from its own ashes, a digital phoenix taking flight on monitors, across networks, and in the realms of virtual space." The computer display is more hospitable to text than the screens of film or television because it offers physical proximity, user control, and a scale appropriate to the body.

The printed book is no longer the chief custodian of the written word. Branding is a powerful variant of literacy that revolves around symbols, icons, and typographic standards, leaving its marks on buildings, packages, album covers, websites, store displays, and countless other surfaces and spaces. With the expansion of the Internet, new (and old) conventions for displaying text quickly congealed, adapting metaphors from print and architecture: window, frame, page, banner, menu. Designers working within this stream of multiple media confront text in myriad forms, giving shape to extended bodies but also to headlines, decks, captions, notes, pull quotes, logotypes, navigation bars, alt tags, and other prosthetic clumps of language that announce, support, and even eclipse the main body of text.

The dissolution of writing is most extreme in the realm of the web, where distracted readers safeguard their time and prize function over form. This debt of restlessness is owed not to the essential nature of computer monitors, but to the new behaviors engendered by the Internet, a place of searching and finding, scanning and mining. The reader, having toppled the author's seat of power during the twentieth century, now ails and lags, replaced by the dominant subject of our own era: the *user*, a figure whose scant attention is our most coveted commodity. Do not squander it.

On electronic writing, see Peter Lunenfeld, *Snap to Grid: A User's Guide to Digital Arts, Media, and Cultures* (Cambridge: MIT Press, 2001); Jay David Bolter, *Writing Space: Computers, Hypertext, and the Remediation of Print* (Mahwah, NJ: Lawrence Erlbaum Associates, 2001), and Stuart Moulthrop, "You Say You Want a Revolution? Hypertext and the Laws of Media," in *The New Media Reader*, ed. Noah Wardrip-Fruin and Nick Monfort (Cambridge: MIT Press, 2003), 691–703.

Hypertext means the end of the death of literature. —STUART MOULTHROP, 1991

DESIGNOBSERVER.COM Website, 2010.
Design: Jessica Helfand, William Drenttel,
Michael Bierut, and Betsy Vardell. *Packing
an enormous volume of content onto its home
page, this design discourse supersite brings
print-quality typography to the screen.*

Kerning is an adjustment of the space between two letters. The characters of the Latin alphabet emerged over time; they were never designed with mechanical or automated spacing in mind. Thus some letter combinations look awkward without special spacing considerations. Gaps occur, for example, around letters whose forms angle outward or frame an open space (*W, Y, V, T*). In metal type, a kerned letter extends past the lead slug that supports it, allowing two letters to fit more closely together. In digital fonts, the space between letter pairs is controlled by a *kerning table* created by the type designer, which specifies spaces between problematic letter combinations.

Working in a page layout program, a designer can choose to use *metric kerning* or *optical kerning* as well as adjusting the space between letters manually where desired. A well-designed typeface requires little or no additional kerning, especially at text sizes.

METRIC KERNING uses the kerning tables that are built into the typeface. When you select metric kerning in your page layout program, you are using the spacing that was intended by the type designer. Metric kerning usually looks good, especially at small sizes. Cheap novelty fonts often have little or no built-in kerning and will need to be optically kerned.

OPTICAL KERNING is executed automatically by the page layout program. Rather than using the pairs addressed in the font's kerning table, optical kerning assesses the shapes of all characters and adjusts the spacing wherever needed. Some graphic designers apply optical kerning to headlines and metric kerning to text. You can make this process efficient and consistent by setting kerning as part of your character styles.

Takes Two

SCALA PRO, WITH KERNING SUPPRESSED
Spacing appears uneven, with gaps around T/a, T/w, and w/o.

Takes Two

SCALA PRO, WITH METRIC KERNING
Spacing appears more even between T/a and T/w.

Takes Two

SCALA PRO, WITH OPTICAL KERNING
Spacing seems more even between T/a, T/w, and w/o.

Warm Type

SCALA PRO ITALIC, WITH KERNING SUPPRESSED
Spacing appears uneven between W/a and T/y.

Warm Type

SCALA PRO ITALIC, WITH METRIC KERNING
Spacing appears more even between W/a and T/y.

Warm Type

SCALA PRO ITALIC, WITH OPTICAL KERNING
Spacing is comparable to metric kerning.

LOVE LETTERS

SCALA PRO ALL CAPITALS, WITH KERNING SUPPRESSED
Spacing is tight between T/T.

LOVE LETTERS

SCALA PRO ALL CAPITALS, WITH METRIC KERNING
Improved spacing between T/T.

LOVE LETTERS

SCALA PRO ALL CAPITALS, WITH OPTICAL KERNING
Improved spacing between T/ T and O/V.

KERNING HEADLINES The subtle differences between metric and optical kerning become more apparent at larger sizes. Most problems occur between capital and lowercase letters. The spacing between *H/a*, *T/a*, and *T/o* improves with optical kerning. The optical kerning applied here in InDesign has created tighter spacing for large text and looser spacing for small text. Look at both effects before choosing a kerning method.

Ha

METRIC KERNING

Ha

OPTICAL KERNING

METRIC VERSUS OPTICAL KERNING

Books And Harlots Have Their Quarrels In Public.

Books And Harlots Can Be Taken To Bed.

Books and harlots—footnotes in one are as banknotes in the stockings of the other.

—WALTER BENJAMIN, 1925

QUADRAAT SANS, WITH METRIC KERNING

Books And Harlots Have Their Quarrels In Public.

Books And Harlots Can Be Taken To Bed.

Books and harlots—footnotes in one are as banknotes in the stockings of the other.

—WALTER BENJAMIN, 1925

QUADRAAT SANS, WITH OPTICAL KERNING

NERD ALERT: *In addition to using optical kerning, the text above has word spacing reduced to 80 percent. With large type, normal word spacing often looks too wide. Adjust word spacing in the Paragraph>Justification menu in InDesign.*

Adjusting the overall spacing of a group of letters is called *tracking* or *letterspacing*. By expanding the tracking across a word, line, or entire block of text, the designer can create a more airy, open field. In blocks of text, tracking is usually applied in small increments, creating a subtle effect not noticeable to the casual reader. Occasionally, a single word or phrase is tracked for emphasis, especially when CAPS or SMALL CAPS are used within a line. Negative tracking, rarely desirable in text sizes, can be used sparingly to help bring up a short line of text. White type on a black background is considered more legible when it is tracked.

SCALY-BREASTED PARTRIDGE
Arborophila chloropus
12 in (30 cm)
Southeast Asia

CRIMSON-HEADED PARTRIDGE
Haematortyx sanguiniceps
10 in (25 cm)
Borneo

BIRDS OF THE WORLD Book, 2007. Author: Les Beletsky. Publisher: The Johns Hopkins University. Art Director: Charles Nix. Designers: Charles Nix, Whitney Grant, and May Jampathom. *This book, set in Adobe Caslon and Caslon 540, uses tracked small capitals for caption headings.*

TRACKING TEXT TYPE

NORMAL TRACKING
Letters do love one another. However, due to their anatomical differences, some letters have a hard time achieving intimacy. Consider the letter *V*, for example, whose seductive valley makes her limbs stretch out above her base. In contrast, *L* solidly holds his ground yet harbors a certain emptiness above the waist. Capital letters, being square and conservative, prefer to keep a little distance from their neighbors.

POSITIVE TRACKING (+20)
Letters do love one another. However, due to their anatomical differences, some letters have a hard time achieving intimacy. Consider the letter *V*, for example, whose seductive valley makes her limbs stretch out above her base. In contrast, *L* solidly holds his ground yet harbors a certain emptiness above the waist. Capital letters, being square and conservative, prefer to keep a little distance from their neighbors.

NEGATIVE TRACKING (-20)
Letters do love one another. However, due to their anatomical differences, some letters have a hard time achieving intimacy. Consider the letter *V*, for example, whose seductive valley makes her limbs stretch out above her base. In contrast, *L* solidly holds his ground yet harbors a certain emptiness above the waist. Capital letters, being square and conservative, prefer to keep a little distance from their neighbors.

TYPE CRIME
TIGHTLY TRACKED TEXT
Letters are tracked too close for comfort.

Books and harlots—both have their type of man, who both lives off and harasses them. In the case of books, critics. WALTER BENJAMIN, 1925

REVERSED TYPE, NO TRACKING

Books and harlots—both have their type of man, who both lives off and harasses them. In the case of books, critics. WALTER BENJAMIN, 1925

REVERSED TYPE, TRACKED +25

Designers most commonly apply tracking to headlines and logos (where kerning adjustments are also frequently required). As text gets bigger, the space between letters expands, and some designers use tracking to diminish overall spacing in large-scale text. Loose or open tracking is commonly applied to capitals and small capitals, which appear more regal standing slightly apart.

TRACKING HEADLINES AND LOGOTYPES

LOVE LETTERS
CAPITALS: NORMAL TRACKING

LOVE LETTERS
CAPITALS: LOOSE TRACKING (+75)

LOVE LETTERS, LOVE LETTERS
SMALL CAPS: NORMAL VS. LOOSE TRACKING (+75)

love letters, *love letters*
LOWER CASE: NORMAL TRACKING

love letters, *love letters*
LOWER CASE: LOOSE TRACKING (+75)

TYPE CRIME: TRACKING LOWERCASE LETTERS
Loosely spaced lowercase letters—especially italics—look awkward because these characters are designed to sit closely together on a line.

EROS Logotype, 1962. Design: Herb Lubalin. *Ultra-tight letterspacing was a hallmark of progressive commercial graphics in the 1960s and 1970s. Here, the letters cradle each other with an intimacy appropriate to the subject matter.*

CRUET & WHISK and THYMES Logotypes, 2006. Design: Duffy & Partners. *The generously tracked capitals in these logotypes give them an affable, antiquarian flavor while imparting an overall lightness to the designs.*

You can express the meaning of a word
or an idea through the spacing, sizing,
and placement of letters on the page.
Designers often think this way when
creating logotypes, posters, or editorial
headlines. The compositions shown here
express physical processes such as
disruption, expansion, and migration
through the spacing and arrangement of
letters. The round *Os* in Futura make it
a fun typeface to use for this project.

Examples of student work from
Maryland Institute College of Art

sition   transiti

Johnschen Kudos

disʳuption   c o m pression

Johnschen Kudos   Johnschen Kudos

ion

t

a

e x p **expansion** i o n

ig

migra m **tion**

Marcos Kolthar   Jason Hogg

elimina ion

o

o

o

o

o o

o

repetition

repetition

Heather Williams   Heather Williams

The distance from the baseline of one line of type to another is called *line spacing*. It is also called *leading*, in reference to the strips of lead used to separate lines of metal type. The default setting in most layout and imaging software is 120 percent of the type size. Thus 10-pt type is set with 12 pts of line spacing. Designers play with line spacing in order to create distinctive typographic arrangements. Reducing the standard distance creates a denser typographic color, while risking collisions between ascenders and descenders. Expanding the line spacing creates a lighter, more open text block. As leading increases, lines of type become independent graphic elements rather than parts of an overall visual shape and texture.

different

folks

different

strokes

TYPE CRIME
*Here, auto spacing yields
an uneven effect.*

different

folks

different

strokes

*Adjusting line spacing with
the baseline shift tool helps create
an even appearance.*

NERD ALERT: A *baseline shift* is a manual adjustment of the horizontal position of one or more characters. Baseline shifts are often used when mixing different sizes or styles of type. The baseline shift tool can be found in the Type tool bar of standard software applications.

VARIATIONS IN LINE SPACING

The distance from the baseline of one line of type to another is called *line spacing*. It is also called *leading*, in reference to the strips of lead used to separate lines of metal type. The default setting in most layout and imaging software is 120 percent of the type size. Thus 10-pt type is set with 12 pts of line spacing. Designers play with line spacing in order to create distinctive layouts. Reducing the standard distance creates a denser typographic color—while risking collisions between ascenders and descenders.

6/6 SCALA PRO
(6 pt type with 6 pts line spacing, or "set solid")

The distance from the baseline of one line of type to another is called *line spacing*. It is also called *leading*, in reference to the strips of lead used to separate lines of metal type. The default setting in most layout and imaging software is 120 percent of the type size. Thus 10-pt type is set with 12 pts of line spacing. Designers play with line spacing in order to create distinctive layouts. Reducing the standard distance creates a denser typographic color—while risking collisions between ascenders and descenders.

6/7.2 SCALA PRO
(Auto spacing; 6 pt type with 7.2 pts line spacing)

The distance from the baseline of one line of type to another is called *line spacing*. It is also called *leading*, in reference to the strips of lead used to separate lines of metal type. The default setting in most layout and imaging software is 120 percent of the type size. Thus 10-pt type is set with 12 pts of line spacing. Designers play with line spacing in order to create distinctive layouts. Reducing the standard distance creates a denser typographic color—while risking collisions between ascenders and descenders.

6/8 SCALA PRO
(6 pt type with 8 pts line spacing)

The distance from the baseline of one line of type to another is called *line spacing*. It is also called *leading*, in reference to the strips of lead used to separate lines of metal type. The default setting in most layout and imaging software is 120 percent of the type size. Thus 10-pt type is set with 12 pts of line spacing. Designers play with line spacing in order to create distinctive layouts. Reducing the standard distance creates a denser typographic color—while risking collisions between ascenders and descenders.

6/12 SCALA PRO
(6 pt type with 12 pts line spacing)

Ancient maps of the world

An

when the world was flat

Avid

inform us, concerning the void

Dream

where America was waiting

Of

to be discovered,

Trans-

Here Be Dragons. James Baldwin

for-

O to be a dragon. Marianne Moore

mation Adrienne Kennedy, *People Who Led to My Plays*

MARGO JEFFERSON

DANCE INK: AN AVID DREAM
OF TRANSFORMATION
Magazine page, 1992.
Designer: Abbott Miller.
Publisher: Patsy Tarr. *The
extreme line spacing allows two
strands of text to interweave.*

Designers experiment with extreme line spacing to create distinctive typographic textures. Open spacing allows designers to play with the space between the lines, while tight spacing creates intriguing, sometimes uncomfortable, collisions.

interminável do embarque, decido respirar um pouco e procurar o sr. Creso com mais calma, outra hora.

PISO OCIDENTAL – EMBARQUE

A área de embarque é chamada de "aquário": um longo corredor com paredes e portas de vidro que separam o pré-embarque das plataformas. O ônibus estaciona nas baias, lá fora, e um funcionário abre as tais portas de vidro, chamando os passageiros. Só então eles passam à região do embarque. Protegem-se, assim, os demais usuários da fumaça emitida pelos veículos, em parte absorvida por um enorme tubo exaustor pintado de amarelo.

Em pé, na plataforma 1, enxerga-se o corredor inteiro, até o fim. Em primeiro plano, um relógio de ponteiros e uma larga escada em caracol que leva ao piso superior. No vão embaixo da escada, algumas lanchonetes e lojas de miudezas encaixam-se com perfeição. De ambos os lados, indicados ao longo do corredor, sucedem-se os números das plataformas 1 a 50, pintados de branco dentro de quadrados verdes, sobrepondo-se ligeiramente uns aos outros como em uma agenda telefônica.

Há poucas crianças vagando pela área. Em compensação, são muitos os seguranças, funcionários de limpeza e vendedores de bebidas caminhando com seus carrinhos. A maioria dos passageiros é composta de adultos que esperam em pé, pois não há lugar para sentar (apenas quatro cadeiras de plástico laranja diante de cada plataforma). Consegue-se escutar remotamente o som dos alto-falantes que tocam "Ovelha negra" em versão acústica e diversas músicas instrumentais, para dar a impressão de que o terminal é calmo. "Mas só pra dar a impressão, mesmo", brinca um dos fiscais da Socicam.

Antes da primeira plataforma par, ergue-se uma sala VIP, como a dos aeroportos. É um espaço envidraçado voltado exclusivamente para o bem-estar dos passageiros das empresas Cometa, 1001 e Catarinense, em viagens a Santa Catarina, Paraná, Rio de Janeiro e Minas Gerais. A abertura das portas é automática e o usuário é recebido por duas moças de saia azul, salto alto e lencinho amarelo, que conferem os bilhetes e aconselham os passageiros a se sentir em casa. Nas paredes, pôsteres de capitais: Curitiba, Florianópolis, São Paulo e Belo Horizonte. No teto, a pintura de um céu azul-escuro com estrelas e o cometa Halley, símbolo da Viação Cometa. Há longas fileiras que somam ao todo 160 cadeiras estofadas em dois tons: marrom-terra e azul-marinho, sob o piso limpíssimo e brilhante. Há duas TVs sintonizadas no canal Globo News, duas máquinas de café e chocolate, uma máquina de refrigerante, quatro aparelhos de ar-condicionado e um galão de água gelada ou natural, "vestido" com um pano branco onde

027

O LIVRO AMERELO DO TERMINAL Book spread, 2008. Designer: Vanessa Barbara with Elaine Ramos and Maria Carolina Sampaio. Publisher: Cosac Naify. *Here, pages of text are set with loose line spacing and printed on thin paper. The vertical placement of the text block varies from spread to spread, allowing text to show through between the lines.*

VISIONARY CITIES: THE
ARCOLOGY OF PAOLO SOLERI
Book, 1970. Design: Paolo
Soleri. *This classic work of
postmodern design uses ultra-
tight line spacing to create
dramatic density on the page.
Produced long before the era of
digital page layout, this book
exploited the possibilities of
phototypesetting and dry
transfer lettering.*

ALIGNMENT

Choosing to align text in justified, centered, or ragged columns is a fundamental typographic act. Each mode of alignment carries unique formal qualities, cultural associations, and aesthetic risks.

Centered text is symmetrical,

like the facade of a classical building.

Centered type often appears on

invitations, title pages, certificates, and tomb stones.

The edges of a centered column

are often dramatically uneven.

Centered lines should be broken to emphasize a key phrase

(such as the name of the bride

or the date of her wedding)

or to allow a new thought to begin on its own line.

Breaking lines in this manner is called

breaking for sense.

Justified text, which has even edges on both the left and right sides of the column, has been the norm since the invention of printing with movable type, which enabled the creation of page after page of straight-edged columns. In metal type setting, the printer justifies each line by hand, using small metal spacers to alter the spaces between words and letters and thus make all the lines the same length. Digital typesetting performs the same labor automatically. Justified type makes efficient use of space. It also creates a clean, compact shape on the page. Ugly gaps can occur, however, when the line length is too short in relation to the size of type used. Hyphenation breaks up long words and helps keep the lines of text tightly packed. Designers often use negative tracking to fit additional characters on a line, or positive tracking to even out a line of type that looks too loose.

CENTERED

Lines of ueven length on a central axis

Centered text is formal and classical. It invites the designer to break a text for sense and create elegant, organic shapes. Centering is often the simplest and most intuitive way to place a typographic element. Used without care, centered text can look staid and mournful, like a tombstone.

JUSTIFIED

Left and right edges are both even

Justified text makes a clean shape on the page. Its efficient use of space makes it the norm for newspapers and books. Ugly gaps can occur, however, as text is forced into lines of even measure. Avoid this by using a line length that is long enough in relation to the size of type. As type gets smaller, more words will fit on each line.

THIS DREARY SHAPE HAS RANDOM LINE BREAKS THAT DON'T RESPOND TO THE RHYTHM OF THE WRITTEN TEXT.

TYPE CRIME
POORLY SHAPED TEXT BLOCK *In most uses, centered text should be broken into phrases with a variety of long and short lines.*

Ugly gaps appear when the designer has made the line length too short, or the author has selected words that are   too   long.

TYPE CRIME
FULL OF HOLES *A column that is too narrow is full of gaps.*

In *flush left/ragged right* text, the left edge is hard and the right edge soft. Word spaces do not fluctuate, so there are never big holes inside the lines of text. This format, which was used primarily for setting poetry before the twentieth century, respects the flow of language rather than submitting to the law of the box. Despite its advantages, however, the flush left format is fraught with danger. Above all, the designer must work hard to control the appearance of the *rag* that forms along the right edge. A good rag looks pleasantly uneven, with no lines that are excessively long or short, and with hyphenation kept to a minimum. A rag is considered "bad" when it looks too even (or too uneven), or when it begins to form regular shapes, like wedges, moons, or diving boards.

Flush right/ragged left is a variant of the more familiar flush left setting. It is common wisdom among typographers that flush right text is hard to read, because it forces the reader's eye to find a new position at the start of each line. This could be true, or it could be an urban legend. That being said, the flush right setting is rarely employed for long bodies of text. Used in smaller blocks, however, flush right text forms effective marginal notes, sidebars, pull quotes, or other passages that comment on a main body or image. A flush or ragged edge can suggest attraction (or repulsion) between chunks of information.

FLUSH LEFT/RAGGED RIGHT
Left edge is hard; right edge is soft

Flush left text respects the organic flow of language and avoids the uneven spacing that plagues justified type. A bad rag can ruin the relaxed, organic appearance of a flush left column. Designers must strive vigilantly to create the illusion of a random, natural edge without resorting to excessive hyphenation.

FLUSH RIGHT/RAGGED LEFT
Right edge is hard; left edge is soft

Flush right text can be a welcome departure from the familiar. Used for captions, side bars, and other marginalia, it can suggest affinities among elements. Because flush right text is unusual, it can annoy cautious readers. Bad rags threaten flush right text just as they afflict flush left, and punctuation can weaken the hard right edge.

A bad rag will fall into weird shapes along the right edge, instead of looking random.

TYPE CRIME
BAD RAG
An ugly wedge shape spoils the ragged edge.

Lots of punctuation (at the ends of lines) will attack, threaten, and generally weaken the flush right edge.

TYPE CRIME
PUNCTUATION EATS THE EDGE *Excessive punctuation weakens the right edge.*

The four modes of alignment (centered, justified, flush left, and flush right) form the basic grammar of typographic composition. Each one has traditional uses that make intuitive sense to readers.

CENTERED

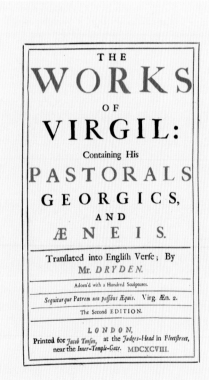

JUSTIFIED

for Coppet. But when the eighty days had passed and the bugaboo was safely on board the *Bellerophon*, she came back to the scenes she loved so well and to what for her was the only heaven: Paris. ¶ She has been called a philosopher and a literary light. But she was only socioliterary. Her written philosophy does not represent the things she felt were true—simply those things she thought it would be nice to say. She cultivated literature, only that she might shine. Love, wealth, health, husband, children—all were sacrificed that she might lead society and win applause. No one ever feared solitude more: she must have those about her who would minister to her vanity and upon whom she could shower her wit. As a type her life is valuable, and in these pages that traverse the entire circle of feminine virtues and foibles she surely must have a place. ¶ In her last illness she was attended daily by those faithful subjects who had all along recognized her sovereignty—in Society she was Queen. She surely now had won her heart's desire, for to that bed from which she was no more to rise, courtiers came and kneeling kissed her hand, and women by the score whom she had befriended paid her the tribute of their tears ✻ She died in Paris at the age of fifty-one.
217

THE WORKS OF VIRGIL Printed for Jacob Tonson, 1698. *Title pages are traditionally set centered. This two-color title page was printed in two passes of the press (note the off-kilter registration of the two colors of ink). Large typefaces were created primarily for use on title pages or in hymn books.*

THE COMPLETE WRITINGS OF ELBERT HUBBARD, VOLUME TWO Printed by the Roycroft Shop, 1908. *This neo-Renaissance book page harkens back to the first century of printing. Not only is the block of text perfectly justified, but paragraph symbols are used in place of indents and line breaks to preserve the solidity of the page.*

FLUSH LEFT

FLUSH RIGHT

L'ENNEMI

Ma jeunesse ne fut qu'un ténébreux orage,
Traversé çà et là par de brillants soleils;
Le tonnerre et la pluie ont fait un tel ravage,
Qu'il reste en mon jardin bien peu de fruits vermeils.

Voilà que j'ai touché l'automne des idées,
Et qu'il faut employer la pelle et les râteaux
Pour rassembler à neuf les terres inondées,
Où l'eau creuse des trous grands comme des tombeaux.

Et qui sait si les fleurs nouvelles que je rêve
Trouveront dans ce sol lavé comme une grève
Le mystique aliment qui ferait leur vigueur?

— O douleur! ô douleur! Le Temps mange la vie,
Et l'obscur Ennemi qui nous ronge le cœur
Du sang que nous perdons croît et se fortifie!

17

132   Technique

things that could not have been done at all had he
stuck to his original idea.

No shields   Trade-markery is a country cousin of heraldry; it
can claim that kin, but native good taste will keep it
from trying to ape its noble relative. I mean that trade-
marks in the form of shields are a joke—as comical as
those mid-Victorian trade devices surrounded by the
Garter. Things like that, in first instances (they are
now meaningless survivals), were efforts on the part of
Trade to sit in the same pew with Race. Under the
modern dispensation, with kings at a discount, the
feudal touch may be dispensed with. One makes this
comment about shields as trade-marks because a cos-
mic law operates to convince every expectant proprietor
of a new trade-mark that he wants his device in the
shape of a shield.

Flexible   A good trade-mark is the thing that lives inside a
boundary line—not the boundary line itself. It should
be possible for the device to step outside its circle, or
triangle, or what not, and still be the same—an unmis-
takable emblem. In other words, marks that depend
for their individuality upon triangular frames, circles,
squares, etc., are weak brethren; they are of a low order
of trade-mark vitality.

Typographic   For the greater number of advertising uses a trade-
flavor   mark design needs to be given a typographic flavor.
It will stand in close relation to type in the usual
advertisement and its stance will be more comfortable
if it is brought into sympathy with type. This means
that the proprietor will have to relax the rigor of his
rule and allow his design (originally rendered in soft
lithographic grays and stipples) to be redrawn in
positive line, with considerable paper showing. It is
not necessary to ape the style of a woodcut in this
effort after typographic flavor; but it is necessary to
echo, to a certain extent, the crisp black lines and

CHARLES BAUDELAIRE/LES FLEURS DU MAL Printed by Bill
Lansing, 1945. *Traditionally, poetry is set flush left, because the line
breaks are an essential element of the literary form. Poetry is not
ususally set centered, except in greeting cards.*

LAYOUT IN ADVERTISING Designed and written by W. A.
Dwiggins, 1928. *In this classic guide to commercial art practices,
Dwiggins has placed callouts or subject cues in the margins. On
the left-hand (verso) page shown here, the cues are set flush right,
drawing them closer to the content they identify.*

Designers sometimes use the archetypal modes of alignment in ways that emphasize their visual qualities. Combining different types of alignment can yield dynamic and surprising layouts.

"Grandma! Grandma! Look at me! I did it!" Oval yelled from the water, her youth taut as a syllogism.

"I saw you darling!" Mother waved. Then she sat back and smiled, nature on her side after all.

"Well sure," Square began— He heard the suck of Circle's chest cavity, speech lobes echoing the startle of her brain's emotive region to vibrate vocal chords so that the up-rush of breath through her body would come out as,

"What?!"

She pushed her sunglasses up onto her head to reveal that her eyes had widened to the size of an animal's before it pounces. And in response, an electro-chemical jolt contracted his muscles to quickly voice "But it's more complicated than that" (accelerando) as he tried to recover.

Tried and failed, he saw, realizing that Mother would take his words as confirmation of Circle's phobia of conceiving. Circle's eyes remained trained on him. "Sometimes more kids just aren't in the cards," he tried.

"What he means," Circle said, emotion beginning to raise veins, "is that we've decided to limit our family."

"Limit your?—"

"It's not like when you and dad were raising a family. Kids cost a lot. The public schools are worthless so you can't even think about sending them there. And anyway, who's going to watch a baby while I'm at work? Square doesn't have time. He can't even figure out the ending to his dumb..."
Dumb?
"...story, watching Oval after school like he does and I don't have time to be around them. Not like you were with us."

a common story

"Well, things have certainly changed," Mother sighed in that exhausted victim tone she adopted whenever she was about to play her "tired blood" card. "In my day, children just came or they didn't. We were just the organ they did it through."

of a common man

"Geez, that's what you want me to go back to?" Circle laughed, her smile an incipient "fear grin" primates often exhibited just before tension broke into fight or flight. "A crap shoot?" This last was meant for him. He decided to let pass the crack about his "dumb" story.

Homo being common to all men

"I only meant—"
and women (obviously)

"Mother, I can't not know what I know!" Her exasperated tone left a pregnant silence at the table. "Excuse me," she said, "I need a refill on my ice." She stood up and there was the shock of her body: a flat athletic torso, muscular shoulders and arms in a cheetah-print swimsuit (a legacy of African, i.e. savage sexuality) that made him want her. "Anybody else want anything?"

45

FLUSH LEFT AND FLUSH RIGHT: VAS: AN OPERA IN FLATLAND Book spread, 2002. Designer: Stephen Farrell. Author: Steve Tomasula. *In this typographic novel, texts and images align left and right against a series of thin rules. Hanging punctuation and boldface letters emphasize the flush edges.*

FLUSH LEFT AND FLUSH RIGHT: INFORMAL Book, 2002. Designer: Januzzi Smith. Author: Cecil Balmond. Photograph: Dan Meyers. *This book is a manifesto for an informal approach to structural engineering and architecture. The text columns juxtapose flush right against flush left alignments, creating a tiny but insistent seam or fissure inside the text and irregular rags along the outer edges.*

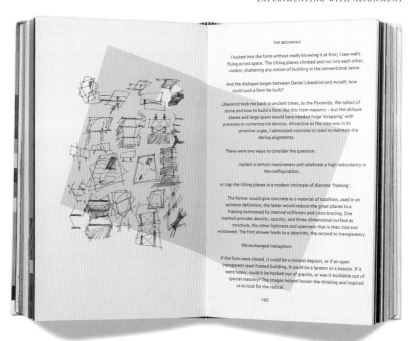

JUSTIFIED: HELLA JONGERIUS Book, 2003. Designers: COMA. Photograph: Dan Meyers. *Transparent paper emphasizes the justified text block. Images hang from a consistent horizontal point, creating a throughline that is visible along the edge of the book.*

Use modes of alignment (flush left, flush right, justified, and centered) to actively interpret a passage of text. The passage here, from Walter Ong's book *Orality and Literacy: The Technologizing of the Word,* explains how the invention of printing with movable type imposed a new spatial order on the written word, in contrast with the more organic pages of the manuscript era. The solutions shown here comment on the conflicts between hard and soft, industrial and natural, planning and chance, that underlie all typographic composition.

Examples of student work from Maryland Institute College of Art

PRINT SITUATES WORDS IN SPACE MORE RELENTLESSLY THAN WRITING EVER DID. writing moves words from the sound world BUT PRINT LOCKS WORDS INTO to a world of visual space, POSITION IN THIS SPACE. CONTROL OF POSITION IS EVERYTHING IN PRINT. PRINTED TEXTS LOOK MACHINE-MADE, AS THEY ARE. in handwriting, control of space tends to be ornamental, TYPOGRAPHIC CONTROL TYPICALLY IMPRESSES MOST BY ITS TIDINESS ornate, as in calligraphy. AND INVISIBILITY: THE LINES PERFECTLY REGULAR, ALL JUSTIFIED ON THE RIGHT SIDE, EVERYTHING COMING OUT EVEN VISUALLY, AND WITHOUT THE AID OF GUIDELINES OR RULED BORDERS THAT OFTEN OCCUR IN MANUSCRIPTS. THIS IS AN INSISTENT WORLD OF COLD, NON-HUMAN, FACTS.

Randomly spaced words break free from a rigidly justified column.
Lu Zhang

PRINT

situates words in space more relentlessly

than writing ever did. Control of position

is everything in print. Printed texts look

machine-made, as they are. Typographic

control typically impresses most by its

WRITING tidiness and invisibility: the lines perfectly

moves words from the sound world regular, all justified on the right side,

to a world of visual space, everything coming out even visually, and

but print locks words without the aid of guidelines or ruled

into position in this space. borders that often occur in manuscripts.

In handwriting, control of space This is an insistent world of cold,

tends to be ornamental, ornate, non-human, facts.

as in calligraphy.

Passages of flush left and flush right text hinge from a central axis.
Johnschen Kudos

Print situates words
in space more
relentlessly than
writing ever did.
Writing moves words from the sound world to a world of visual space,
but print locks
words into position
in this space.
Control of position
is everything in
print. Printed texts
look machine-made,
as they are.
In handwriting, control of space tends to be ornamental, ornate.
Typographic control
typically impresses
most by its tidiness
and invisibility: the
lines perfectly regular,
all justified on the This is an insistent
right side, everything world of cold,
coming out even non-human, facts.
visually, and without
the aid of guidelines
or ruled borders that
often occur in
manuscripts.

Long, centered lines are bridges between narrow, ragged columns.
Benjamin Lutz

relentlessly than writing ever did. Writing moves words from the sound world to a world of visual space, but print locks words into position in this space. Control of position is everything in print. Printed texts look machine-made, as they are. In handwriting, control of space tends to be ornamental, ornate, as in calligraphy. Typographic control typically impresses most by its tidiness and invisibility: the lines perfectly regular, all justified on the right side, everything coming out even visually, and without the aid of guidelines or ruled borders that often occur in manuscripts. This is an insistent world of cold, non-human, facts.

Print situates words in space more

The beginning of the paragraph is moved to the end.
Daniel Arbello

Print situates words in space more relentlessly than writing ever did. Writing moves words from the sound world to a world of visual space, but print locks words into position in this space.

Control of position is everything in print.

Printed texts look machine-made, as they are. In handwriting, control of space tends to be ornamental, ornate, as in calligraphy. Typographic control typically impresses most by its tidiness and invisibility: the lines perfectly regular, all justified on the right side, everything coming out even visually, and without the aid of guidelines or ruled borders that often occur in manuscripts. THIS IS AN INSISTENT WORLD OF COLD, NON-HUMAN, FACTS.

A single line slides out of a justified block.
Kapila Chase

Print situates words in space more relentlessly than writing ever did.

Writing moves words from the sound world to a world of

VISUAL SPACE

but print locks words into position in this space. Control of position is everything in print. Printed texts look machine-made, as they are.

In handwriting, control of space tends to be ornamental, ornate, as in calligraphy.

Typographic control typically impresses most by its tidiness and invisibility: the lines perfectly regular, all justified on the right side, everything coming out even visually, and without the aid of guidelines or ruled borders that often occur in manuscripts.

This is an insistent world of cold, non-human, facts.

Elements break away from a justified column.
Efrat Levush

Print situates words in space more relentlessly than writing ever did. Writing moves words from the

sound world to a world of visual space, but print locks words into position in this space.

Control of position is everything in print. Printed texts look

machine-made, as they are. In handwriting, control of space tends to be

ornamental, ornate, as in calligraphy. Typographic control typically impresses most

by its tidiness and invisibility: the lines perfectly regular, all justified on the right side,

everything coming out even visually, and without the aid of guidelines or ruled borders that often occur

in manuscripts. This is an insistent world of cold, non-human, facts.

Text is forced into a grid of ragged squares.
Kim Bender

Roman letters are designed to sit side by side, not on top of one another. Stacks of lowercase letters are especially awkward because the ascenders and descenders make the vertical spacing appear uneven, and the varied width of the characters makes the stacks look precarious. (The letter *I* is a perennial problem.) Capital letters form more stable stacks than lowercase letters. Centering the column helps to even out the differences in width. Many Asian writing systems, including Chinese, are traditionally written vertically; the square shape of the characters supports this orientation. The simplest way to make a line of Latin text vertical is to rotate the text from horizontal to vertical. This preserves the natural affinity among letters sitting on a line while creating a vertical axis.

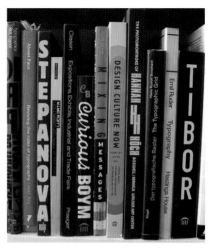

BOOK SPINES *Stacked letters sometimes appear on the spines of books, but vertical baselines are more common. Starting from the top and reading down is the dominant direction in the United States.*

v
e
r
t
i
g
o

TYPE CRIME
STACKED LOWERCASE

v
e
r
t
i
g
o

SMALL CAPS, STACKED

V
E
R
T
I
G
O

V
E
R
T
I
G
O

VERTIGO
A FILM BY ALFRED HITCHCOCK

top to bottom

VERTIGO
A FILM BY ALFRED HITCHCOCK

bottom to top

VERTIGO
A FILM BY ALFRED HITCHCOCK

both directions

VERTICAL BASELINES *There is no fixed rule determining whether type should run from top to bottom or from bottom to top. It is more common, however, especially in the United States, to run text on the spines of books from top to bottom. (You can also run text up and down simultaneously.)*

MEXICAN STREET SIGNS
Photographs by Andrea Marks. *Stacked letters often appear on commercial street signs, which often employ thin, vertical slices of space. The letters in these signs were drawn by hand. Wide characters and squared-off Os stack better than narrow letters with traditional rounded forms. In some instances, the letters have been specially aligned to create vertical relationships, as in the "Optica" sign at right, painted on a sliver of flat molding inside a door frame.*

SIMPATICO

BEVERLY D'ANGELO

JAMES GAMMON

MARCIA GAY HARDEN

ED HARRIS

FRED WARD

WELKER WHITE

STARTS
NOVEMBER 1

THE
PUBLIC
THEATER

425 LAFAYETTE STREET
(212) 598-7150

WRITTEN AND
DIRECTED BY
SAM SHEPARD

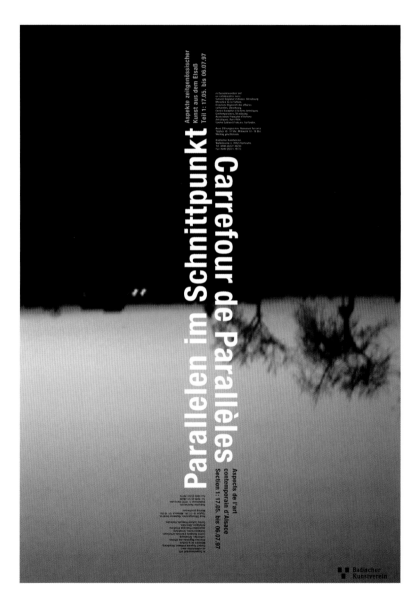

SIMPATICO Poster for the Public Theater, 1994. Designer: Paula Scher/ Pentagram. *Type set on a vertical baseline creates movement across the poster. The theater's logo, which also employs a vertical baseline, can be easily placed on street banners.*

PARALLELEN IM SCHNITTPUNKT (CROSSING PARALLELS) Poster, 1997. Designer: Gerwin Schmidt. Publisher: Art-Club Karlsruhe. *The axes of type and landscape intersect to create posters that are simple, powerful, and direct. The text is mirrored in German and French.*

I N THE BEGINNING of a text, the reader needs an invitation to come inside. Enlarged capitals, also called *versals*, commonly mark the entrance to a chapter in a book or an article in a magazine. Many medieval manuscripts are illuminated with elaborately painted rubrics. This tradition continued with the rise of the printing press. At first, initials were hand-painted onto printed pages, making mass-produced books resemble manuscripts, which were more valuable than printed books. Initials soon became part of typography. A printer could set them together with the main text in wood blocks or cast lead characters, or add them with a separate process such as engraving. Today, enlarged caps are easily styled as part of a publication's typographic system.

A VIEW OF THE MONUMENTS Book page, eighteenth century. *This page was printed in two passes: letterpress type with engraved illustrations.*

NEW YORK TIMES BOOK REVIEW Newspaper page, 2009. Art director: Nicholas Blechman. Illustrator: Ellen Lupton. *The dropped capital is a separate illustration placed in the layout.*

IN THIS PARAGRAPH, the enlarged capital sits on the same baseline as the text that follows. This simple solution is easy to implement on both page and screen. Setting the first few words of the text block in SMALL CAPITALS helps smooth the transition between the initial and the text.

AN ENLARGED LETTER cut into the text block is called a *dropped capital* or *drop cap*. This example was produced using the Drop Caps feature in InDesign. The software automatically creates a space around one or more characters and drops them the requested number of lines. The designer can adjust the size and tracking of the capital to match it to the surrounding text. Similar solutions can be implemented on the web in CSS. The space around the capital is rectangular, which can be visually awkward, as seen here with the sloping silhouette of the letter *A*.

WAS IT THE BEST OF TIMES, the worst of times, or just Times New Roman? The dropped capital used here (The Serif Bold) was positioned as a separate element. A text wrap was applied to an invisible box sitting behind the capital, so that the text appears to flow around the intruding right prow of the *W*. Likewise, the left prow extends out into the margin, making the character feel firmly anchored in the text block. Hand-crafted solutions like this one cannot be applied systematically.

GRAB YOUR READER BY THE CAHUNAS AND NEVER EVER LET GO DESIGNERS SOMETIMES ADAPT the drop cap convention for other purposes. An illustration or icon can appear in place of a letterform. Purely typographic alternatives are also possible, such as inserting a title or subtitle into space carved from the primary text block. Such devices mobilize a familar page structure for diverse and sometimes unexpected uses.

Paragraphs do not occur in nature. Whereas sentences are grammatical units intrinsic to the spoken language, paragraphs are a literary convention designed to divide masses of content into appetizing portions.

Indents have been common since the seventeenth century. Adding space between paragraphs (*paragraph spacing*) is another standard device. On the web, a paragraph is a semantic unit (the `<p>` tag in html) that is typically displayed on screen with space inserted after it.

A typical indent is an *em space*, or a *quad*, a fixed unit of space roughly the width of the letter's cap height. An em is thus proportional to the size of the type; if you change the point size or column width, the indents will remain appropriately scaled. Alternatively, you can use the tab key to create an indent of any depth. A designer might use this technique in order to align the indents with a vertical grid line or other page element. Avoid indenting the very first line of a body of text. An indent signals a break or separation; there is no need to make a break when the text has just begun.

Despite the ubiquity of indents and paragraph spacing, designers have developed numerous alternatives that allow them to shape content in distinctive ways.

NERD ALERT: Use the Space After Paragraph feature in your page layout program to insert a precise increment of space between paragraphs. Skipping a full line often creates too open an effect and wastes a lot of space. Get in the habit of inserting a full paragraph return (Enter key) only at the end of paragraphs; insert a line break when you don't want to add additional space (Shift + Enter).

The table is covered with a table cloth which itself is protected by a plastic table cloth. Drapes and double drapes are at the windows. We have carpets, slipcovers, coasters, wainscoting, lampshades. Each trinket sits on a doily, each flower in its pot, and each pot in its saucer.
  Everything is protected and surrounded. Even in the garden, each cluster is encircled with wire netting, each path is outlined by bricks, mosaics, or flagstones.
  This could be analyzed as an anxious sequestration, as an obsessional symbolism: the obsession of the cottage owner and small capitalist not only to possess, but to underline what he possesses two or three times. There, as other places, the unconscious speaks in the redundancy of signs, in their connotations and overworking.

— *Jean Baudrillard, 1969*

INDENT AND LINE BREAK

The table is covered with a table cloth which itself is protected by a plastic table cloth. Drapes and double drapes are at the windows. We have carpets, slipcovers, coasters, wainscoting, lampshades. Each trinket sits on a doily, each flower in its pot, and each pot in its saucer.

Everything is protected and surrounded. Even in the garden, each cluster is encircled with wire netting, each path is outlined by bricks, mosaics, or flagstones.

This could be analyzed as an anxious sequestration, as an obsessional symbolism: the obsession of the cottage owner and small capitalist not only to possess, but to underline what he possesses two or three times. There, as other places, the unconscious speaks in the redundancy of signs, in their connotations and overworking.

— *Jean Baudrillard, 1969*

LINE BREAK AND 1/2 LINE SPACE (PARAGRAPH SPACING)

The table is covered with a table cloth which itself is protected by a plastic table cloth. Drapes and double drapes are at the windows. We have carpets, slipcovers, coasters, wainscoting, lampshades. Each trinket sits on a doily, each flower in its pot, and each pot in its saucer.

Everything is protected and surrounded. Even in the garden, each cluster is encircled with wire netting, each path is outlined by bricks, mosaics, or flagstones.

This could be analyzed as an anxious sequestration, as an obsessional symbolism: the obsession of the cottage owner and small capitalist not only to possess, but to underline what he possesses two or three times. There, as other places, the unconscious speaks in the redundancy of signs, in their connotations and overworking.

— *Jean Baudrillard, 1969*

OUTDENT (HANGING INDENTATION) AND LINE BREAK

The table is covered with a table cloth which itself is protected by a plastic table cloth. Drapes and double drapes are at the windows. We have carpets, slipcovers, coasters, wainscoting, lampshades. Each trinket sits on a doily, each flower in its pot, and each pot in its saucer.   Everything is protected and surrounded. Even in the garden, each cluster is encircled with wire netting, each path is outlined by bricks, mosaics, or flagstones.   This could be analyzed as an anxious sequestration, as an obsessional symbolism: the obsession of the cottage owner and small capitalist not only to possess, but to underline what he possesses two or three times. There, as other places, the unconscious speaks in the redundancy of signs, in their connotations and overworking.

— *Jean Baudrillard, 1969*

EXTRA SPACE INSIDE LINE, WITHOUT LINE BREAK

The table is covered with a table cloth which itself is protected by a plastic table cloth. Drapes and double drapes are at the windows. We have carpets, slipcovers, coasters, wainscoting, lampshades. Each trinket sits on a doily, each flower in its pot, and each pot in its saucer. ■ Everything is protected and surrounded. Even in the garden, each cluster is encircled with wire netting, each path is outlined by bricks, mosaics, or flagstones. ■ This could be analyzed as an anxious sequestration, as an obsessional symbolism: the obsession of the cottage owner and small capitalist not only to possess, but to underline what he possesses two or three times. There, as other places, the unconscious speaks in the redundancy of signs, in their connotations and overworking.

— *Jean Baudrillard, 1969*

SYMBOL, WTHOUT INDENT OR LINE BREAK

The table is covered with a table cloth which itself is protected by a plastic table cloth. Drapes and double drapes are at the windows. We have carpets, slipcovers, coasters, wainscoting, lampshades. Each trinket sits on a doily, each flower in its pot, and each pot in its saucer.

Everything is protected and surrounded. Even in the garden, each cluster is encircled with wire netting, each path is outlined by bricks, mosaics, or flagstones.

This could be analyzed as an anxious sequestration, as an obsessional symbolism: the obsession of the cottage owner and small capitalist not only to possess, but to underline what he possesses two or three times. There, as other places, the unconscious speaks in the redundancy of signs, in their connotations and overworking.

— *Jean Baudrillard, 1969*

TYPE CRIME: TOO MANY SIGNALS *Using paragraph spacing and indents together squanders space and gives the text block a flabby, indefinite shape.*

Different kinds of content invite different approaches to marking paragraphs. In early printed books, paragraphs were indicated with a symbol, such as ||, with no additional space or line break. In the seventeenth century, it became standard to indent the first line of a paragraph and break the line at the end. Commercial printing tends to embrace fragmentation over wholeness, allowing readers to sample bits and pieces of text. Modern literary forms such as the interview invite designers to construct inventive typographic systems.

Dominus Salomoni secundò apparens, iubet sua seruare præcepta, addita comminatione nisi seruata fuerint. Salomon plures ædificat ciuitates, gentes sibi facit tributarias, & classe in Ophir missa plurimum auri recipit.

C A P.   I X.

[1] **A** ᴄᴛᴠᴍ est autem cùm perfecisset Salomon ædificium domus Domini , & ædificium regis , & omne quod optauerat & volurat facere, [2] apparuit ei Dominus ᴀ secundò || sicut apparuerat ei in Gabaon. [3] Dixítque Dominus ad eum , Exaudiui *2.Par.7. c. 11.* orationem tuam & deprecationem tuam, quam de- *Sup.3.4.5.* precatus es coram me: sanctificaui domū hanc quam ædificasti , vt ponerem nomen meum ibi in sempiternum , & erunt oculi mei & cor meum ibi cunctis diebus. [4] Tu quoque si ambulaueris coram me, si- *David 2.* cut ambulauit * pater tuus , in simplicitate cordis & in æquitate: & feceris omnia quæ præcepi tibi, & legitima mea & iudicia mea seruaueris,[5] ponam thro- *2.Re.7.b.12* num regni tui super Israel in sempiternum, ||sicut lo- *c.16.* cutus sum Dauid patri tuo, dicens , Non auferetur *1.Pa.22. b.* vir de genere tuo de solio Israel. [6] Si autem auer- *10.* sione auersi fueritis vos & filij vestri, non sequentes me , nec custodientes mandata mea , & ceremonias meas quas proposui vobis, sed abieritis & colueritis deos alienos , & adoraueritis eos : [7] auferam Israel de superficie terræ quam dedi eis, & templum quod ʙ sanctificaui nomini meo proiiciam à conspectu meo, erítque Israel in prouerbium , & in fabulam cunctis populis. [8] Et domus hæc erit in exemplum : omnis qui transierit per eam, stupebit & sibilabit, & dicet, ||Quare fecit Dominus sic terræ huic & domui huic? *Dt.29.d.* [9] Et respondebunt , Quia dereliquerunt Dominum *24.* Deum suum , qui eduxit patres eorum de terra-Æ- *Iere.22.b.8.* gypti , & secuti sunt deos alienos , & adorauerunt eos,& coluerunt eos : idcirco induxit Dominus super eos omne malum hoc. [10] || Expletis autem an- *2.Par.8.a.t* nis viginti postquàm ædificauerat Salomon duas domos , id est , domum Domini & domum regis. [11] (Hiram rege Tyri præbente Salomoni ligna cedrina & abiegna , & aurum iuxta omne quod opus habuerat:)tunc dedit * Salomon Hiram viginti op- *rex L* pida in terra-Galilææ. [12] Et egressus est Hiram de Tyro,vt videret oppida quæ dederat ei Salomon, & non placuerunt ei , [13] & ait , Hæcine sunt ciuitates quas dedisti mihi , frater? Et appellauit eas Ter- ᴄ ram-chabul , vsque in diem hanc. [14] Misit quoque Hiram

ʙɪʙʟᴇ Page detail, c. 1500. *In this beautiful arrangement, the dense, unbroken text column contrasts with a flurry of surrounding details, including a dropped capital, marginal notes, and the triangular chapter summary.*

ALL BUILT-IN FIXTURES are furnished with nickel hardware and 1½-inch casing, to be used as a casing or as a ground for the finished casing.

Stock carried in pine (unfinished).

All ironing boards carried in stock are 12 inches wide—any width made to order.

"PEERLESS" equipment is very simple to install, will require no special arrangements of your plans and will make your house or apartment a real home, a good investment and add a distinction you could not acquire otherwise.

Hoosier Cabinets furnished in oak or flat white finish. Also with aluminum or porceliron table slides.

ᴄᴏᴍᴍᴇʀᴄɪᴀʟ ᴘᴀᴍᴘʜʟᴇᴛ, 1911. *This busy design entreats the reader with an overload of signals: indents, line breaks, paragraph spacing, and ornaments.*

dominate its board?

I'd be interested to know what Maxwell Anderson and David Ross think about the possibility of changing the membership of museum boards so that they more fully represent the communities they claim to serve. Can we imagine a Whitney Museum board that is not a rich man's club?

Irving Sandler

There are diverse museum audiences. A significant constituency consists of artists. They need what they see to make art. In talking to artists, at least of my generation, everyone has told me of the importance of the Museum of Modern Art's permanent collection in the development of their art. I would hope that museums could serve all of their diverse audiences, but the health of art and its future depends on how they meet the needs of artists.

Maurice Berger

Dan, you wrote: "Because of this feeling of being excluded, I believe that one of the most important commitments any museum professional can make is to try to reach out and connect to the public through continuous lectures, gallery tours, workshops, and the difficult but necessary writing of readable wall and brochure texts."

This is a very important point, yet I suspect that you may be the exception rather than the rule. All too often, I have found (as a consultant to a number of museums) resistance on the part of many curators to examining and improving their pedagogical skills. Indeed, education departments are often marginal to or left out of the curatorial process. On Thursday, I will open a two-day session on museum education, public address, and pedagogy.

Irving, you wrote: "A significant constituency consists of artists. They need what they see to make art. . . . I would hope that museums could serve all of their diverse audiences, but the health of art and its future depends on how they meet the needs of artists."

A very important observation—the museum as a space of education, inspiration, and motivation for other artists.

Maxwell L. Anderson

Alan asked about the possibility of opening up major museum boards. It took me quite some time to persuade the Whitney Museum board that it would be logical to have a seat for an artist. I was lucky enough to have three artists on the board of Toronto's Art Gallery of Ontario, a much larger museum spanning from the Renaissance to the present with a budget comparable to the Whitney's.

The concern expressed by the Whitney's board was that having an artist could create conflicts of interest. I noted that it might well be a conflict of interest to have trustees who actively collected in the general areas that the museum does, but that I trust members to recuse themselves when discussions warrant it.

Eventually, I was given the green light by the Nominating Committee to invite Chuck Close, who graciously accepted over a bottle of Glenlivet in his studio, and proved to be a superb trustee. Chuck has helped keep the conversation alive and focused on the museum's mission. His term was up this June.

My nominee to succeed him would have provided a return engagement to mine a current, in this case the Whitney, but that was not to be. Chuck's term has been extended, and he will be terrific as long as he cares to stay on. My preference was to alternate, at the end of each three-year term, between a more senior artist and a midcareer artist.

As far as other positions on boards, the prevailing desire of most nominating committees is to have trustees with the means necessary to fuel a campaign and support the annual fiscal burden of the operating budget. One can understand the impulse. On the other hand, across the nation there is still an unfilled need for greater ethnic diversity and better representation of various segments of an artistic spectrum—in the Whitney's case, for example, for more collectors of contemporary art.

For the makeup of a board to change, there has to be an overarching will to do it. That is not the impulse around the United States today. When times are tight, whatever will there might be is put to the side in a quest to find people with proven capacity to give.

Mary Kelly

Over the years, I have noticed how the same work, shown in different contexts, draws vastly different audiences, in terms of numbers and responses, and perhaps this is why I placed emphasis on the issue of reception in my earlier remarks. Of course, in making a work, there is a subjective investment that presupposes an audience, or put another way, the desire of the other. I think artists are always speaking, consciously or unconsciously, to very specific people—friends, lovers, patrons, collectors, and sometimes to certain communities—professional, political, social, generational, or geographic, but this is never the same audience constructed by the exhibition. Considered as a "statement," you could say an exhibition is formulated by a curator/author who is given the

Museums of Tomorrow: A Virtual Discussion
Issues in Cultural Theory 8
12–13 October

MUSEUMS OF TOMORROW: A VIRTUAL DISCUSSION Book spread, 2004. Designed by Franc Nunoo-Quarcoo and Karen Howard. *Outdents (instead of indents) mark paragraph breaks in this multi-authored text.*

DESIGN BEYOND DESIGN Book spread, 2004. Designed and edited by Jan van Toorn. *Lines and blocks of text slide into the margin to mark changes of voice in an ongoing conversation.*

discussion

hasn't been any talking about artistic practice and political practice. So how can artists and graphic designers intervene? At the same time, it is not for the others that one intervenes, it is with the others and for oneself. That is very important; we should not be paternalistic missionaries. I think that politics itself is an art, politics is the art of managing conflicts, the art of relations of force, and therefore necessarily involves the people who possess the power of expression. For let me remind you that expression and the orderly transfer of ideas play a very, very important role in conflicts.

Member of the audience
I would like to ask Jörg Petruschat how he sees the relation between social conflict and artistic practice, especially in relation to design.

Jörg Petruschat
I can hear..., but today it's the seventh of november and... at school I had to learn russian. I'll try it.
I came here for three reasons. I see that revolution in technology served to cement the social status quo. Many designers hope to change the world when they go to technologies and I think that is a big illusion. And my duty is not to say to you what you have to do in future, but my duty is to think about what I see in the present. And I think it's an illusion to run behind the technology changes in the hope of changing the social status quo. In my opinion we should not make the mistake of thinking that we are the greatest because we are the latest. We have to look into the history and the problems of history because the situation, as I showed, from the fifteenth down to the nineteenth century has many similarities with the situation today. That's the first.
The second is that technology is a political structure, it transmits a kind of power, of economic power, and this is a new form that we cannot touch in our everyday life. This technology functions behind a façade. So the political is also structural in this case.
When designers think there are possibilities to change the world in contact with these technological systems they think like Walter Gropius, that the computer's only an instrument. I think that is false. The computer is not only an instrument but a big structure with many standards, and standards affect everyday life. That's the third reason.

Member of the audience
I enjoyed Susan's talk very much. But I have some doubts. Are you really saying: I want to go back to the original meaning of the word aesthetics, to go back to perception, and I want to see how perception is displaced in our culture?

Susan Buck-Morss
I do think that there is this opacity of representation, in other words, the way art is not just communication, the way that there's something

friday 7 november

else going on there. Either it's the medium itself, or it's something else that is extremely important. That's the most political we can do better to concentrate on that, than to think about exactly what message is getting across in the sense of a representational message, a direct message. But when you speak about aesthetics and an aesthetics problematic, I think it's what the avant-garde can only hope to do now. I think the avant-garde legitimated its leadership in the past by thinking it knew where history was going. I think this notion of history in progress is very dangerous. You can't be elitist if you know where we're going and you know what's holding us. I really agree with Benjamin that one has to argue radical but give up absolutely the notion of progress or automatic progress.
What does that leave for an avant-garde? That is my question and I was trying to argue as one part of political art, but not all of political art. And in this avant-garde possibility I was thinking about interruption in a temporal sense, or displacement. Maybe it is a very important kind of space where not very pleasant things happen. I do think that it's still possible, and for me rather fruitful, to think of a tradition of avant-garde art and how that could be reformulated, not in the way that would say what political art should be about, but something that gives some description and direction.

Lorraine Wild
My question... do you think that in the context of what you're talking about, that it keeps being useful to talk about art, even at all as the definition of what is actually avant-garde or necessary at the moment? I was thinking about that when you opened up with the installation by Ramirez in Tijuana's public plaza, that in fact is a building that demonstrates a code. You could actually not call that art at all, you could call that an informational exhibition, but that somehow this nomenclature that we attach to the activity immediately sets it out into a different round, makes it more difficult to talk about; and that encrusted with the whole idea of cultural hierarchy that in fact works against the very thing.

Susan Buck-Morss
Well, I mean it's interesting, what you say. What the difference is between the word design and the word art. Art is the code word in late western bourgeois society for disinterested interest, for non-instrumental practice. And so I am trying to occupy that or to use it. In fact you're talking about public space of communication; you're not actually talking about anything that obeys the conventional definitions of art. Somehow, we get stuck with this almost retrogressive notion of art, but then actually that very same definition has been used to prevent or tends to create a wall when it comes to this sort of activi-

90   91

CAPTIONS

The placement and styling of captions affect the reader's experience as well as the visual economy and impact of page layouts. Some readers are primarily attracted to pictures and captions, while others prefer to follow a dominant written narrative, consulting illustrations in support of the text. From a reader's perspective, close proximity of captions and images is a welcome convenience. Placing captions adjacent to pictures is not always an efficient use of space, however. Designers should approach such problems editorially. If captions are essential to understanding the visual content, keep them close to the pictures. If their function is merely documentary, adjacency is more easily sacrificed.

EL BANCO DE UNO | Signage proposal | Agency: Saffron | Design: Joshua Distler, Mike Abbink, Gabor Schreier, Virginia Sardón

EL BANCO DE UNO
Signage proposal
Agency: Saffron
Design: Joshua Distler, Mike Abbink, Gabor Schreier, Virginia Sardón

EL BANCO DE UNO
Signage proposal
Agency: Saffron
Design: Joshua Distler, Mike Abbink, Gabor Schreier, Virginia Sardón

EL BANCO DE UNO
Signage proposal
Agency: Saffron
Design: Joshua Distler, Mike Abbink, Gabor Schreier, Virginia Sardón

1 Newspaper, 2009. Design: Nick Mrozowski. © www.ionline.pt. *Captions tell a story in this layout from the Portuguese newspaper i.*

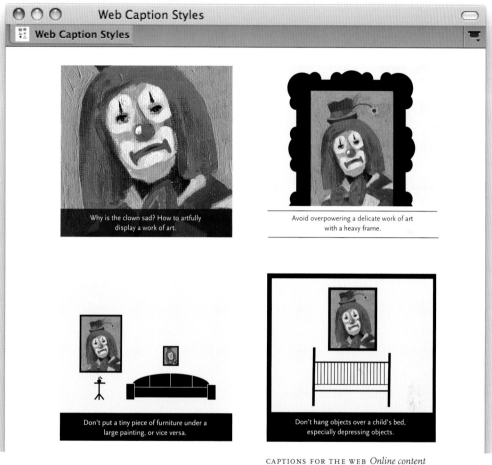

CAPTIONS FOR THE WEB *Online content management systems coordinate pictures and captions in a database. Designers use rules, frames, overlays, and color blocks to visually connect images and captions, creating coherent units. Shown here are four different ways to style captions for the web.*

INTERACTIVE WEB CAPTIONS Guardian.co.uk, 2009. Design director: Mark Porter. *A secondary caption reveals itself when users rolls over this image on the* Guardian's *home page.*

A typographic *hierarchy* expresses the organization of content, emphasizing some elements and subordinating others. A visual hierarchy helps readers scan a text, knowing where to enter and exit and how to pick and choose among its offerings. Each level of the hierarchy should be signaled by one or more cues, applied consistently across a body of text. A cue can be spatial (indent, line spacing, placement) or graphic (size, style, color). Infinite variations are possible.

Writers are trained to avoid redundancy as seen in the expressions "future plans" or "past history." In typography, some redundancy is acceptable, even recommended. For example, paragraphs are traditionally marked with a line break *and* an indent, a redundancy that has proven quite practical, as each signal provides backup for the other. To create an elegant economy of signals, try using no more than three cues for each level or break in a document.

Emphasizing a word or phrase within a body of text usually requires only one signal. *Italic* is the standard form of emphasis. There are many alternatives, however, including **boldface**, SMALL CAPS, or a change in color. A full-range type family such as Scala has many weight and style variations designed to work together. You can also create emphasis with a **different font**. If you want to mix font families, such as Scala and **Futura**, adjust the sizes so that the x-heights align.

BOLD, ITALIC, UNDERLINED CAPS!

TYPE CRIME
TOO MANY SIGNALS
*Emphasis can be created
with just one shift.*

EXPRESSING HIERARCHY

I	Division of angels	Division of angels	DIVISION OF ANGELS		
	A. Angel	Angel	*Angel*		*angel*
	B. Archangel	Archangel	*Archangel*	DIVISION	*archangel*
	C. Cherubim	Cherubim	*Cherubim*	OF ANGELS	*cherubim*
	D. Seraphim	Seraphim	*Seraphim*		*seraphim*
II	Ruling body of clergy	Ruling body of clergy	RULING BODY OF CLERGY		
	A. Pope	Pope	*Pope*		*pope*
	B. Cardinal	Cardinal	*Cardinal*	RULING BODY	*cardinal*
	C. Archbishop	Archbishop	*Archbishop*	OF CLERGY	*archbishop*
	D. Bishop	Bishop	*Bishop*		*bishop*
III	Parts of a text	Parts of a text	PARTS OF A TEXT		
	A. Work	Work	*Work*		*work*
	B. Chapter	Chapter	*Chapter*	PARTS OF	*chapter*
	C. Section	Section	*Section*	A TEXT	*section*
	D. Subsection	Subsection	*Subsection*		*subsection*

SYMBOLS, INDENTS, AND LINE BREAKS   INDENTS AND LINE BREAKS ONLY   FONT CHANGE, INDENTS, AND LINE BREAKS   ALIGNMENT, FONT CHANGE, AND LINE BREAKS

MAIN HEAD ———— COMMON TYPOGRAPHIC DISEASES

MAIN TEXT ———— Various forms of dysfunction appear among populations exposed to typography for long periods of time. Listed here are a number of frequently observed afflictions.

TYPOPHILIA An excessive attachment to and fascination with the shape of letters, often to the exclusion of other interests and object choices. Typophiliacs usually die penniless and alone.

TYPOPHOBIA The irrational dislike of letterforms, often marked by a preference for icons, dingbats, and—in fatal cases—bullets and daggers. The fears of the typophobe can often be quieted (but not cured) by steady doses of Helvetica and Times Roman.

SUBSECTIONS ———— TYPOCHONDRIA A persistent anxiety that one has selected the wrong typeface. This condition is often paired with OKD (optical kerning disorder), the need to constantly adjust and readjust the spaces between letters.

TYPOTHERMIA The promiscuous refusal to make a lifelong commitment to a single typeface—or even to five or six, as some doctors recommend. The *typothermiac* is constantly tempted to test drive "hot" new fonts, often without a proper license.

COMMON TYPOGRAPHIC DISEASES

There are endless ways to express the hierarchy of a document.

Various forms of dysfunction appear among populations exposed to typography for long periods of time. Listed here are a number of frequently observed afflictions.

Typophilia An excessive attachment to and fascination with the shape of letters, often to the exclusion of other interests and object choices. Typophiliacs usually die penniless and alone.

Typophobia The irrational dislike of letterforms, often marked by a preference for icons, dingbats, and—in fatal cases—bullets and daggers. The fears of the typophobe can often be quieted (but not cured) by steady doses of Helvetica and Times Roman.

Typochondria A persistent anxiety that one has selected the wrong typeface. This condition is often paired with OKD (optical kerning disorder), the need to constantly adjust and readjust the spaces between letters.

Typothermia The promiscuous refusal to make a lifelong commitment to a single typeface—or even to five or six, as some doctors recommend. The *typothermiac* is constantly tempted to test drive "hot" new fonts, often without a proper license.

COMMUNICATING HIERARCHY Complex content requires a deeply layered hierarchy. In magazines and websites, a typographic format is often implemented by multiple users, including authors, editors, designers, and web producers. If a hierarchy is clearly organized, users are more likely to apply it consistently. Designers create *style guides* to explain the princples of a hierarchy to the system's users and demonstrate how the system should be implemented.

SOLIDARIETÀ INTERNAZIONALE Magazine redesign, 2009. Design: Sezione Aurea. *Publications often commission design firms to create new formats that can be implemented by staff designers and editors. This redesign uses the typefaces Myriad and Utopia, designed by Robert Slimbach. A comprehensive style guide serves to communicate the new format to the magazine's staff.*

STRUCTURAL HIERARCHY Designers and editors should organize content structurally rather than stylistically, especially in digital documents. When creating style sheets in a page layout program, label the elements with terms such as "title," "subtitle," and "caption" rather than "bold," "tiny," or "apple green Arial." In CSS, elements such as em (emphasis), strong, and p (paragraph) are structural, whereas i (italic), b (bold), and br (break) are visual. As a body of content is translated into different media, the styles should continue to refer to the parts of the document rather than to specific visual attributes.

Structural hierarchies help make websites understandable to search engines and accessible to diverse users. A document should have only one h1 heading, because search engines apply the strongest value to this level of the document. Thus to conform with web standards, designers should apply heading levels (h1, h2, and so on) structurally, even when they choose to make some levels look the same. Using structural, semantic markup is a central principle of web standards.

For more on web standards, see Jeffrey Zeldman with Ethan Marcotte, *Designing with Web Standards,* third edition (Berkeley, CA: New Riders, 2009).

THE CITY Website, 2010. Designer: Graham Stinson. *The City is a social networking site that helps churches and non-profits engage in community activities. Auto-detection determines whether the reader is using a desktop or mobile phone and then re-routes layout characteristics in order to create a custom view. Each layout references a different CSS file; the main HTML for each page remains the same.*

HIERARCHY AND ACCESSIBILITY The web was invented in order to provide universal access to information, regardless of a person's physical abilities or access to specialized hardware or software. Many users lack the browsers or software plug-ins required for displaying certain kinds of files, while visually impaired users have difficulty with small type and non-verbal content. Creating structural hierarchies allows designers to plan alternate layouts suited to the software, hardware, and physical needs of diverse audiences.

Sometimes good typography is heard, not seen. Visually impaired users employ automated screen readers that linearize websites into a continuous text that can be read aloud by a machine. Techniques for achieving successful linearization include avoiding layout tables; consistently using alt tags, image captions, and image descriptions; and placing page anchors in front of repeated navigation elements that enable users to go directly to the main content. Various software programs allow designers to test the linearization of their pages.

CLAPHAMINSTITUTE.ORG Website, 2003. Designer: Colin Day/Exclamation Communications. Publisher: The Clapham Institute. *This site was designed to be accessible to sighted and non-sighted users. Below is a linearized version of the home page. A visually impaired reader would hear this text, including the alt tags for each image. The "skip to content" anchor allows users to avoid listening to a list of navigation elements.*

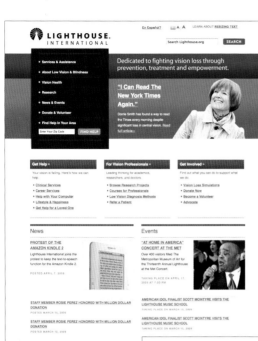

LIGHTHOUSE.ORG Website, 2010. Design: Dan Mall and Kevin Sharon/Happy Cog. Front-end code: Jenn Lukas. Information architecture: Kevin Hoffman. Accessibility research and testing: Angela Colter and Jennifer Sutton. *The visual layout of this website* (LEFT) *is optimized for sighted users, while the source order of the code* (BELOW) *is optimized for the visually impaired, allowing users to linearize the text with an automated screen reader. For example, in the visual display, the navigation menu appears immediately below the logo. In the source code, however, the organization name is followed directly by the tagline, preventing the top of the page from clogging up with navigation elements. Such differences between the visual display and the source order are kept to a minimum because not everyone who uses a screen reader is blind, and some people with disabilities who navigate via source order can see the visual layout with their eyes. If the visual layout differs too much from the source code, these users would be confused. The relationship between the visual layout and the source order is also optimized for search engines.*

```
<body class="home">
<div id="content-wrap">

<div id="header">

        <p class="language"><a href="#">En Espa&ntilde;ol?</a></p>

        <p class="move"><a href="#content">Skip to main content</a></p>

        <h1>
                <img src="/i/logo.gif" alt="" class="hide" />
                <a href="/" title="home">Lighthouse International</a>
        </h1>

        <div class="home-intro">

                <p class="mission"><strong>Dedicated to fighting vision loss through prevention, treatme

                        <div class="home-feature">
                                <img src="/i/content/dorrie-smith.png" alt="Dorrie Smith, blog author and Lighth

                                <h2><a href="/services-assistance/help-with-computers-technology/dorries-sight/i

                                <p>Dorrie Smith has found a way to read the Times every morning despite signific
                        </div>

                        <div id="home-empty-repeat"></div>
                </div>

                <form action="/results/" method="post" id="search">
                        <fieldset>
                                <legend><label for="searchtext" class="move-js">Search Lighthouse.org</label></l

                                <p>
                                        <input type="text" id="searchtext" name="searchtext" class="filled" valu
                                        <input type="image" src="/i/widgets/search.gif" alt="Search" />
                                </p>
                        </fieldset>
                </form>

                <div id="secondary">
                        <ul>
                                <li class="first"><a href="/services-assistance/">Services &amp; Assistance</a><
                                <li><a href="/low-vision-and-blindness/">About Low Vision &amp; Blindness</a></l
                                <li><a href="/vision-health/">Vision Health</a></li>
                                <li><a href="/research/">Research</a></li>
                                <li><a href="/news-events/">News &amp; Events</a></li>
                                <li><a href="/donate-volunteer/">Donate &amp; Volunteer</a></li>
                                <li class="form-wrap">
                                        <form action="/listings/" method="post" id="find-help">
                                                <p>
                                                        <label for="searcharea">Find Help In Your Area</label>
                                                        <input type="text" id="searcharea" name="searcharea" val
                                                        <input type="image" src="/i/widgets/find-help.gif" alt="
                                                </p>
                                        </form>
```

...g des Kaisers
abgebildet:

„Ich habe es nicht gewollt."

Bei Soissons wurden die feindlichen Reih'n
Von den tapfern Deutschen geschlagen,
Da stellt nach der Schlacht Kaiser Wilhelm sich ein,
Um den Helden ein Dankwort zu sagen.

Und wo der geliebte Herrscher erscheint,
Erheben sich grüßend die Hände.
Aus tausend kräftigen Stimmen vereint
Gab's ein Jubelgeschrei ohne Ende.

Nachdem schritt der Kaiser, der sichtlich bewegt,
Auf das Feld, wo vor wenigen Stunden
Die Helden zur ewigen Ruh man gelegt,
Die den Tod auf dem Schlachtfeld gefunden.

Am Grab eines Jünglings stand der Kaiser gebannt—
Kaum „Siebzehn" — im Grab bei den Alten,—
Der Herrscher von Wehmut jetzt übermannt
Konnt' der Tränen sich nicht mehr enthalten.

Er betete Worte — kerndeutsch — treu wie Gold,
Vor denen ein Weltall sich beuge:
„Gott Vater im Himmel — ich hab's nicht gewollt.
Du weißt — Du bist mein Zeuge."

Paul Hambroek
Oberleutnant a. D.

(Mit Genehmigung des Generalkommandos.)

Karl Kraus zählt Wilhelm II.
zu „den Schwerverbrechern
auf dem Thron" mit der
„Beteuerung, daß sie es nicht
gewollt haben, woran sie,
da sie es taten, doch schuldig
sind" [F 595,2].

1920; F 531,52f.

→ gemeinsames **Vorgehen**

→ etwas zum **Vortrag** bringen

→ in die **Falle** gehen

→ ich habe alles reiflich **erwogen**

→ im **Lauf** des Abends

→ ein **Laut** auf den Lippen

→ zum **Schluß**

→ zu **Mantua** in Banden Der treue
   Hofer war

→ **Gesellschaft** mit beschränkter
   Haftung / G. m. b. H.

→ **vorlieb** nehmen

seit der Thronbesteigung!) — —

— — So erlebte ich, daß er einen doch in
Major, den Adjutanten des Kronprinzen, gan
O h r z o g, ihm e i n e n t ü c h t i g e n S c h l a g
g a b und sagte: — —

— — empfing er in Tempelhof im Salo
minister und den Chef des Militärkabinettes mit
alten Esel glaubt, daß ihr alles besser wiß

————————

*) Deutsche Verlagsanstalt, Stuttgart, 192.

Und daß das »gemeinsame Vorgehen« für den
war, »sobald Kraus die Satire auf Kaiser Wilhelm
werde«, beweist eine Vertrautheit der Innsb
Programm, die ich selbst am Nachmittag noch ni
ihnen in die Falle gegangen! Aber wenn einer
Innsbruck auf Demonstrationen ausgehen, bis
Abends eine Ahnung von dem Vorhandensein
will ich dem Wilhelm glauben, daß er es nicht ge
Josef, daß er alles reiflich erwogen hat. Die Wah
einer vagen Kenntnis meiner Gesinnung, aber v
die ihre auszuleben, in den Saal geführten Ind
Abends ein Dutzend weit besserer Anlässe — e
zwei Diebsgenerale — hatten vorübergehen lass
der Laut auf den Lippen erstarb, und erst zum
über die eigene Unregsamkeit ihnen Bewußts
ihre Anwesenheit legitimierten, indem sie

WÖRTERBUCH DER REDENSARTEN/KARL KRAUS, DIE FACKEL
Book, 1999. Designer: Anne Burdick. Publisher:
Österreichische Akademie der Wissenschaften. *This book
presents essays from the journal* Die Fackel, *published by the
Viennese writer Karl Kraus from 1899 to 1936. The journal's text
appears in the center of each page. This text is sometimes
represented with an image of the original publication and
sometimes filtered through the modern typography of the new
edition. In the beige-colored margins, different styles and sizes of
type indicate different modes of editorial commentary.*

RADAR Magazine, 2008. Designed by Luke Hayman/Pentagram and Kate Elazegui/Radar. *Mass-market magazine covers often combine a big photograph, a big headline, and a big logo with a swarm of teasers about articles to be found inside. Radar's covers present feature stories front and center while enticing readers with numerous compact headlines. In contrast, the magazine's table of contents provides a more leisurely overview. Here, the typographic hierarchy emphasizes the articles' titles and uses the page numbers as easy-to-find anchors.*

THE BELIEVER Magazine, front and back covers, 2009. Design: Dave Eggers. Illustrations: Charles Burns. *The busy but readable covers of this literary magazine use slab serif text in multiple sizes and weights to advertise the content found inside. The line illustrations integrate comfortably with the text. A full table of contents appears on the back cover, providing readers with an easy-to-use interface. Influenced by nineteenth-century almanacs, the design of* The Believer *uses borders and frames to draw attention to the content and create a memorable visual identity.*

Michael Bierut, Kerrie Powell, Sunnie Guglielmo

Michael Bierut, Justin Weyers

YALE SCHOOL OF ARCHITECTURE Posters, 2003–2006.
Designers: Michael Bierut and team/Pentagram. *Produced
over a series of years for a single client, these posters apply diverse
typographic treatments and hierarchies to similar bodies of content.
The black-and-white palette creates consistency over time.*

Michael Bierut

Michael Bierut, Genevieve Panuska

Michael Bierut, Jacqueline Kim

Michael Bierut, Andrew Mapes

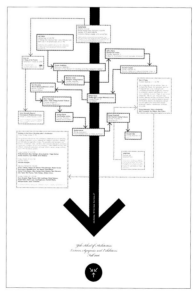

Michael Bierut, Michelle Leong, Sasha Fernando

Choose a text that has a recurring structure, such as a table of contents, a news aggregator, or a calendar of events. Analyze the structure of the content (main title, subtitles, time, location, body text, and so on) and create a visual hierarchy that expresses this structure. Make it easy for readers to find the information they want. For example, in a crime report some readers might scan for location, looking for data about their neighborhood, while others might be more drawn to the lurid details of particular crimes. Use changes in size, weight, leading, style, and column structure to distinguish the levels of the hierarchy. Make a style sheet (in a page layout program for print or in CSS for the web) in order to create several variations quickly.

Crime Blotter

Callie Neylan, Betsy Martin

Crime Blotter

06 00 AM
EAST VILLAGE
Noun Found Smothered by Adjectives *Message lost in dense cloud of confused signals.*

11 30 AM
UPPER EAST SIDE
Verb Defrauded by Misplaced Modifier *Missing the point revenge is sought by victim.*

07 00 PM
WILLIAMSBURG
Flood of Clichés Wreaks Havoc *Hipster kicks bucket after biting bullet and butterfly.*

Callie Neylan, Betsy Martin

Crime Blotter

6:00AM | EAST VILLAGE
Noun Found Smothered by Adjectives
Message lost in dense cloud of confused signals.

11:30AM | UPPER EAST SIDE
Verb Defrauded by Misplaced Modifier
Missing the point, revenge is sought by victim.

7:00PM | WILLIAMSBURG
Flood of Clichés Wreaks Havoc
Hipster kicks bucket after biting bullet.

Katie Burk, Paulo Lopez

`<h1>`
`<h2>`
`<h3>`

Crime Blotter

6:00am **East Village**

Noun Found Smothered by Adjectives

Message lost in dense cloud of confused signals.

`<class="time">`

11:30am **Upper East Side**

Verb Defrauded by Misplaced Modifier

Missing the point, revenge is sought by victim.

7:00pm **Williamsburg**

Flood of Clichés Wreaks Havoc

Hipster kicks bucket after biting bullet.

`<p>`

These typographic variations were generated in CSS using the structural hierarchy presented above.

Examples of work by staff designers in a workshop at National Public Radio, 2010.

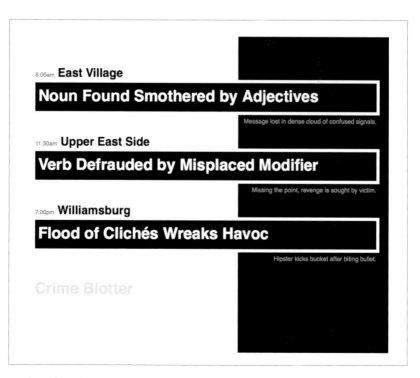

David Wright, Nelson Hsu

In the real world of graphic design, managing large quantities of text is a routine challenge. Designers use the principles of hierarchy, alignment, and page layout to make content easy to scan and enjoyable to read. You can try this exercise with any long list of entries: calendar events, dictionary definitions, pithy quotes, classified ads, or a page from a college course catalog. Numbering the elements in the list gives you a graphic element to manipulate. Design a poster that presents the content in a visually interesting way. Work with style sheets to test different type treatments quickly and consistently.

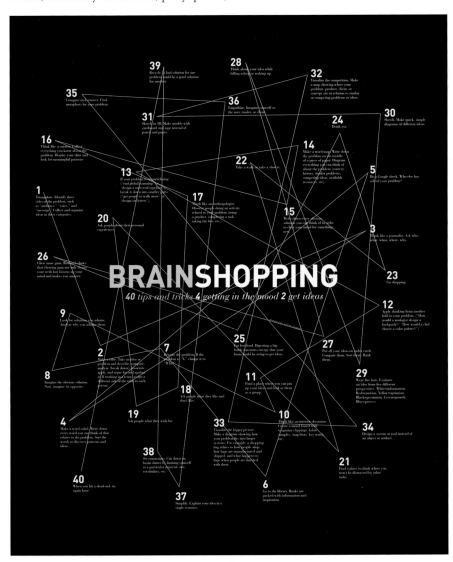

Sabrina Kogan

Examples of student work from Maryland Institute College of Art.

Becky Slogeris

Andy Mangold

{GRID}

HISTORIA NATURALIS
Book, 1472. Printed by
Nicolas Jenson, Venice
Collection of the Walters Art
Museum, Baltimore. *This book
features an elegant, unbroken
text block set in one of the
earliest roman typefaces. The
page has no line breaks or
indents.*

GRID

A GRID BREAKS SPACE OR TIME INTO REGULAR UNITS. A grid can be simple or complex, specific or generic, tightly defined or loosely interpreted. Typographic grids are all about control. They establish a system for arranging content within the space of a page, screen, or the built environment. Designed in response to the internal pressures of content (text, image, data) and the outer edge or frame (page, screen, window), an effective grid is not a rigid formula but a flexible and resilient structure, a skeleton that moves in concert with the muscular mass of information.

Grids belong to the technological framework of typography, from the concrete modularity of letterpress to the rulers, guides, and coordinate systems employed in graphics applications. Although software generates illusions of smooth curves and continuous tones, every digital image or mark is constructed—ultimately—from a grid of neatly bounded blocks. The ubiquitous language of the GUI (graphical user interface) creates a gridded space in which windows overlay windows in a haphazard way.

In addition to their place in the background of design production, grids have become explicit theoretical tools. Avant-garde designers in the 1910s and 1920s exposed the mechanical grid of letterpress, bringing it to the polemical surface of the page. In Switzerland after World War II, graphic designers built a total design methodology around the typographic grid, hoping to construct with it a new and rational social order.

The grid has evolved across centuries of typographic development. For graphic designers, grids are carefully honed intellectual devices, infused with ideology and ambition, and they are the inescapable mesh that filters, at some level of resolution, nearly every system of writing and reproduction.

in librum Job · LVI

LATIN BIBLE Book page, 1497. Printed by Anton Koberger. *A two-column grid engulfs a second set of columns. Each page is a dense mass incised with narrow gutters and open spaces where illuminated capitals would have been added by hand. The layout changes from page to page.*

GRID AS FRAME

Alphabetic writing, like most writing systems, is organized into columns and rows of characters. Whereas handwriting flows into connected lines, the mechanics of metal type impose a stricter order. Each letter occupies its own block, and the letters congregate in orderly rectangles. Stored in gridded cases, the characters become an archive of elements, a matrix of existing forms from which each page is composed.

Until the twentieth century, grids served as frames for fields of text. The margins of a classical book page create a pristine barrier around a flush, solid block of text. A page dominated by a solitary field of type remains today's most common book format, although that perfect rectangle is now broken with indents and line breaks, and the margins are peppered with page numbers and running heads (text indicating the book or chapter title).

In addition to the classical norm of the single-column page, various alternative layouts existed during the first centuries of printing, from the two-column grid of Gutenberg's Bible to more elaborate layouts derived from the medieval scribal tradition, where passages of scripture are surrounded by scholarly commentary. Polyglot (multilingual) books display a text in several languages simultaneously, demanding complex divisions of the surface.

Such formats permit multiple streams of text to coexist while defending the sovereignty of the page-as-frame. The philosopher Jacques Derrida has described the frame in Western art as a form that seems to be separate from the work, yet is necessary for marking its difference from everyday life. A frame or pedestal elevates the work, removing it from the realm of the ordinary. The work thus depends on the frame for its status and visibility.

Typography is, by and large, an art of framing, a form designed to melt away as it yields itself to content. Designers focus much of their energy on margins, edges, and empty spaces, elements that oscillate between present and absent, visible and invisible. With print's ascent, margins became the user interface of the book, providing space for page numbers, running heads, commentary, notes, and ornaments.

The frame...disappears, buries itself, effaces itself, melts away at the moment it deploys its greatest energy. The frame is in no way a background...but neither is its thickness as margin a figure. Or at least it is a figure that comes away of its own accord. —JACQUES DERRIDA, 1987

כפר בראשית א

GENESIS. Translat.B.Hierony. *Creatio.*

CAPVT PRIMVM.

IN principio creauit Deus cælum & terrã. Terra autem erat inanis & vacua: & tenebræ erant super faciê abyssi: & spiritus Dei ferebatur super aquas. Dixitq; Deus, Fiat lux. Et facta est lux. Et vidit Deus lucem quòd esset bona:& diuisit lucem à tenebris. Appellauitq; lucem diem;& tenebras nocte. Factumq; est vespere & mane dies vnus. Dixit quoque Deus, Fiat firmamentũ in medio aquarum; & diuidat aquas ab aquis. Et fecit Deus firmamentum, diuisitq; aquas quæ erant sub firmamento, ab his quæ erant super firmamentũ. Et factum est ita. Vocauitq; Deus firmamentũ, cælum: & factum est vespere, & mane dies secundus. Dixit verò Deus, Congregentur aquæ quæ sub cęlo sunt, in locum vnum; & appareat arida.Et factum est ita. Et vocauit Deus aridã, terram:congregationesq; aquarum appellauit maria. Et vidit Deus quòd esset bonum. Et ait, Germinet terra herbã virentem & facientem semen; & lignum pomiferũ faciens fructũ iuxta genus suum, cuius semen in semetipso sit super terram.Et factũ est ita. Et protulit terra herbam virentẽ, & facientẽ semen iuxta genus suũ;lignumq; faciens fructũ; & habens vnumquodq; sementem secundũ speciem suam. Et vidit Deus quòd esset bonum. Et factum est vespere & mane dies tertius. Dixit autẽ Deus, Fiant luminaria in firmamento cæli; & diuidant diem ac noctẽ; & sint in signa & tẽpora & dies & annos;Vt luceat in firmamento cæli, & illuminent terrã.Et factum est ita. Fecitq; Deus duo luminaria magna: luminare maius, vt præsset diei: & luminare minus,vt præesset nocti: & stellas. Et posuit eas Deus in firmaméto cæli, vt luceret super terrã;Et præessent diei ac nocti;& diuiderent lucem ac tenebras. Et vidit Deus quòd esset bonũ. Et factum est vespere, & mane dies quartus. Dixit etiam Deus,Producant aquæ reptile animæ viuentis, & volatile super terram sub firmamento cæli.

תרגום אונקלוס

בקדמין

CAPVT PRIMVM.

IN principio fecit Deus cælum & terra. At terra erat inuisibilis et incôposita, et tenebræ super abyssum: spiritus Dei ferebatur su per aquam. Et dixit Deus, Fiat lux, & facta est lux. Et vidit Deus lucê, quòd bona: & diuisit Deus inter lucem, & inter tenebras. Et vocauit Deus lucê diê: & tenebras vocauit noctê: & factû est vespere, & factû est maine, dies vnus. Et dixit Deus, Fiat firmamentû in medio aquæ: & sit diuisû inter aquâ, & aquã. Et fecit Deus firmamêtû: & diuisit Deus inter aquã quæ erat sub firmamêto: & inter aquã quæ super firmamêtû. Et vocauit Deus firmamentû cælû: & vidit Deus, quòd bonû. Et factû est vespere, & factû est mane, dies secûdus. Et dixit Deus, Cõgregetur aqua quæ sub cælo, in cõgregatione vnâ, & appareat arida. Et factû est ita: & cõgregata est aqua quæ sub cælo, in cõgregationê suã: & apparuit arida. Et vocauit Deus aridã, terrã: et cõgregationes aquarû, vocauit maria. Et vidit Deus quòd bonû. Et dixit Deus, Germinet terra herba fæni seminante semê secundû genus et secundû similitudinê: & lignû pomiferû faciens fructû, cuius semen ipsius in ipso secundû genus super terrã. Et factum est ita. Et protulit terra herbã fæni seminante semen secundû genus & secundû similitudinê: & lignu pomiferû faciens fructû, cuius semê eius in ipso, secundû genus super terrã. Et vidit Deus quòd bonû. Et factû est vespere, & factû est mane, dies tertius. Et dixit Deus: Fiant luminaria in firmamento cæli, vt luceant super terrã, ad diuidendum inter diê, & inter noctê, & sint in signa, & in têpora, & in dies, & in annos. Et sint in illuminatione in firmamento cæli, vt luceant super terram. Et factum est ita. Et fecit Deus duo luminaria magna: luminare magnû in principatus diei: & luminare minus in principatû noctis: et stellas. Et posuit eas Deus in firmamêto cæli: vt lucerêt super terram: Et præessent diei, & nocti, & diuiderent inter lucê et inter tenebras: & vidit Deus quòd bonû. Et factû est vespere, & factû est mane, dies quartus. Et dixit Deus, Producant a- quæ reptilia animarû viuentiû: & volatilia volatia super terrã, secundû firmamenti cæli: & factû est ita.

CHALDAICÆ PARAPHRASIS TRANSLATIO.
CAPVT PRIMVM.

IN principio creauit Deus cælum & terram. Terra autem erat deserta & vacua; & tenebræ super faciem abyssi: & spiritus Dei inflabat super faciem aquarum. Et dixit Deus, Sit lux; & fuit lux. Et vidit Deus lucem quòd esset bona. Et diuisit Deus inter lucem & inter tenebras. Appellauitque Deus lucem diem, & tenebras vocauit noctem. Et fuit vespere & fuit mane dies vnus. Et dixit Deus, Sit firmamentum in medio aquarum: & diuidat inter aquas & aquas. Et fecit Deus firmamentum: & diuisit inter aquas quæ erant sub- ter firmamentum, & inter aquas quæ erant super firmamentum; & fuit ita. Et vocauit Deus firmamentum cælum: Et fuit vespere & fuit mane, dies secundus. Et dixit Deus, Congregentur aquæ quæ sub cælo sunt, in locum vnum: & appareat arida. Et fuit ita. Et vocauit Deus aridam terram: & locum congregationis aquarum appellauit maria. Et vidit Deus quòd esset bonum. Et dixit Deus, Germinet terra ger- minationem herbæ, cuius filius sementis seminatur: arboremque fructiferam facientem fructus secundum genus suum; cuius filius sementis in ipso sit super terram. Et fuit ita. Et produxit terra germen herbæ, cuius filius sementis seminatur secundum genus suum; & arborem facientem fructus, cuius filius sementis in ipso secundum genus suum. Et vidit Deus quòd esset bonum. Et fuit vespere & fuit mane, dies tertius. Et dixit Deus, Sint luminaria in firmamento cæli, vt diuidant inter diem & noctem: & sint in signa & in tempora: & vt numerentur per ea dies & anni. Et sint in luminaria in firmamento cæli ad illuminandum super terram: & fuit ita. Et fecit Deus duo luminaria magna: lu- minare maius, vt dominaretur in die: & luminare minus, vt dominaretur in nocte: & stellas. Et posuit eas Deus in firmamento cæli ad illuminan- dum super terram. Et vt dominentur in die & in nocte: & vt diuiderent inter lucê & tenebras: & vidit Deus quòd esset bonum. Et fuit vespere & fuit mane, dies quartus. Et dixit Deus, Serpant aquæ reptile animæ viuêtis: & auem quæ volat super terrã super faciê aëris firmamenti cælorum.

A 2

BIBLIA POLYGLOTTA Book spread, 1568. Printed by Christopher Plantin, Antwerp. *Plantin's polyglot Bible is zoned for five different translations (Hebrew, Greek, Aramaic, Syriac, and Latin). Each zone is proportioned to accommodate the typographic texture of a particular script. The page is a dense rectangle cut into parts. The pieces— though highly individualized— fit together into a unified whole. Reproduced from William Dana Orcutt*, In Quest of the Perfect Book *(New York: Little, Brown and Co., 1926).*

148 SUPPLEMENT DE L'ANT. EXPLIQ. Liv. VI.

CHAPITRE SECOND.

*I. La colonne de Pompée. II. On ne convient pas sur ses mesures. III. Colonne
d'Alexandre Severe.*

.. I. LA fameuse colonne de Pompée est auprès d'Alexandrie : on ne sait
pour quelle raison elle porte le nom de Pompée ; je croirois volontiers
que c'est par quelque erreur populaire. Plusieurs voiageurs en ont parlé , tous
conviennent qu'elle est d'une grandeur énorme. Deux des plus modernes
en ont donné le dessein & les mesures ; mais ils different considerablement
entre eux sur la hauteur du piedestal, de la colonne & du chapiteau : cepen-
dant tous deux disent qu'ils l'ont mesurée.

,, Pour ce qui est de la colonne, dit l'un , (c'est Corneille Brun p. 241.)
,, elle est sur un piedestal quarré , haut de sept ou huit pieds & large de qua-
,, torze à chacune de ses faces. Ce piedestal est posé sur une base quarrée ,
,, haute d'environ un demi pied , & large de vingt, faite de plusieurs pierres
,, maçonnées ensemble. Le corps de la colonne même n'est que d'une seule
,, pierre , que quelques-uns croient être de granit ; d'autres disent que c'est
,, une espece de pâte ou de ciment, qui avec le tems a pris la forme de pierre.
,, Pour moi je crois que c'est une vraie pierre de taille, du moins autant que
,, j'ai pu le reconnoitre par l'épreuve que j'en ai faite. Et si cela est vrai, com-
,, me personne presque n'en doute , il y a sujet de s'étonner comment on a
,, pu dresser une pierre de cette grandeur : car après l'avoir mesurée , j'ai trou-
,, vé qu'elle a quatre-vingt-dix pieds de haut , & que sa grosseur est telle, que
,, six hommes peuvent à peine l'embrasser ; ce qui revient , selon la mesure
,, que j'en ai prise, à trente-huit pieds. Au haut il y a un beau chapiteau pro-
,, portionné à la grosseur de la colonne, mais fait d'une piece separée.

L'autre , qui est M. Paul Lucas, en parle en cette maniere : ,, Un de mes
,, premiers soins fut d'aller examiner la colonne de Pompée, qui est près d'A-
,, lexandrie du côté du couchant , & je croi qu'il seroit difficile de rien ajou-

---

CAPUT SECUNDUM.

*I. Columna Pompeii. II. De ejus mensuris non conve-
nit inter eos qui istæc loca adierunt. III. Columna
Alexandri Severi.*

I. CEleberrima illa Pompeii columna prope
Alexandriam erigitur. Cur Pompeii columna
vocetur ; ignoratur. Libenter crederem hujusmodi
denominationem ex populari errore manavisse. Ex
peregrinantibus omnes enormis magnitudinis esse
narrant. Duo recentiores & figuram & mensuras
dederunt , at inter illos non convenit de stylobatæ,
columnæ & capitelli magnitudine. Attamen ambo
dicunt se mensuras excepisse.

,, Quantum ad columnam , inquit Cornelius
,, Brunius p. 241. ea imposita est quadrato styloba-
,, tæ cujus altitudo est septem octove pedum, la-
,, tera vero singulis in faciebus sunt quatuordecim
,, pedum. Stylobates autem ille quadratæ basi im-
,, ponitur , altitudine dimidii pedis, ex lapidibus
,, plurimis structa basis est , longitudinis circum-
,, quaque viginti pedes habens. Columna ex uno
,, lapide est , plurimi putant ex marmore granito
,, esse , alii vero quasi cæmentum & compactam
,, materiam esse, quæ procedente tempore , formam
,, lapidis sumserit. Puto ego esse lapidem quantum
,, saltem experiri licuit. Quod si ita sit , id autem
,, nemo hodie in dubium vocat ; plane mirum
,, quo pacto tantum lapidem erigere potuerint.
,, Nam cum mensuram duxissem , nonaginta pedes
,, altitudinis habere comperi , tantæque ejus est spis-
,, situdo , ut sex viri simul vix illam amplecti pos-
,, sint , id quod ad mensuram a me sumtam redu-
,, citur , circuitus enim ejus est triginta & octo
,, pedum. In culmine capitellum est ex uno lapide
,, secundum columnæ proportionem.

Alius , nempe Paulus Lucas , columnam sic des-
cribit. ,, Ubi primum potui columnam Pompeii
,, adii , quæ prope Alexandriam est versus oc-
,, cidentem. Difficile autem esset ejus mensuras

---

mount Perazim,[1] he shall be wroth as *in* [g]the valley of Gibeon, that he may do his work, [r]his strange work; and bring to pass his act, his strange act.

22 Now therefore [s]be ye not mockers, [t]lest your bands be made strong: for I have heard from the Lord God of hosts, [u]a consumption, even determined upon the whole earth.

23 ¶ Give [v]ye ear, and hear my voice; hearken, and hear my speech.

24 Doth the ploughman plough all day to sow? doth he open and [w]break the clods of his ground?

25 When he hath made plain the face thereof, doth he not cast abroad the fitches,[2] and scatter the cummin, and cast in[3] the principal wheat, and the appointed barley, and the rye,[4] in their place?[5]

26 For[6] [x]his God doth instruct him to discretion, *and* doth teach him.

27 For the fitches are not [y]thrashed with a thrashing-instrument, neither is a cart-wheel turned about upon the cummin; but [z]the fitches are beaten out with a staff, and the cummin with a rod.

28 [a]Bread-*corn* is bruised;[8] because he will not ever be thrashing it, nor break *it with* [b]the wheel of his cart, nor bruise it *with* his horsemen.

29 This also [c]cometh forth from the Lord of hosts, *which* is wonderful in counsel, *and* excellent in working.

CHAPTER XXIX.

God's heavy judgments upon Jerusalem, 1—6. The unsatiableness of her enemies, 7, 8. The senselessness, 9—12, and deep hypocrisy of the Jews, 13—17. A promise of sanctification to the godly, 18—24.

WOE[9] to Ariel, to Ariel, the[10] city *where* David dwelt! [a]add ye year to year; let them kill[11] sacrifices.

2 Yet [b]I will distress Ariel, and there shall be heaviness and sorrow: and[c] it shall be unto me as Ariel.[12]

3 And I will [d]camp against thee round about, and will lay siege against thee with a mount, and I will raise forts against thee.

4 And [e]thou shalt be brought down, *and* shalt speak out of the ground, and thy speech shall be low out of the dust, and thy voice shall be, as

(748)

of one that hath a familiar spirit, out of the ground, and thy speech shall whisper[1] out of the dust.[2]

5 Moreover, [f]the multitude of thy strangers shall be like small dust, and the multitude of the terrible ones *shall be* [g]as chaff that passeth away; yea, it shall be [h]at an instant suddenly.

6 Thou shalt be [i]visited of the Lord of hosts with thunder, and with earthquake, and great noise, with storm and tempest, and the flame of devouring fire.

7 And [k]the multitude of all the nations that fight against Ariel, even all that fight against her and her munition, and [l]that distress her, shall be [m]as a dream of a night-vision.

8 It shall even be[3] [n]as when an hungry *man* dreameth, and, behold, he eateth; but he awaketh, and his soul is empty: or as when a thirsty *man* dreameth, and, behold, he drinketh; but he awaketh, and, [o]behold, *he is* faint, and his soul hath appetite: so shall the multitude of all the nations be that fight against mount Zion.

9 ¶ Stay yourselves, [p]and wonder; cry[4] ye out, and cry: [q]they are drunken,[5] but not with wine; they stagger, but not with strong drink.

10 For [r]the Lord hath poured out upon you the spirit of deep sleep, and [s]hath closed your eyes: the prophets and your rulers,[6] [t]the seers, hath he covered.

11 And the vision of all[7] is become unto you as the words of a [u]book [w]that is sealed, which *men* deliver to one that is learned, saying, Read this, I pray thee: and he saith, [x]I cannot; for it *is* sealed.

12 And the book[9] is delivered to him that is not learned, saying, Read this, I pray thee: and he saith, [y]I am not learned.

13 ¶ Wherefore the Lord[10] said, [z]Forasmuch as this people draw near *me* with their mouth, and with their lips do honour me, but have removed their heart far from me, and [a]their fear[11] toward me is taught by the precept of men:

14 Therefore, behold, [b]I will proceed[9] to do a marvellous work among

this people, *even* a marvellous work and a wonder; *a*for the wisdom of their wise *men* shall perish, and the understanding of their prudent *men* shall be hid.

15 Woe unto them that *b*seek deep to hide their counsel from the Lord, and*c* their works are in the dark, and they say, *d*Who seeth us? and who knoweth us?

16 Surely[1] *e*your turning of things upside down shall be esteemed *f*as the potter's clay: for shall the work say of him that made it, He made me not? *g*or shall the thing framed say of him that framed it, He had no understanding?

17 ¶ *Is* it not *h*yet a very little while and *i*Lebanon*2* shall be turned into a fruitful field, and *k*the fruitful field shall be esteemed as a forest?

18 And in that day shall *l*the deaf hear the words of the book, and the eyes of the blind shall see out of obscurity, and out of darkness.

19 The *m*meek also shall increase*3* *their* joy in the Lord, and *n*the poor among men shall *o*rejoice in the Holy One of Israel.

20 For *p*the terrible one is brought to nought, and *q*the scorner is consumed, *r*and all that watch*4* for iniquity are cut off:

21 That *s*make a man*5* an offender for a word, *t*and lay a snare for him that reproveth in the gate, *u*and turn aside the just for a thing of nought.

22 Therefore thus saith the Lord, who*6* redeemed Abraham, concerning the house of Jacob, *w*Jacob shall not now be ashamed, neither shall his face now wax pale.

23 But when he seeth his children, the*x* work of mine hands, in the midst of him, they shall *y*sanctify my name, and sanctify the Holy One of Jacob, and shall *z*fear the God of Israel.

24 They *a*also that erred in spirit shall come*7* to understanding, and they that murmured shall learn doctrine.

CHAPTER XXX.

The prophet threateneth the people for their confidence in Egypt, 1–7, and contempt of God's word, 8–17. God's mercies toward his church, 18–26. God's wrath, and the people's joy in the destruction of Assyria, 27–33.

WOE to *a*the rebellious children, saith the Lord, *b*that take coun-

sel, but not of me; and that *c*cover with a covering, but not of my Spirit, that they may *d*add sin to sin:

2 That *e*walk to go down into Egypt, *f*and have not asked at my mouth; to strengthen themselves in the strength of Pharaoh, and to trust in *g*the shadow of Egypt!

3 Therefore shall *h*the strength of Pharaoh be your shame, and the trust in the shadow of Egypt *i*your confusion.

4 For *k*his princes were at *l*Zoan, and his ambassadors came to *m*Hanes.

5 They were all *n*ashamed of a people *that* could not profit them, nor be an help nor profit, but a shame, and also a reproach.

6 The *o*burden of the *p*beasts of the south:*2* *q*into the land of trouble and anguish, from whence *come* the young and old lion, *r*the viper and fiery flying serpent, they will carry their *s*riches upon the shoulders of young asses, and their treasures upon the bunches of camels, to a people *that* shall not profit *them*.

7 For *t*the Egyptians shall help in vain, and to no purpose: therefore have I cried concerning*3* this, *u*Their strength*4* *is* to sit still.

8 ¶ *v*Now go, *w*write it before them in a table,*5* and note it in a book, that it may be for the*6* time to come for ever and ever;

9 That *x*this *is* a rebellious people, *y*lying children, children *that* *z*will not hear the law of the Lord:

10 Which *a*say to the seers, See not; and to the prophets, Prophesy not unto us right things, *b*speak unto us smooth things, prophesy *7*deceits:

11 Get *b*you out of the way, turn aside out of the path, *c*cause the Holy One of Israel to cease from before us.

12 Wherefore thus saith the Holy One of Israel, *d*Because ye despise this word, *e*and trust in *9*oppression and perverseness, and stay thereon:

13 Therefore this iniquity shall be to you *f*as a breach ready to fall, swelling out*10* in a high wall, whose breaking *g*cometh suddenly at an instant.

14 And *h*he shall break it as the

(749)

Center reference column

A.M.3291. B.C.713.

c ch.19.3,11-14; Job 5,
13; Je.8.7-9; John9.29.
d Ps. 1. 1; 73.11; 22.28; 1
Co.1.19-24.
b ch.30.1; Job22.13,14;
Ps. 10.11-13; 139.1-4;
Je.23.24; Eze.8.12.
a Job 24. 13-17; 34. 22;
John3.19.
d ch.47.10; Ps.73.11.
1 Rather, 'Oh your
perverseness! Shall
the potter be regarded as the clay'? *i* s
as if he had no more
understanding and
skill than his work.
Paul employs the
same allusion but
for a different purpose, Ro. 9.20. The
points of comparison
are the nothingness
of man, the infinity
of God.
e ch.24.1; Je.47.6.
f ch. 45.9,10; Ro. 9.19-
21.
g Ps.94.8,9.
k ch. 63. 18; Hag. 2.6;
He.10.37.
i ch.32.15,33.1,2;Ho.1.
9,10;Ro.11.11-17.
2 There shall be
changes as great as
if Lebanon should
become a cultivated
region, or as if a well-
tilled field should
grow up into a
forest.
k Hos. 3. 4; Mic. 3. 12;
Eze.11.1,3; Ro.11.19-
27.
l ch. 35. 24; Mat. 11. 5;
Mar. 7.37; John 5.45;
Ac.26.18;Ep.1.17-19;
1Pe.2.9;Re.3.18.
m ch.61.1;Ps.25.9;Mat.
5.3;11.29; Ga.5.22,23;
Ja.3.13-18; 1Pe.2.1-3.
3 Heb. *add*.
n ch. 41. 17; Zep.3.
12,18; Mat.5.3,11.5; 1
Co.1.26-29.
o ch. 61. 10; Hab. 3.18;
Ph.3.1,4,4.
p ch.49.25;Hab.1.6,7.
q ch.28.14-22.
r Mic. 2.1; Mar. 2. 6,7;
Lu.6.7.
4 That is, who anxiously seek for opportunities to commit
iniquity.
s Mat.22.15.
5 Heb. *the latter day*.
t The connection requires that this
should be understood
of those who administer justice; and the
sense is probably correctly expressed by
Noyes, 'Who condemned the poor man
in his cause.' So
also Rosenmüller,
Gesenius, & Henderson.
t Je.18.18; Am.5.10,7.
10-17.
u Pr.18.21; Eze.13.19;
Mat. 26.15; Ac. 3.14;
Ja.5.6.
x ch.41.8,9,14; Ge. 48.
16;Lu.1.68;1Pe.1.18,
19; Re.5.9.
6 This is a poetical
introduction of Jacob
as the ancestor of
the Jewish people,—
as if the venerable
patriarch were looking upon his children.
Their deportment
had been such as
would suffuse a father's cheeks with
shame; henceforward in the reformation that should occur he should not be
ashamed of them, but
should look on them
with approbation.—
Barnes.
y ch. 44. 23-26; 49. 7.
&c.; 61.7-11; Je.30.5-
7, 10; Eze. 39. 25-29;
Joel 2. 27; Ro. 11. 11,
&c.
z ch.29.23;50.21;Ep.2.
10.
a ch.3.16;Mat.6.9; Re.
11.13-17.
a Ho.3.3;Re.13.4.
b ch. 28. 7; Zec. 12.10;
Mat.21.38-32; Lu.15.
17-19;Ac.2.37,6.7.
7 Heb. *know understanding.*

CHAP. XXX.
A.M.3291. B.C.713.
a ver.9; ch.65.2; De.9.
7,24; Eze. 2.3; 12. 2,3;
Ac.7.51,52.
*b*ch.8.19;1Jo.10.13,14.

c ch. 4.5;Jer. , 28.15
1 The idea which best
suits the connection
here is that suggested
by Lowth, in accordance with the Septuagint, and the
Syriac, and adopted
by Rosenmüller, Gesenius, &c., 'to make
a libation; that is, to
make a covenant, or
compact.
d ch. 1.5,5.18; Hos.13.
2;Ti.3.13.
e ch.20.5,6;31.1-3;Eb.
17.4; Je.37.5; Eze.29.
6,7.
f Nu. 27.21; Jos. 9.14;
Je.42.2,20.
g ch. 19.1;Jo.9.15.
h Jer.37.5,7.11,12.
16.
i ch.19.11;Nu.13.22.
m Je.43.7, *Tahpanhes;*
Eze. 30. 18, *Tehaphnehes.*
n ch.30.5,6.
o ch.46.1,2.
p 1Ki.10.2.
2 The prophet sees
the caravan, or the
beasts of the ambassadors heavily laden
with rich treasures
travelling southward
towards Egypt, and
cries out, 'O the
heavy burden, the
load of treasures
going to the south.'
—*Barnes.*
q ch.9.4; De.1.29; Je.
11.4.
r Nu.21.6,7;De.8.15.
s ch.9.1.
t ch.31.1-3.
3 Or, *to her.*
u ver. 15; ch. 7.4; Ps.
14.13; La.3.26; Ho.5.
13.
4 The word rendered
'strength,' *Rahab*, is
a proper name of
Egypt,and the phrase
rendered 'to sit still,'
is a part of the name
which the prophet
gave to her, 'I have
called her *Rahab*, the
inactive.'
v ch.8.1; Je.36. 2,23-32;
51.60;Hab.2.2.
5 Heb. *the better day*,
ch. 2.2;Nu.24.14. De.
4.30; Job 19.25; Eze.
38. 16; Ho. 3.5; 1 Ti.
4.1.
w ver.1;ch.1.4: De.32.
29; Je.44.3-47; Ac.7.
51.
x ch.59.3,Jo.9.5,5; Ho.
13.
y 1Ch. 36. 13,16; Ne.9.
29,30; Je.7.13; Zec.7.
11,12.
z 1Ki.11.29;2Ch.16.10;
Je.3. 31; 26.11, 20-23;
29.27; 38. 4; Am.2.12;
7.13;Mic.2.6;Ac.4.17,
18;1Ti.3.15,16.
a 1Ki.22.6-13,27; Je.6.
13,14; Eze.13.7-10,18-
22;John 7.7.
7 'No man professedly
desires to be deceived; but many a man
is willing to put himself under that kind
of teaching which is
deceit, and which he
might know to be
deceit and falsehood
if he would examine
it.'
b Am.7.13.
c John 13.7,8,24; Pp.4.
4.
6 They said they were
weary of the name of
the Holy One of Israel, (ver. 11,) and
of the perpetual reiteration of his commands. Isaiah, as if
to shew them how
little he was disposed
to comply with their
prejudices, makes an
immediate appeal to
that name again.
d ch. 5. 24; 31. 1,3; Am.
2. 4; Lu 10. 16; 1Th.
4.8.
e ch.28.15;Je.13.25.
9 *Or, fraud.*
f Eze. 13. 10-15; Mat.
17.3,5.1,3.
g Ps.2.9;Je.19.10,11.

LES MOTS EN LIBERTÉ FUTURISTES: LETTRE D'UNE JOLIE FEMME À UN MONSIEUR PASSEISTE Poem, 1912. Author: F. T. Marinetti. *In this Futurist poem, Marinetti attacked the conventions of poetry and the restrictions imposed by the mechanical grid of letterpress. The rectilinear pressures of the grid are nonetheless evident in the composed work.*

MERZ-MATINÉEN Poster, 1923. Designer: El Lissitzky. *The Russian Constructivist artist and designer traveled extensively in Europe in the 1920s, where he collaborated with other members of the international avantgarde, including the Dadaist Kurt Schwitters. This precisely assembled poster for a Dada event is organized and activated by the rectilinear grid of letterpress.*

FORTOLIET Postcard, 1925. Designer: Piet Zwart. Collection of Elaine Lustig Cohen. *The Dutch graphic designer Piet Zwart was influenced by the De Stijl movement as well as Constructivism. In the visual identity he created for Fortoliet, a flooring company, Zwart built monumental letters out of typographic rules.*

DIVIDING SPACE

In the nineteenth century, the multi-columned, multimedia pages of newspapers and magazines challenged the supremacy of the book and its insular edge, making way for new typologies of the grid. By questioning the protective function of the frame, modern artists and designers unleashed the grid as a flexible, critical, and systematic tool. Avant-garde artists and poets attacked the barriers between art and everyday life, creating new objects and practices that merged with urban experience.

Leading the assault against print's traditional syntax was F. T. Marinetti, who established the Futurist movement in 1909. Marinetti devised poems that combined different styles and sizes of type and allowed lines of text to span multiple rows. Marinetti's ingenius manipulations of the printing process work against—but inside—the constraints of letterpress, exposing the technological grid even while trying to overturn it. Dada artists and poets performed similar typographic experiments, using letterpress printing as well as collage, montage, and various forms of photomechanical reproduction.

Constructivism, which originated in the Soviet Union at the end of the 1910s, built on Futurist and Dada typography, bringing a more rational approach to the attack on typographic tradition. El Lissitzky employed the elements of the print shop to emphasize the mechanics of letterpress, using printer's rules to make the technological matrix actively and physically present. Constructivism used rules to divide space, throwing its symmetry into a new kind of balance. The page was no longer a fixed, hierarchical window through which content might be viewed, but an expanse that could be mapped and articulated, a space extending beyond the edge.

For Dutch artists and designers, the grid was a gateway to the infinite. The paintings of Piet Mondrian, their abstract surfaces crossed by vertical and horizontal lines, suggest the expansion of the grid beyond the limits of the canvas. Theo van Doesburg, Piet Zwart, and other members of the Dutch De Stijl group applied this idea to design and typography. Converting the curves and angles of the alphabet into perpendicular systems, they forced the letter through the mesh of the grid. Like the Constructivists, they used vertical and horizontal bars to structure the surface of the page.

Typography is mostly an act of dividing a limited surface. —WILLI BAUMEISTER, 1923

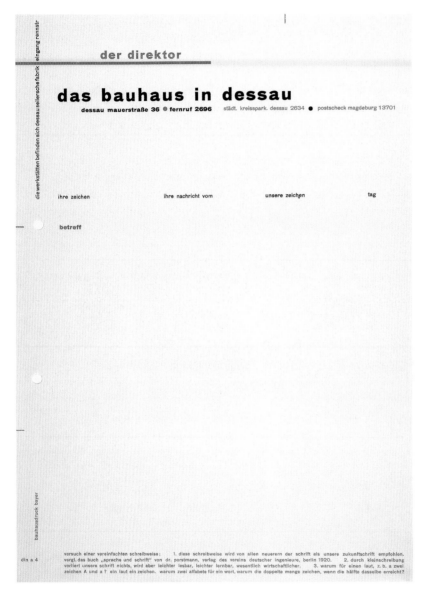

DAS BAUHAUS IN DESSAU
Letterhead, 1924. Designer:
Herbert Bayer. Collection of
Elaine Lustig Cohen. *Herbert
Bayer's letterheads for the
Bauhaus are manifestos for a
new typographic order. Rather
than provide a decorative frame
or a centered title, Bayer treated
the entire page as a surface to be
divided. Points, short hatches,
and lines of type indicate axes
for folding the sheet and
positioning text. This letterhead
also promotes Bayer's idea that
all letters should be lowercase,
a point expounded in small
print across the bottom.*

The new typography not only contests the classical "framework"
but also the whole principle of symmetry. —PAUL RENNER, 1931

Jan Tschichold's book *The New Typography*, published in Germany in 1928, took ideas from Futurism, Constructivism, and De Stijl and conveyed them as practical advice for commercial printers and designers. Functionally zoned letterheads using standard paper sizes were central to Tschichold's practical application of modernism. Whereas Futurism and Dada had aggressively attacked convention, Tschichold advocated design as a means of discipline and order, and he began to theorize the grid as a modular system based on standard measures.

By describing the expansion of space in all directions, the modern grid slipped past the classical frame of the page. Similarly, modern architecture had displaced the centered facades of classical building with broken planes, modular elements, and continuous ribbons of windows. The protective frame became a continuous field.

 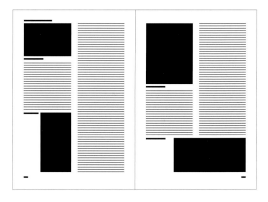

THE NEW TYPOGRAPHY
Diagram, 1928
(redrawn). Designer and
author: Jan Tschichold

Tschichold's diagram of good and bad magazine design advocates staggering images in relation to content instead of forcing text to wrap around blocks moored at the center of the page. Explaining this experiment, Tschichold wrote that his redesigned pages would be even more effective if the photographic halftones (called "blocks") were produced in fixed rather than arbitrary sizes.

I have intentionally shown blocks of different and "accidental" widths, since this is what usually has to be contended with (although in the future, with standard block-sizes, it will happen less often).
—JAN TSCHICHOLD, 1928

ZAHN-NOPPER Store identity, 1961–63. Designer: Anton Stankowski. *This identity system demonstrates a programmatic approach to design, using a limited set of elements to construct diverse yet genetically linked solutions. The system is governed by flexible rules for construction rather than a fixed logotype.*

GRID AS PROGRAM

Classics of Swiss design theory include Josef Müller-Brockmann, *Grid Systems in Graphic Design* (Switzerland: Ram Publications, 1996; first published in 1961) and *The Graphic Artist and His Design Problems* (Switzerland: Arthur Niggli Ltd., 1961); and Karl Gerstner, *Designing Programmes* (Switzerland: Arthur Niggli, 1964). See also Emil Ruder, *Typography* (New York: Hastings House, 1981; first published in 1967).

During the post–World War II period, graphic designers in Switzerland honed ideas from the New Typography into a total design methodology. It was at this time that the term *grid* (*Raster*) became commonly applied to page layout. Max Bill, Karl Gerstner, Josef Müller-Brockmann, Emil Ruder, and others were practitioners and theorists of a new rationalism that aimed to catalyze an honest and democratic society. Rejecting the artistic clichés of self expression and raw intuition, they aspired to what Ruder called "a cool and fascinating beauty."

Gerstner's book *Designing Programmes* (1964) is a manifesto for systems-oriented design. Gerstner defined a design "programme" as a set of rules for constructing a range of visual solutions. Connecting his methodology with the new field of computer programming, Gerstner presented examples of computer-generated patterns that were made by mathematically describing visual elements and combining them according to simple rules.

Expanding on the pioneering ideas of Bayer, Tschichold, Renner, and other designers of the avant garde, the Swiss rationalists rejected the centuries-old model of the page-as-frame in favor of a continuous architectural space. Whereas a traditional book would have placed captions, commentary, and folios within a protective margin, the rationalist grid cut the page into multiple columns, each bearing equal weight within the whole, suggesting an indefinite progression outward. Pictures were cropped to fit the modules of the grid, yielding shapes of unusual proportion. Constructing ever more elaborate grids, the Swiss designers used the confines of a repeated structure to generate variation and surprise. Such grids could be activated in numerous ways within a single publication, always referring back to the root structure.

This approach, which quickly became known as "Swiss design," found adherents (and detractors) around the world. Many American designers dismissed Swiss rationalism as irrelevant to a society driven by pop culture and hungry for rapidly transforming styles. Programmatic thinking is now being revived, however, as designers today confront large-scale information projects. The need is greater than ever for flexible "programs" designed to accommodate dynamic bodies of content.

The typographic grid is a proportional regulator for composition, tables, pictures, etc.... The difficulty is: to find the balance, the maximum of conformity to a rule with the maximum of freedom. Or: the maximum of constants with the greatest possible variability."
—KARL GERSTNER, 1961

14. Eingangshalle

15. Treppe

2 Mehrfamilienhäuser im Doldertal Zürich

Räumliche Organisation

Situation: Die beiden Mehrfamilienhäuser liegen im Villenviertel, auf halber Höhe des westwärts abfallenden „Zürichberg" [4]. Längs dem Grundstück verläuft auf der Nordwestseite eine öffentliche Parkanlage mit einem dichten Baumbestand. Die Zufahrtsstrasse genannt „Doldertal "hat ein Gefälle von 10% und ist nicht durchgehend. Die Schrägstellung der Blöcke zur Baulinie ergibt eine verbesserte Südlage für die Wohnräume, eine Abdrehung der Schlafräume von der Strasse und eine lockere Gesamtanlage, ohne gegenüberliegende Schmalseiten. [5]   (Siehe auch baugesetzliche Sonderheiten.) Raumprogramm: Es ist versucht worden, die Vorzüge des Einfamilienhauses soweit als möglich auf die Etagenwohnung zu übertragen (freies, schallsicheres Wohnen, Einbeziehung der Landschaft, grosse Wohnterrassen, weitgehende innere Ausstattung). Im Untergeschoss: Gedeckter Vorplatz mit zwei Garagen, Eingangshalle mit Treppenaufgang, Abstellräume, Vorratskeller, Waschküche und Trockenraum, die beiden letztern nur im untern Haus. Unter der Eingangshalle mit besonderm Eingang [9] (7) liegen Heizung und Kohlenraum. Im Parterre: eine Vierzimmerwohnung mit Mädchenzimmer und ein Einzimmer-Appartment mit direktem Eingang vom Garten. Im Obergeschoss: eine 5/6-Zimmerwohnung mit Mädchenzimmer. Zu dieser

Wohnung gehört noch ein auf Höhe Dachgeschoss liegendes Sonnenbad [12] (16), durch eine Eisentreppe von der Terrasse erreichbar. In beiden Wohnungen liegen Treppe und Küche ausserhalb der eigentlichen Wohnfläche (Schallisolation); dennoch hat die Küche eine betriebstechnisch zentrale Lage (Verbindung mit der Terrasse, je eine Durchreiche nach Essplatz und Treppenhaus.) Im Dachgeschoss ein grosses und ein kleines Atelier, Abstellräume im Treppenbau.

Technische Durchbildung
(vgl. Technische Details)

Konstruktionsprinzip: Eisenskelett, Eisenbeton-Zwischendecken, Fassadenausmauerung mit gebrannten Hohlsteinen, hintermauert mit Gipsdielen. Die Fassaden sind konstruktiv von den Zwischendecken getrennt. Das zurückgesetzte Dachgeschoss besteht aus Holz mit einer äussern Eternitverkleidung. Zur Fertigstellung des Äussern sind ausschliesslich Materialien mit unterhaltsloser Oberfläche verwendet worden: Edelputz (weisser Zement, Natursteinpartikeln, ohne Farbbeigabe); Eternit für Rolladenkasten, Brüstungen, Sonnen-Storen-Vordach und Dachgeschoßaufbau; lackiertes Holz für Rolladen und Garagentore; Kupfer für sämtliche Spenglerarbeiten; feuerverzinktes Eisen für Fensterbleche, Geländer. Gestrichen sind lediglich die Fenster und gewisse Metallteile aus architektonischen Gründen. Fensterflächen: Horizontal-Schiebefenster in Föhrenholz in den Woh-

nungen. Grösse des Normalfensters 310 × 120 cm, zusammengebaut mit dem Rolladenkasten; fester Teil einwärts klappbar zum Reinigen. Die Südfenster des Wohnraumes sind mit der Brüstung zusammengebaut (vgl. [21], [22], [23]). Die Küchenfenster sind doppelt, alle übrigen Fenster am Bau einfach verglast. Die Ateliers haben durchgehende 45 cm hohe Oberlichter unter der Decke mit Lüftungsklappen, sowie gewisse fest verglaste Fenster mit normaler Brüstung. Verglasung: Wohnungsfenster Spiegelglas 6/7 mm, Atelier-Oberlichter Rohglas, Treppenhausfenster Drahtglas. Sonnenschutz: für die Wohnzimmerfenster vor der Fassade gehängte Sonnenstoren [21] (44), für die Schlafzimmer Roll-Jalousien. Heizung: Jedes Haus hat seine eigene Warmwasserheizung für Kleinkaliberkoks, die gleichzeitig für die Warmwasserbereitung benützt wird. Pro Haus ein Warmwasserboiler mit 1000 Liter Inhalt. Wohnungsausstattung: Die beiden Häuser sind für anspruchsvolle Mieter, jedoch ohne Luxus ausgestattet. Die Zimmer sind dementsprechend geräumig dimensioniert (Wohnraum 35,00 m², Terrasse 20,00 m²). Die Skelettkonstruktion erlaubt jederzeit eine den Wünschen der Mieter entsprechende Variabilität des Grundrisses. Im Wohnraum befindet sich ein offener Kamin und ein breites Fensterbrett für Blumen. Eingebaute Schränke im Korridor, in den Zimmern, kleiner Abstellraum. Fussböden: In den Wohnungen Holzmosaik (Esche im Wohnraum, Eiche in den übrigen Räumen und im Korridor.

2 Mehrfamilienhäuser im Doldertal Zürich   52

16. Teilansicht von Südwest mit Eingang und Garagen

In den Küchen sind Steinzeugplatten, versuchsweise Linoleum; in den Bädern Terrazzo, schwarz, mit weissen Marmorkörnern. Die Treppentritte und Podeste bestehen ebenfalls aus Terrazzo (Tritte fertige Platten, Podeste im Bau gegossen und geschliffen). Die Stirnseiten der Tritte und die Sockel sind mit weissen, hartglasierten Platten belegt [14]. Die Böden der Ateliers sind mit hellgrauem Linoleum belegt. Wandbehandlung: Gipsverputz in sämtlichen Räumen, Kalkabrieb in Küchen, Bädern und Aborten. Die Wände der Zimmer sind mit Leimfarbe gestrichen, mit Ausnahme derjenigen in den Wohnräumen und Gängen (tapeziert mit Grundpapier und Leimfarbanstrich, oder Ölfarbanstrich auf Stoffbespannung). In den Ateliers Verkleidung der Wände in Holzkonstruktion mit Sperrplatten (gewachste finnische Birke).
Im Treppenhaus: Aussenwand stoffbespannt, mit Ölfarbe gestrichen, mittlere Brüstungswand gespachtelt und Hochglanz mit Ripolin gestrichen; der Handlauf in Eisen, im Feuer weiss emailliert. Fenstersimse: Diese bestehen in allen Räumen der Wohnungen aus perforierten, 3 cm starken Schieferplatten. Ausstattung der Bäder und Küchen: Grösse des Bades in den Wohnungen 6 m² mit Badwanne, Bidet und zwei Lavabos, W.C. Der Spiegel über den Lavabos ist gegen die festverglaste Fensterfläche gehängt (Licht auf das Gesicht). Die Küchen sind vollständig ausgestattet, je eine Durchreiche ins Treppenhaus und in den Wohn-Essraum, zweiteiliger Aufwaschtisch in Chrom-

nickel-Stahlblech, Kühlschrank, Arbeitsflächen in Ahornholz. Elektrische Beleuchtung: Diese ist in allen Wohn- und Schlafräumen, Gängen, Küchen, Ateliers eine indirekte.

Ökonomische Angaben
Die beiden Häuser sind Privatbesitz von Herrn Dr. S. Giedion, Zentralsekretär der Internationalen Kongresse für Neues Bauen. Die Baukosten inkl. Architektenhonorar betragen: 43,5 Maurerstunden · pro m³ umbauten Raumes bei total 1985 m³ pro Haus, offene Halle im Parterre zur Hälfte gerechnet. Die durchschnittlichen Baukosten für normale Wohnbauten in Zürich, ohne besonderen Ausbau, betragen 38 bis 40 Maurerstunden pro m³ umbauten Raumes. (1 Mstd.= Fr. 1.72 1935/36)

Ästhetischer Aufbau
Die Schrägstellung der Blöcke ergibt einerseits eine lockere Gesamtanlage und erhöht anderseits deren plastische Selbständigkeit. Der zweigeschossige Charakter der Häuser (Baubestimmung der betreffenden Zone) wird durch das Loslösen des Baukörpers vom Terrain und durch das Zurücksetzen des Dachgeschosses gewahrt. Dieser Eindruck wird verstärkt durch die vom Hauptbau abweichende Konstruktion des Dachgeschosses (Holz und Eternit). In der Südfassade ist durch Weglassen der gemauerten Brüstungen ein äusseres Zusammenfassen von Wohnraum und Wohnterrasse erreicht. In der räumlichen Gliederung treten vielfach schräg verlaufende Wände auf, wodurch eine gewisse Auflockerung der Rechtwinkligkeit erreicht wird. Die Eingangshalle ganz in Glas hat eine freie Form und lässt den Durchblick in den rückwärtsliegenden Park frei.
Der Garten reicht über die weitergeführten Gartenplatten (Granit) bis zum Treppenaufgang. In den Wohnräumen und Ateliers reichen die Fenster bis zur Decke, in den Schlafräumen ist ein Sturz von 40 cm. In der Dimensionierung von Bauteilen und Ausstattungsdetails ist eine dem betreffenden Material entsprechende Sparsamkeit sowie eine organische und gepflegte Formgebung beobachtet worden. Materialbehandlung und Farbgebung: Aussen wirken die Baustoffe in ihrer natürlichen Struktur und Farbe: Edelputz (weisser Zement mit roten, schwarzen und glimmernden Steinsplittern), Eternit, lackiertes Holz, Eisenteile feuerverzinkt, mit Aluminiumfarbe gestrichen. Farbe an folgenden Stellen: Fensterrahmen dunkelgrau, Geländerrohre, Abdeckbleche weissgrau, die sichtbaren Kellermauern und Säulen sind normal verputzt und hellgrau gestrichen. Im Innern: Die Wände im Treppenhaus, in den Gängen und Nebenräumen sind weissgrau, ebenso das gesamte Holzwerk, Radiatoren, Leitungen. Die Wände der Wohn- und Schlafräume sind hell getönt (beige, rosa, hellblau, grau). Besondere farbige Akzente kommen weder aussen noch innen vor; es ist damit der wechselnden Bewohnung des Miethauses Rechnung getragen worden.

53   2 Mehrfamilienhäuser im Doldertal Zürich

DIE NEUE ARCHITEKTUR/
THE NEW ARCHITECTURE
Book, 1940. Designer: Max Bill.
Author: Max Roth. Photograph:
Dan Meyers.

Designed by Max Bill in 1940, this book is considered the first use of a systematic modular grid. Each image is sized to fit the column structure—as Jan Tschichold had predicted in 1928—filling one, two, or three zones. Acknowledging the originality of its layout, the author credits Bill as "the creator of the typographical structure of the book."

Der New-York-Times-Prospekt zeigt die Lösung einer komplexen Aufgabe; zeigt, wie eine Idee, ein Text und die typographische Darstellung über mehrere Phasen hinweg integriert werden. Darüber hinaus kann sich die Aufgabe stellen, Prospekte wie diesen wiederum mit andern Werbemitteln und Drucksachen zu integrieren. Denn heute brauchen Firmen mehr und mehr nicht bloss hier einen Prospekt, da ein Plakat, dort Inserate usw. Heute braucht eine Firma etwas anderes: Eine Physiognomie, ein optisches Gesicht.

Die Beispiele dieser Seiten geben die Physiognomie der boîte à musique, eines Grammophongeschäfts in Basel, wieder. Die boîte à musique hat ein Signet und einen firmeneigenen Stil – und doch wieder nicht, wenn man unter dem einen ein starres, nachträglich überall dazugesetztes Zeichen und unter dem andern ein bloss ästhetisches Prinzip versteht. Vielmehr: Die einmal definitiv festgelegten, aber jeweils den verschiedenen Funktionen und Proportionen angepassten Elemente selber bilden das Signum und den Stil in einem.

Abbildung 13 zeigt die Struktur. Fixiert sind die Elemente Schrift und Rahmen; ferner die Verbindung von beiden und das Prinzip der Variabilität: der Rahmen kann, ausgehend von der Ecke unten rechts, nach oben sowie nach links beliebig um ganze Einheiten vergrössert werden. Einen in sich proportional hervorragenden Fall gibt es nicht. Es gibt nur wertgleiche Varianten; und hervorragend ist die Variante dann, wenn sie der jeweiligen Aufgabe am besten angemessen ist.

Abbildung 14 zeigt die Neujahrskarte mit gleichzeitig verschieden proportionierten Varianten; 15 den Briefbogen, wo das Signum dem (gegebenen) Din A4 Format angepasst ist; 16 und 17 Inserate, wieder entsprechend dem zur Verfügung stehenden Insertionsraum bemessen; 18 ein Geschenkbon.

13

56.57

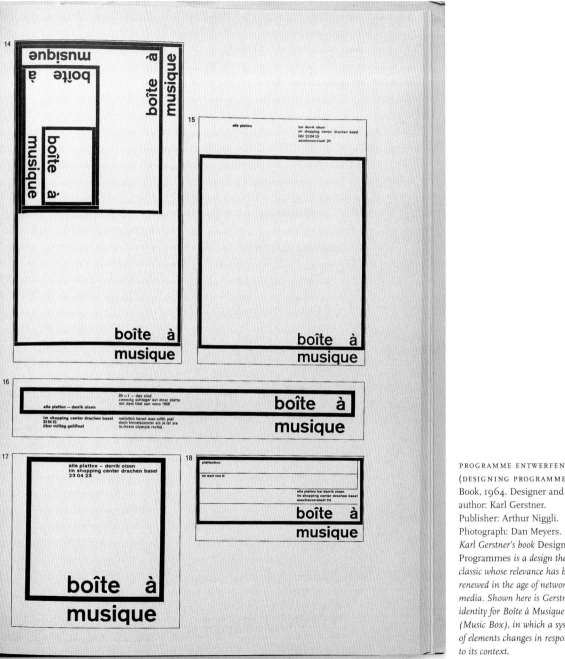

PROGRAMME ENTWERFEN (DESIGNING PROGRAMMES) Book, 1964. Designer and author: Karl Gerstner. Publisher: Arthur Niggli. Photograph: Dan Meyers. *Karl Gerstner's book* Designing Programmes *is a design theory classic whose relevance has been renewed in the age of networked media. Shown here is Gerstner's identity for Boîte à Musique (Music Box), in which a system of elements changes in response to its context.*

GRID AS TABLE

Tables and graphs are a variant of the typographic grid. A table consists of vertical columns and horizontal rows, each cell occupied by data. A graph is a line mapped along the *x* and *y* axes of a grid, each dimension representing a variable (such as time and stock value, shown below). As explained by Edward Tufte, the leading critic and theorist of information design, tables and graphs allow relationships among numbers to be perceived and rapidly compared by the eye. In tables and graphs, the grid is a cognitive tool.

Tables are a central aspect of web design. The table feature was incorporated into HTML code in 1995 so that web authors could present tabular data. Graphic designers, eager to give shape to the web's wide and flacid text bodies, quickly devised unauthorized uses for the HTML table, transforming this tool for representing data into nothing more, nor less, than a typographic grid. Designers have used the table feature to control the placement of images and captions and to build margins, gutters, and multicolumn screens. Designers also use tables to combine multiple styles of alignment—such as flush left and flush right—within a document, and to construct elegantly numbered and bulleted lists.

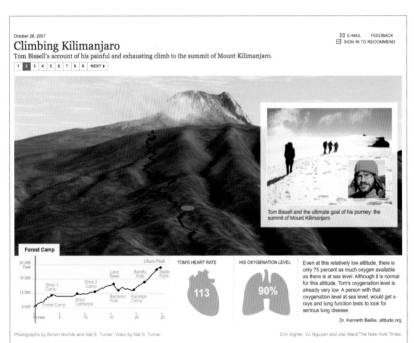

CLMBING KILIMANJARO (BELOW) Interactive information graphic, 2007. Graphics director: Steve Duenes/NYTimes.com. Courtesy of the New York Times. *This interactive three-dimensional travelogue traces Tom Bissell's harrowing climb to the top of Mount Kilimanjaro. The fever graph plots the distance Bissell traveled in relation to the changing elevation. The graphic coordinates his path with photographs shot along the way and an ongoing account of Bissell's rising heart rate and plummeting oxygenation level.*

On the aesthetics and ethics of information design, see Edward Tufte, *Envisioning Information* (Cheshire, Conn.: Graphics Press, 1990).

On designing accessible websites, see Jeffrey Zeldman with Ethan Marcotte, *Designing with Web Standards*, third edition (Berkeley, CA: New Riders, 2009) and Patrick Lynch and Sarah Horton, *Web Style Guide: Basic Design Principles for Creating Web Sites* (New Haven: Yale University Press, 2001). See also the site www.webstyleguide.com.

By creating cells that span multiple columns and rows, designers build layout structures that bear little relation to the logically ordered fields of a data chart. A master table typically establishes areas for navigation, content, and site identity, and each region contains a smaller table—or tables—inside itself. Grids propagate inside of grids.

Advocates of web standards reject such workarounds as spurious and unethical design tactics. Visually driven, illogical layout tables can cause problems for sight-impaired users, who implement various devices to translate digital pages into sound, cell by cell, row by row. Assistive screen readers "linearize" digital text into a stream of spoken words. Accessibility experts encourage web designers to "think in linear terms" wherever possible, and to make sure their tables make sense when read in a continuous sequence. Accessible websites also consider the needs of users working with older software or text-only browsers. Linear thinking helps not only sight-impaired audiences but also the users of mobile devices, where space is tight.

MICA.EDU Website, 2004. Designers: Carton Donofrio Partners. Publisher: Maryland Institute College of Art. *HTML tables, with their borders gently expressed, are an element of this neatly gridded webpage. Here, the table element is used not as a secret grid but as a structure for organizing content in columns and rows.*

HTML, the mark-up system that allowed the Internet to become a global mass medium, is the virtual counterpart to letterpress, which mechanized the production of the book and cleared the ground for a world culture of print. Like letterpress, HTML is a text-hungry medium that can be coaxed, with some resistance, to display images.

HTML coexists with other languages on the web, just as alternative technologies appeared alongside letterpress. Lithography, invented for the manufacture of images in the eighteenth century, soon incorporated words in addition to pictures, just as letterpress made space in its mechanical grid for woodcuts, engravings, and photographic halftone blocks. In the twentieth century, lithography replaced letterpress as the world's dominant printing method; used with digital or photographic typesetting, it conveys text and pictures with equal comfort.

Lithography is not governed by grids as relentlessly as letterpress; neither is Flash, the animation software that became a common web-design tool at the turn of the twentieth century. Flash was originally designed for the creation of vector-based cartoons. Although Flash's primary purpose was pictorial, designers were soon using it to construct the interfaces of entire websites. The Flash sites that became, in the late 1990s, icons of a new web aesthetic were more cinematic than typographic, often featuring a painterly mix of word and image. They were soon supplanted by template-driven sites built dynamically by content management systems. In such sites, elements are placed via CSS (Cascading Style Sheets); the resulting designs have a structured appearance that is predictable over time.

Hand-coding HTML is as slow and deliberate as setting metal type. Empty table cells are used to define areas of open space, but HTML makes these collapse if the cells are truly empty, causing the grid to implode. The transparent images that often fill these spaces are virtual equivalents to the blank spacing material of metal type.

THE CHOPPING BLOCK Website (detail), 2004. Designers: Thomas Romer, Jason Hillyer, Charles Michelet, Robert Reed, and Matthew Richmond/The Chopping Block. *This website reprises the design of early twentieth-century fruit-crate labels, which were produced as lithographic prints that merge text and image. The webpage is animated, loading elements over time.*

JOSHUADAVIS.COM Website, 2009. Designer: Joshua Davis. *In this template-driven site, elements are automatically arranged in a uniform grid.*

RETURN TO UNIVERSALS

William Gibson's 1984 novel *Neuromancer* envisions cyberspace as a vast ethereal grid. Gibson's data cowboy leaves behind the "meat" of his body and drifts off into a "transparent 3d chessboard extending to infinity." In Gibson's novel, this chessboard grid is projected on an internal surface of the mind, bound by no screen or window.

The grid as infinite space—defying edges and dominated by the mind rather than the body—is a powerful instrument within modernist theory, where it is a form both rational and sublime. In the early twentieth century, avant-garde designers exposed the grid in order to dramatize the mechanical conditions of print. After World War II, Swiss designers built a total design methodology around the grid, infusing it with ideological intentions. The grid was their key to a universal language. With the postmodern turn toward historical, vernacular, and popular sources in the 1970s and 1980s, many designers rejected the rationalist grid as a quaint artifact of Switzerland's own orderly society.

The rise of the Internet has rekindled interest in universal design thinking. The web was invented in the early 1990s (in Switzerland) to let scientists and researchers share documents created with different software applications. Its inventor, Tim Berners-Lee, never guessed that the web would become a design-driven medium connecting vast numbers of differently abled and divergently motivated people around the globe.

Universal design systems can no longer be dismissed as the irrelevant musings of a small, localized design community. A second modernism has emerged, reinvigorating the utopian search for universal forms that marked the birth of design as a discourse and a discipline nearly a century earlier. Against the opacity and singularity of unique visual expressions—grounded in regional preferences and private obsessions—ideas of commonality, transparency, and openness are being reborn as information seeks once again to shed its physical body.

On the invention of the web, see Tim Berners-Lee, *Weaving the Web* (New York: HarperCollins, 1999). For a contemporary account of universal design thinking, see William Lidwell, Kritina Holden, and Jill Butler, *Universal Principles of Design* (Gloucester, Mass.: Rockport Publishers, 2003). See also William Gibson, *Neuromancer* (New York: Ace Books, 1984).

To produce designs that are objectively informative is primarily a socio-cultural task. —JOSEF MÜLLER-BROCKMANN, 1961

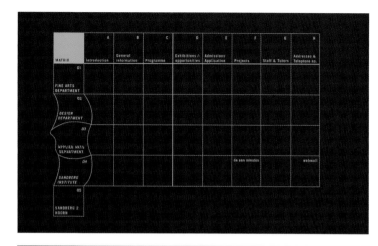

WWW.SANDBERG.NL
Website, 2003. Designer:
Luna Maurer. Publisher:
Sandberg Institute. *The grid is
a navigation device that warps
and changes as the user rolls
over it. The vertical axis
represents departments in the
school, and the horizontal axis
represents types of program
information. As the user passes
over the grid, cells fill with light
and appear to lift away from
the screen, indicating the
availability of information at
that intersection.*

GOLDEN SECTION

The golden section, which appears in nature as well as in art and design, has many surprising properties. For example, when you remove a square from a golden rectangle, the remainder is another golden rectangle, a process that can be infinitely repeated to create a spiral.

No book about typography would be complete without a discussion of the *golden section*, a ratio (relationship between two numbers) that has been used in Western art and architecture for more than two thousand years. The formula for the golden section is a : b = b : (a+b).

This means that the smaller of two elements (such as the shorter side of a rectangle) relates to the larger element in the same way that the larger element relates to the two parts combined. In other words, side *a* is to side *b* as side *b* is to the sum of both sides. Expressed numerically, the ratio for the golden section is 1 : 1.618.

Some graphic designers are fascinated with the golden section and use it to create various grids and page formats—indeed, entire books have been written on the subject. Other designers believe that the golden section is no more valid as a basis for deriving sizes and proportions than other methods, such as beginning from standard industrial paper sizes, or dividing surfaces into halves or squares, or simply picking whole-number page formats and making logical divisions within them.

A grid can be simple or complex, specific or generic, tightly defined or loosely interpreted. Typographic grids are all about control. They establish a system for arranging content within the space of page, screen, or built environment. Designed in response to the internal pressures of content (text, image, data) and the outer edge or frame (page, screen, window), an effective grid is not a rigid formula but a flexible and resilient structure, a skeleton that moves in concert with the muscular mass of content. Grids belong to the technological framework of typography, from the concrete modularity of letterpress to the ubiquitous rulers, guides, and coordinate systems of graphics applications. Although software generates illusions of smooth curves and continuous tones, every digital image or mark is constructed—ultimately—from a grid of neatly bounded blocks. The ubiquitous language of the gui (graphical user interface) creates a gridded space in which windows overlay windows. In addition to their place in the background of design production, grids have become explicit theoretical tools. Avant-garde designers in the 1910s and 1920s exposed the mechanical grid of letterpress, bringing it to the polemical surface of the page. In Switzerland after World War II, graphic designers built a total design methodology around the typographic grid, hoping to build from it a new and rational social order. The grid has evolved across centuries of typographic evolution. For graphic designers, grids are carefully honed intellectual devices, infused with ideology and ambition, and they are the inescapable mesh that filters, at some level of resolution, nearly every system of writing and reproduction. A grid can be simple or complex, specific or generic, tightly defined or loosely interpreted. Typographic grids are all about control. They establish a system for arranging content within the space of page, screen, or built environment. Designed in response to the internal pressures of content (text, image, data) and the outer edge or frame (page, screen, window), an effective grid is not a rigid formula but a flexible and resilient structure, a skeleton that moves in concert with the muscular mass of content. Grids belong to the technological framework of typography, from the concrete modularity of letterpress to the ubiquitous rulers, guides, and coordinate systems of graphics applications. Although software generates illusions of smooth curves and continuous tones, every digital image or mark is constructed—ultimately—from a grid of neatly bounded blocks. The ubiquitous language of the gui (graphical user interface) creates a gridded space in which windows overlay windows. In addition to their

Golden rectangle of text on
8.5 x 11-inch page (U.S. standard)

A grid can be simple or complex, specific or generic, tightly defined or loosely interpreted. Typographic grids are all about control. They establish a system for arranging content within the space of page, screen, or built environment. Designed in response to the internal pressures of content (text, image, data) and the outer edge or frame (page, screen, window), an effective grid is not a rigid formula but a flexible and resilient structure, a skeleton that moves in concert with the muscular mass of content. Grids belong to the technological framework of typography, from the concrete modularity of letterpress to the ubiquitous rulers, guides, and coordinate systems of graphics applications. Although software generates illusions of smooth curves and continuous tones, every digital image or mark is constructed—ultimately—from a grid of neatly bounded blocks. The ubiquitous language of the gui (graphical user interface) creates a gridded space in which windows overlay windows. In addition to their place in the background of design production, grids have become explicit theoretical tools. Avant-garde designers in the 1910s and 1920s exposed the mechanical grid of letterpress, bringing it to the polemical surface of the page. In Switzerland after World War II, graphic designers built a total design methodology around the typographic grid, hoping to build from it a new and rational social order. The grid has evolved across centuries of typographic evolution. For graphic designers, grids are carefully honed intellectual devices, infused with ideology and ambition, and they are the inescapable mesh that filters, at some level of resolution, nearly every system of writing and reproduction. A grid can be simple or complex, specific or generic, tightly defined or loosely interpreted. Typographic grids are all about control. They establish a system for arranging content within the space of page, screen, or built environment. Designed in response to the internal pressures of content (text, image, data) and the outer edge or frame (page, screen, window), an effective grid is not a rigid formula but a flexible and resilient structure, a skeleton that moves in concert with the muscular mass of content. Grids belong to the technological framework of typography, from the concrete modularity of letterpress to the ubiquitous rulers, guides, and coordinate systems of graphics applications. Although software generates illusions of smooth curves and continuous tones, every digital image or mark is constructed—ultimately—from a grid of neatly bounded blocks. The ubiquitous language of the gui (graphical user interface) creates a gridded space in which windows overlay windows. In addition to their

Golden rectangle of text on
A4 page (European standard, 210 x 297 mm)

Commercial printers generally prefer to work with pages trimmed to even measures rather than with obscure fractions. However, you can float golden rectangles within a page of any trim size.

For a more detailed account of design and the golden section, see Kimberly Elam, *Geometry of Design* (New York: Princeton Architectural Press, 2001). For an emphasis on applying the golden section to typography, see John Kane, *A Type Primer* (London: Laurence King, 2002).

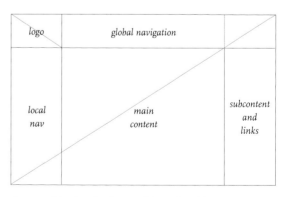

logo   global navigation

local nav   main content   subcontent and links

It may well be absurd to base a website on the golden section, but here, nonetheless, is a design for one. This wire frame diagram describes a webpage that is 500 x 809 pixels. The "golden screen" is then divided with squares and golden rectangles.

SINGLE-COLUMN GRID

A grid can be simple or complex, specific or generic, tightly defined or loosely interpreted. Typographic grids are all about control. They establish a system for arranging content within the space of page, screen, or built environment. Designed in response to the internal pressures of content (text, image, data) and the outer edge or frame (page, screen, window), an effective grid is not a rigid formula but a flexible and resilient structure, a skeleton that moves in concert with the muscular mass of content. Grids belong to the technological framework of typography, from the concrete modularity of letterpress to the ubiquitous rulers, guides, and coordinate systems of graphics applications. Although software generates illusions of smooth curves and continuous tones, every digital image or mark is constructed—ultimately—from a grid of neatly bounded blocks. The ubiquitous language of the gui (graphical user interface) creates a gridded space in which windows overlay windows. In addition to their place in the background of design production, grids have become explicit theoretical tools. Avant-garde designers in the 1910s and 1920s exposed the mechanical grid of letterpress, bringing it to the polemical surface of the page. In Switzerland after World War II, graphic designers built a total design methodology around the typographic grid, hoping to build from it a new and rational social order. The grid has evolved across centuries of typographic evolution. For graphic designers, grids are carefully honed intellectual devices, infused with ideology and ambition, and they are the inescapable mesh that filters, at some level of resolution, nearly every system of writing and reproduction. A grid can be simple or complex, specific or generic, tightly defined or loosely interpreted. Typographic grids are all about control. They establish a system for arranging content within the space of page, screen, or built environment. Designed in response to the internal pressures of content (text, image, data) and the outer edge or frame (page, screen, window), an effective grid is not a rigid formula but a flexible and resilient structure, a skeleton that moves in concert with the muscular mass of content. Grids belong to the technological framework of typography, from the concrete modularity of letterpress to the ubiquitous rulers, guides, and coordinate systems of graphics applications. Although software generates illusions of smooth curves and continuous tones, every digital image or mark is constructed—ultimately—from a grid of neatly bounded blocks. The ubiquitous language of the gui (graphical user interface) creates a gridded space in which windows overlay windows. In addition to their place in the background of design production, grids have become explicit theoretical tools. Avant-garde designers in the 1910s and 1920s exposed the mechanical grid of letterpress, bringing it to the polemical surface of the page. In Switzerland after World War II, graphic designers built a total design methodology around the typographic grid, hoping to build from it a new and rational social order. The grid has evolved across centuries of typographic evolution. For graphic designers, grids are carefully honed intellectual devices, infused with ideology and ambition, and they are the inescapable mesh that filters, at some level of resolution, nearly every system of writing and reproduction. A grid can be simple or complex, specific or generic, tightly defined or loosely interpreted. Typographic grids are all about control. They establish a system for arranging content within the space of page, screen, or built environment. Designed in response to the internal pressures of content (text, image, data) and the outer edge or frame (page, screen, window), an effective grid is not a rigid formula but a flexible and resilient structure, a skeleton that moves in concert with the muscular mass of content. Grids belong to the technological framework of typography, from the

This standard, 8.5 x 11-inch page has even margins all the way around. It is a highly economical, but not very interesting, design.

A grid can be simple or complex, specific or generic, tightly defined or loosely interpreted. Typographic grids are all about control. They establish a system for arranging content within the space of page, screen, or built environment. Designed in response to the internal pressures of content (text, image, data) and the outer edge or frame (page, screen, window), an effective grid is not a rigid formula but a flexible and resilient structure, a skeleton that moves in concert with the muscular mass of content. Grids belong to the technological framework of typography, from the concrete modularity of letterpress to the ubiquitous rulers, guides, and coordinate systems of graphics applications. Although software generates illusions of smooth curves and continuous tones, every digital image or mark is constructed—ultimately—from a grid of neatly bounded blocks. The ubiquitous language of the gui (graphical user interface) creates a gridded space in which windows overlay windows. In addition to their place in the background of design production, grids have become explicit theoretical tools. Avant-garde designers in the 1910s and 1920s exposed the mechanical grid of letterpress, bringing it to the polemical surface of the page. In Switzerland after World War II, graphic designers built a total design methodology around the typographic grid, hoping to build from it a new and rational social order. The grid has evolved across centuries of typographic evolution. For graphic designers, grids are carefully honed intellectual devices, infused with ideology and ambition, and they are the inescapable mesh that filters, at some level of resolution, nearly every system of writing and reproduction. A grid can be simple or complex, specific or generic, tightly defined or loosely interpreted. Typographic grids are all about control. They establish a system for arranging content within the space of page, screen, or built environment. Designed in response to the internal pressures of content (text, image, data) and the outer edge or frame (page, screen, window), an effective grid is not a rigid formula but a flexible and resilient structure, a skeleton that moves in concert with the muscular mass of content. Grids belong to the technological framework of typography, from the concrete modularity of letterpress to the ubiquitous rulers, guides, and coordinate systems of graphics applications. Although software generates illusions of smooth curves and continuous tones, every digital image or mark is constructed—ultimately—from a grid of neatly bounded blocks. The ubiquitous language of the gui (graphical user interface) creates a gridded space in which windows overlay windows. In addition to their place in the background of design production, grids have become explicit theoretical tools. Avant-garde designers in the 1910s and 1920s exposed the mechanical grid of letterpress, bringing it to

This page is an inch shorter than a standard U.S. letter. The text block is a square, leaving margins of varying dimension.

Every time you open a new document in a page layout program, you are prompted to create a grid. The simplest grid consists of a single column of text surrounded by margins.

By asking for page dimensions and margin widths from the outset, layout programs encourage you to design your page from the *outside in.* (The text column is the space left over when the margins have been subtracted.)

Alternatively, you can design your page from the inside out, by setting your margins to zero and then positioning guidelines and text boxes on a blank page. This allows you to experiment with the margins and columns rather than making a commitment as soon as you open a new document. You can add guidelines to a master page after they meet your satisfaction.

GRID SYSTEMS   PAGE ONE

A grid can be simple or complex, specific or generic, tightly defined or loosely interpreted. Typographic grids are all about control. They establish a system for arranging content within the space of page, screen, or built environment. Designed in response to the internal pressures of content (text, image, data) and the outer edge or frame (page, screen, window), an effective grid is not a rigid formula but a flexible and resilient structure, a skeleton that moves in concert with the muscular mass of content. Grids belong to the technological framework of typography, from the concrete modularity of letterpress to the ubiquitous rulers, guides, and coordinate systems of graphics applications. Although software generates illusions of smooth curves and continuous tones, every digital image or mark is constructed—ultimately—from a grid of neatly bounded blocks. The ubiquitous language of the gui (graphical user interface) creates a gridded space in which windows overlay windows. In addition to their place in the background of design production, grids have become explicit theoretical tools. Avant-garde designers in the 1910s and 1920s exposed the mechanical grid of letterpress, bringing it to the polemical surface of the page. In Switzerland after World War II, graphic designers built a total design methodology around the typographic grid, hoping to build from it a new and rational social order. The grid has evolved across centuries of typographic evolution. For graphic designers, grids are carefully honed intellectual devices, infused with ideology and ambition, and they are the inescapable mesh that filters, at some level of resolution, nearly every system of writing and reproduction. A grid can be simple or complex, specific or generic, tightly defined or loosely interpreted. Typographic grids are all about control. They establish a system for arranging content within the space of page, screen, or built environment. Designed in response to the internal pressures of content (text, image, data) and the outer edge or frame (page, screen, window), an effective grid is not a rigid formula but a flexible and resilient structure, a skeleton that moves in concert with the muscular mass of content. Grids belong to the technological framework of typography, from the concrete modularity of letterpress to the ubiquitous rulers, guides, and coordinate systems of graphics applications. Although software generates illusions of smooth curves and continuous tones, every digital image or mark is constructed—ultimately—from a grid of neatly bounded blocks. The ubiquitous language of the gui (graphical user interface) creates a gridded space in which windows overlay windows. In addition to their place in the background of design production, grids have become explicit theoretical tools. Avant-garde designers in the 1910s and 1920s exposed the mechanical grid of letterpress, bringing it to

grid systems   page one

A grid can be simple or complex, specific or generic, tightly defined or loosely interpreted. Typographic grids are all about control. They establish a system for arranging content within the space of page, screen, or built environment. Designed in response to the internal pressures of content (text, image, data) and the outer edge or frame (page, screen, window), an effective grid is not a rigid formula but a flexible and resilient structure, a skeleton that moves in concert with the muscular mass of content. Grids belong to the technological framework of typography, from the concrete modularity of letterpress to the ubiquitous rulers, guides, and coordinate systems of graphics applications. Although software generates illusions of smooth curves and continuous tones, every digital image or mark is constructed—ultimately—from a grid of neatly bounded blocks. The ubiquitous language of the gui (graphical user interface) creates a gridded space in which windows overlay windows. In addition to their place in the background of design production, grids have become explicit theoretical tools. Avant-garde designers in the 1910s and 1920s exposed the mechanical grid of letterpress, bringing it to the polemical surface of the page. In Switzerland after World War II, graphic designers built a total design methodology around the typographic grid, hoping to build from it a new and rational social order. The grid has evolved across centuries of typographic evolution. For graphic designers, grids are carefully honed intellectual devices, infused with ideology and ambition, and they are the inescapable mesh that filters, at some level of resolution, nearly every system of writing and reproduction. A grid can be simple or complex, specific or generic, tightly defined or loosely interpreted. Typographic grids are all about control. They establish a system for arranging content within the space of page, screen, or built environment. Designed in response to the internal pressures of content (text, image, data) and the outer edge or frame (page, screen, window), an effective grid is not a rigid formula but a flexible and resilient structure, a skeleton that moves in concert with the muscular mass of content. Grids belong to the technological framework of typography, from the concrete modularity of letterpress to the ubiquitous rulers, guides, and coordinate systems of graphics applications. Although software generates illusions of smooth curves and continuous tones, every digital image or mark is constructed—ultimately—from a grid of neatly bounded blocks. The ubiquitous language of the gui (graphical user interface) creates a gridded space in which windows overlay windows. In addition to their place in the background of design production, grids have become explicit theoretical tools. Avant-garde designers in the 1910s and 1920s exposed the mechanical grid of letterpress, bringing

In this symmetrical double-page spread, the inside margins are wider than the outside margins, creating more open space at the spine of the book.

Books and magazines should be designed as *spreads* (facing pages). The two-page spread, rather than the individual page, is the main unit of design. Left and right margins become inside and outside margins. Page layout programs assume that the inside margins are the same on both the left- and right-hand pages, yielding a symmetrical, mirror-image spread. You are free, however, to set your own margins and create an asymmetrical spread.

In this asymmetrical layout, the left margin is always wider than the right margin, whether it appears along the inside or outside edge of the page.

MULTICOLUMN GRID

There are numerous ways to use a basic column grid. Here, one column has been reserved for images and captions, and the others for text.

In this variation, images and text share column space.

While single-column grids work well for simple documents, multicolumn grids provide flexible formats for publications that have a complex hierarchy or that integrate text and illustrations. The more columns you create, the more flexible your grid becomes.
You can use the grid to articulate the hierarchy of the publication by creating zones for different kinds of content. A text or image can occupy a single column or it can span several. Not all the space has to be filled.

Elements of varying width are staggered within the structure of the grid.

Grid systems

刷

The typographic grid is a proportional regulator for composition, tables, pictures, etc. It is a formal programme to accommodate x unknown items.

The typographic grid is a proportional regulator for composition, tables, pictures, etc. It is a formal programme to accommodate x unknown items. The typographic grid is a proportional regulator for composition, tables, pictures, etc. It is a formal programme to accommodate x unknown items.

A grid can be simple or complex, specific or generic, tightly defined or loosely interpreted. Typographic grids are all about control. They establish a system for arranging content within the space of page, screen, or built environment. Designed in response to the internal pressures of content (text, image, data) and the outer edge or frame (page, screen, window), an effective grid is not a rigid formula but a flexible and resilient structure, a skeleton that moves in concert with the muscular mass of content. Grids belong to the technological framework of typography, from the concrete modularity of letterpress to the ubiquitous rulers, guides, and coordinate systems of graphics applications. Although software generates illusions of smooth curves and continuous tones, every digital image or mark is constructed—ultimately—from a grid of neatly bounded blocks. The ubiquitous language of the gui (graphical user interface) creates a gridded space in which windows overlay windows. In addition to their place in the background of design production, grids have become explicit theoretical tools. Avant-garde designers in the 1910s and 1920s exposed the mechanical grid of letterpress, bringing it to the polemical surface of the page. In Switzerland after World War II, graphic designers built a total design methodology around the typographic grid, hoping to build from it a new and rational social order. The grid has evolved across centuries of typographic evolution. For graphic designers, grids are carefully honed intellectual devices, infused with ideology and ambition, and they are the inescapable mesh that filters, at some level of resolution, nearly every system of writing and reproduction. A grid can be simple or complex, specific or generic, tightly defined or loosely interpreted. Typographic grids are all about control. They establish a system for arranging content within the space of page, screen, or built environment. Designed in response to the internal pressures of content (text, image, data) and the outer edge or frame (page, screen, window), an effective grid is not a rigid formula but a flexible and resilient

The typographic grid is a proportional regulator for composition, tables, pictures, etc. It is a formal programme to accommodate x unknown items.

The typographic grid is a proportional regulator for composition, tables, pictures, etc. It is a formal programme to accommodate x unknown items.

The typographic grid is a proportional regulator for composition, tables, pictures, etc. It is a formal programme to accommodate x unknown items.

A grid can be simple or complex, specific or generic, tightly defined or loosely interpreted. Typographic grids are all about control. They establish a system for arranging content within the space of page, screen, or built environment. Designed in response to the internal pressures of content (text, image, data) and the outer edge or frame (page, screen, window), an effective grid is not a rigid formula but a flexible and resilient structure, a skeleton that moves in concert with the muscular mass of content. Grids belong to the technological framework of typography, from the concrete modularity of letterpress to the ubiquitous rulers, guides, and coordinate systems of graphics applications. Although software generates illusions of smooth curves and continuous tones, every digital image or mark is constructed—ultimately—from a grid of neatly bounded blocks. The ubiquitous language of the gui (graphical user interface) creates a gridded space in which windows overlay windows. In addition to their place in the background of design production, grids have become explicit theoretical tools. Avant-garde designers in the 1910s and 1920s exposed the mechanical grid of letterpress, bringing it to the polemical surface of the page. In Switzerland after World War II, graphic designers built a total design methodology around the typographic grid, hoping to build from it a new and rational social order. The grid has evolved across centuries of typographic evolution. For graphic designers, grids are carefully honed intellectual devices, infused with ideology and ambition, and they are the inescapable mesh that filters, at some level of resolution, nearly every system of writing and reproduction. A grid can be simple or complex, specific or generic, tightly defined or loosely interpreted. Typographic grids are all about control. They establish a system for arranging content within the space of page, screen, or built environment. Designed in response to the internal pressures of content (text, image, data) and the outer edge or frame (page, screen, window), an effective grid is not a rigid formula but a flexible and resilient

A horizontal band divides a text zone from an image zone. Elements gravitate toward this line, which provides an internal structure for the page.

HANG LINE In addition to creating vertical zones with the columns of the grid, you can also divide the page horizontally. For example, an area across the top can be reserved for images and captions, and body text can "hang" from a common line. In architecture, a horizontal reference point like this is known as a *datum*.

Columns of text hang from a datum, falling downward with an uneven rag across the bottom.

Ifang Leisalpa
(Schloss),
2090 Meter

und verdichtet, wie dies im Betonbau üblich ist. Da der Beton
bei diesem Vorgang die Vor- und Rücksprünge der Rückseite
der Steinplattenwand umfliesst, entstand eine vorzügliche
Verzahnung und Verbindung der beiden Materialien Kunststein
(Beton) und Naturstein.

Allerdings konnten die Wände nicht in ihrer ganzen Höhe
auf einmal hintergossen werden. Das musste in Höhenetappen
von 50 cm erfolgen. Erst wenn der Beton einer Lage eine bestimm-
te Festigkeit erreicht und sich mit dem Mauerwerk verbunden
hatte, konnte die nächste Lage von 50 cm darüber betoniert
werden. Eine höhere Schüttmasse von flüssigem Beton hätte
die freistehenden Steinplattenwände seitlich weggedrückt.

Insgesamt wurden für die Wände der Therme 450 m³ oder
1300 Tonnen Valser Quarzitplatten zu 3100 m² Wandfläche in
20 Schichten pro m² verarbeitet. Die Länge aller verwendeten
Plattenstreifen zusammen ergibt ein Total von 62.000 Lauf-
metern, was der Strecke von Vals nach Haldenstein entspricht.

Peter Zumthor

Valser Quarzit	Boden	Fugen und Mörtelmasse	Grotten
Druckfestigkeit: etwa 217 N/mm² Rohdichte: 2.698 kg/m³ Wasseraufnahme-koeffizient: Masse –% 0,25 Gefräste Stein-platten: Stärken 6, 3, 4, 7 und 3,1cm Toleranz: 1 mm Breiten: 12–30 cm Längen: bis 3,20 m über 60.000 lfm Fugenbreite: etwa 2 mm	Breiten der Bahnen: 8–110 cm Längen: bis 3,20 m, je Platte zum Teil über 3 m² in einer Stärke von 2 cm Oberflächen: poliert, gefräst, gestockt, ge-schliffen in allen Möglichkeiten und einer Fugen-breite von 1 mm	EMACO R 304 BARRA 80 Firma MBT	Eckverbin-dungen, Schwel-len, Sturzplatten, Treppenunter-sichte und Tritte, Sitze als einzel-ne Werkstücke gefertigt	minimale Toleranzen (weit unter SIA-Norm) beim Schneiden und Vermauern der Steine, wie zum Beispiel auf 6 m Höhe weniger als 5 mm Toleranz	Trinkstein: polierte Quader aufeinander-geschichte Grösse etwa 0,5–1 m³ Quellgrotte: gebrochener Stein im Innern Schwitzstein: eingefärbter und polierter Beton Steininsel: grossformatige gespaltene Platten bis zu 3 m² je Platte

STEIN UND WASSER, WINTER 2003|04 Booklet, 2003. Designer: Clemens Schedler/Büro für konkrete Gestaltung. Publisher: Hotel Therme, Switzerland. *This publication for a spa in Switzerland uses a five-column grid. The main text fills a four-column block, and the smaller texts occupy single columns.*

General
Non-Fiction

Art

Photography

Collector's
Editions

Film

Architecture

220 × 156 mm
8⅝ × 6⅛ inches
240 pp
c.80 b&w illus.

Paperback
0 7148 3164 6

£ **14.95** UK
$ **24.95** US
€ **24.95** EUR
$ **39.95** CAN
$ **49.95** AUS

Béla Bartók

Kenneth Chalmers

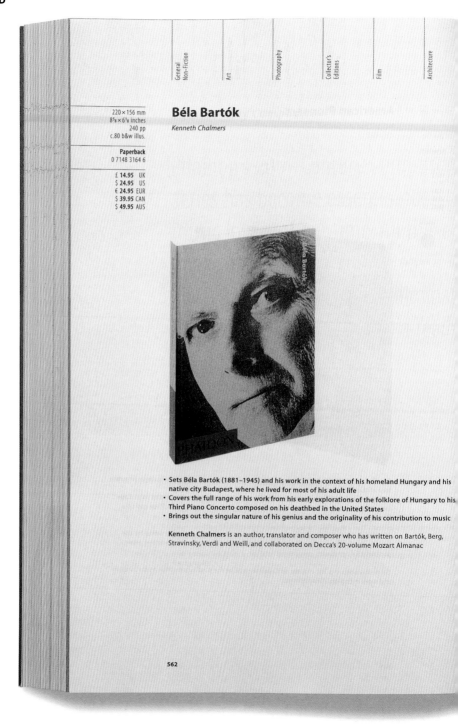

- Sets Béla Bartók (1881–1945) and his work in the context of his homeland Hungary and his native city Budapest, where he lived for most of his adult life
- Covers the full range of his work from his early explorations of the folklore of Hungary to his Third Piano Concerto composed on his deathbed in the United States
- Brings out the singular nature of his genius and the originality of his contribution to music

Kenneth Chalmers is an author, translator and composer who has written on Bartók, Berg, Stravinsky, Verdi and Weill, and collaborated on Decca's 20-volume Mozart Almanac

562

20 × 156 mm
× 6⅛ inches
240 pp
180 b&w illus.

Paperback
7148 3203 0

£ 14.95 UK
$ 24.95 US
€ 24.95 EUR
$ 39.95 CAN
$ 49.95 AUS

The Beatles

Allan Kozinn

- Follows the extraordinary development of the four self-taught musicians from Liverpool
  from their beginnings until the break-up in 1970
- Examines why the innovative music of the Beatles – created, at least initially, as ephemera –
  has remained so durable
- Considers not only the commercially released disks but also studio outtakes, demos,
  unreleased recordings and broadcast performances
- Sets the group's evolution against the backdrop of the popular culture explosion of the 1960s

Allan Kozinn has written musical criticism for the *New York Times* since 1977 and won ASCAP
awards for his work, including the book *Mischa Elman and the Romantic Style*

'A well-rounded, readable account. Makes a convincing case for putting the Beatles on the
shelf between Bartók and Boulez.' *(The Sunday Times)*

PHAIDON: FALL 2003
Catalogue, 2003. Designer:
Hans Dieter Reichert.
Publisher: Phaidon.
Photograph: Dan Meyers. *This
catalogue for a book publisher
provides a rational and elegant
structure for displaying hundreds
of different books, each one
presented as a physical object
annotated with documentary
data. The margins act as a
navigational interface for the
catalogue. Divisions occur both
horizontally and vertically.*

563

If/Then   **Discovery in Digital Craft**   Malcolm McCullough   134
keyboards, digital and musical

3/8

> Play serves learning though experimentation without risk. Learning occurs through quick, imprecise actions, conducted within understood rules of a game, and free from threat or consummation. Play does not use up so much as build.

military-industrial world of computing, one important way to do so is to play.

Play takes many forms. For example, it can be individual or social. According to one classic taxonomy, individual play includes pursuit of sensations, exercise of motor apparatus and experimentation with higher mental powers. This mental play includes exercise of attention, emotion and will. Attention play includes tests of memory, imagination, focus and reason. On the other hand, social play includes fighting and rivalry, loving and courtship, imitation and status seeking. Imitative play includes movements, drama, behavioural constructions and emulation of inner states. [2]

Crafts and craft learning embrace quite a range of these playful forms. Arguably, no productive process combines so many so well. Sensation, skilled motion, attention, involvement, will — all must be balanced, and this is the basis for craft as recreation. Craft learning is a form of imitative social learning. Movements are physical skills taught directly, whether by demonstration or coaching. Drama is a lesser component here, although it may be understood in the willful suspension of disbelief that allows participation in an abstract medium. Constructions are the artifacts. They are the plastic play, the visual examples, the operational learning. Finally the inner state is the patience, reflectivity and intent that distinguish the master.

Play serves learning though experimentation without risk. Play often lacks any immediately obvious aim other than the pursuit of stimulation, but functions almost instinctively to serve the process of development. Learning occurs through quick, imprecise actions, conducted within understood rules of a game, and free from threat or consummation. Play does not use up so much as build. One thing it

builds is common sense. Play's endlessly variable series of awkward, exaggerated motions seeks out the approximate arena for later development of true competence.

There is much to be said for play in a medium. If a medium is defined by its affordances and constraints, then learning consists of exploring these properties. Experimentation is especially useful for becoming familiar with constraints: we learn from our mistakes. We must accept that beginning work in a new medium will be full of setbacks. There will also be fortuitous discoveries, however particularly of affordances. Design is not only invention, but also sensitivity to a medium. Craft cannot be merely in service of technique, or of inappropriately conceived ends. The craftsman must begin to feel something about the artifacts, and only certain moves will feel right.

Of course when it comes to computation, we all must learn. In a sense, we're all children— the medium is *that* new. And of course, the most fluent experts here are often quite young. As all of us learn about this promising new domain, a chain of developments should be clear: play shapes learning; learning shapes the mind; mental structures shape software; and software data structures afford work and play.

Structure and Improvisation

The master at play improvises. Consider the jazz pianist. In *Ways of the Hand — The Organization of Improvised Conduct* (1978), the musician David Sudnow gives us a rare description of otherwise tacit knowledge in action. Improvising on a piece takes much more talent than simply playing from a notation or learning by rote, Sudnow explains. Moreover, improvising begins with a sense of structure, from which it builds a cognitive map. For example, the 'way in' to an arpeggio is mentally mapped. The structure of the keyboard presents a physical map of a chord, which may be modified in countless ways by physical moves. One could play the adjacent keys, for example, or one could translate by any arbitrary interval. One could transpose or invert. One could change the order in which the notes were played, or the

2 Karl Groos, *The Play of Man*. New York: Appleton and Co., 1901

the same pitches as the first, the doubled back and went fast again, but over different pitches... There were innumerable variations possible; looking at 'structure' in this way and corresponding to various continuity practices, ways of the hand were cultivated that were suited to the performance of such manoeuvres... Transposition of such a figure to a new segment and correct repetition with respect to pitch, without slowing it down or slowing down parts of it, involved coping with the topography of the terrain by the hand as a negotiative organ with various potentials and limitations. [3]

tempo, or the attack and decay. Of course one could substitute dominant, major and minor chords.

Sudnow argues that because these variations are sequences of physical positions, they are learned as active skills no longer necessary to be understood at a mental level. Each becomes a handful. That the hand gets a hold of a variation on a chord is indicated by observed tendencies to start into particular sequences with certain fingers on certain keys. The manoeuvre is known by the hand, and the mind only maps the way in. The ability to modify the run note by note — which would require conscious attention — only comes later. Even without attentive intellectual guidance, however, the natural tendency of the hand is not to repeat itself, even in a series of figural repetitions. Thus once a sufficient repertoire of runs is learned, this tendency inherently ensures a richness to the sound. The hand searches its territory for sequences, which process replaces a faithfulness to the score, and that makes jazz. For example:

> The new run could be in various other ways only 'essentially related' to the preceding run. Say then first started slow and went up fast, then doubled back and went fast again, while the second started slowly and came back down through

Although jazz is the obvious case, it is hardly alone. Improvisation plays a role in many contemporary practices, and in many traditional crafts. Few of these worlds employ such a singular instrument as the piano; few are able to turn so much over to the hands, but all involve playful response to a structure. For example, of industrial design, Herbert Read insisted that "Art implies values more various than those determined by practical necessity." [4] As a modernist and industrialist, he felt admiration for fundamental structural laws, such as the golden section also admired by his contemporary Le Corbusier. He was convinced, however, that metrical irregularities based on a governing structure, rather than slavish adherence to the laws in their precision, was the basis for pleasurable expression. He cited Ruskin's line that "All beautiful lines are drawn under mathematical laws organically transgressed." [5] He held that this was the case even in the useful (industrial) arts.

Consider the case of processing a digital photograph. The makeup of the raster image file, the various tone scale and filtration operators, provides a very clear structure in which to work but demands no particular order of operation. The complex microstructure of the sampled pixels provides a sub-

> The natural tendency of the hand is not to repeat itself, even in a series of figural repetitions. Thus once a sufficient repertoire of runs is learned, this tendency inherently ensures a richness to the sound. The hand searches its territory for sequences, which process replaces a faithfulness to the score, and that makes jazz.

3 David Sudnow, *Ways of the Hand—The Organization of Improvised Conduct*, Cambridge, MA: Harvard University Press, 1978, p 7
4 Herbert Read, *Art and Industry—The Principles of Industrial Design* New York: Horizon Press, 1954 [1934]
5 *Ibid.*

IF/THEN PLAY: DESIGN IMPLICATIONS OF NEW MEDIA Book, 1999. Designers: Mevis and Van Deursen. Editor: Jan Abrams. Publisher: Netherlands Design Institute. Photograph: Dan Meyers. *In this book about new media, a two-column grid contains the main body of text. The pull quotes, running across two columns, are framed in thinly ruled boxes that suggest the overlapping "windows" on a computer screen. The top margin, which resembles the tool bar in a browser, provides an interface to the book.*

wild wirkende, dem Lennéschen Ideal folgende, baumreiche Naturgarten weicht englischen Rasenflächen, die sich mit nur noch wenigen Baum- und Strauchgruppen und gepflegten Blumenbeeten abwechseln. Mit dieser Veränderung, so der dritte Direktor des Zoos, Heinrich Bodinus, soll es möglich werden, den belebenden und erwärmenden Strahlen der Sonne Zutritt zu verschaffen. Anders als zuvor finden sich in den Berliner Zeitungen nun immer häufiger positiv gefärbte Erlebnisberichte. Vorläufiger Höhepunkt und nicht zu unterschätzender rite de passage für die breite Anerkennung des Gartens war das DREI-KAISER-TREFFEN im Herbst 1872: Kaiser Wilhelm, Kaiser Alexander II. von Rußland und Kaiser Franz-Joseph von Österreich-Ungarn werden in einem zwanzig Wagen umfassenden Zug über das Zoogelände kutschiert. Obwohl der Zoo zu dieser Zeit noch außerhalb der Stadt gelegen ist, ist dessen neuartige Gestaltung schon ein Zeichen dafür, daß die preußische Hauptstadt um die Anbindung an die Kultur der großen europäischen Metropolen bemüht ist. Die Bevölkerungszahl Berlins steigt mit der industriellen Entwicklung jener Jahre erheblich, und dem Zoo kommt (neben den Stadtparks) zunehmend ein Erholungswert zu, der durch eine Reihe von technischen Neuerungen gesteigert werden kann: eine Dampfmaschine sorgt für Wasserzirkulation und verwandelt die früher im Sommer überlriechenden Gewässer des Gartens in belebte Weiher. Hinzu kommt die Erleichterung von An- und Abreise. Ab 1875 verbindet eine Pferdebahnlinie Berlin mit dem Zoo. Im Jahre 1884 folgt die Installation elektrischer Beleuchtung, die eine Ausdehnung der Öffnungszeiten bis in die Abendstunden zuläßt. Kinderspielhallen und -plätze werden eingerichtet. Wo sonst könnten sie sicher vor dem Getümmel der Weltstadt in frischer Luft ihre Glieder üben und ihre Lungen weiten? heißt es im Programmheft des Jahres 1899. ‖ Der Zoo entwickelt sich deutlich zu einem integralen Bestandteil der städtischen Kultur. Anders als in den Stadtparks — etwa dem Humboldthain — stellt hier der Eintrittspreis sicher, daß die das Vergnügen schmälernden Obdachlosen und Bettler vor den Toren bleiben. Zoofreunde werben um die Gunst von Kolonialoffizieren, die helfen sollen, die Tierbestände zu erhöhen und die in der Folge tatsächlich zunehmend als Donatoren fungieren. Forschungsreisen und Expeditionen in viele Regionen der Erde — häufig unter maßgeblicher Regie der Zoodirektoren — führen zur Entdeckung bislang unbekannter Tierarten. Die intensive Kooperation von Zoo und Naturkundemuseum setzt sich fort, so daß der Bestand des Museums 1894 auf etwa 2 Mio. Tiere, darunter etwa 150 000 Wirbeltiere, angewachsen ist. ‖ Der Berliner Zoo wird in den letzten Jahrzehnten des 19. Jahrhunderts zu einem repräsentativen Treffpunkt und zu einem Raum, in dem sich preußische Mentalität wenn auch nicht aufhebt, so doch relativiert. Fremdartige Tierwelt und eine Architektur des Orient, des Fernen Osten und der Savannen, verbindet sich, in einiger Entfernung vom hektischen und geschäftigen Leben der Stadt, zu einem den Stadtbewohnern bis dahin unbekannten Ambiente. Hier entwickelt sich Natur zum Unterhaltungsgegenstand. Die von Zirkussen, Menagerien und Märkten bekannten sensationellen und theatralischen Aspekte gehen mit dem zoologischen Erkenntnisinteresse eine eigenartige Symbiose ein. Getragen wird diese Entwicklung nicht zuletzt 90 von ökonomischen Zwängen: immer wieder kämpft die Zoogesellschaft um ihre Existenz. ‖ Der Zoo wird zu einem der Plätze der Stadt, wo sich Vorahnungen einer noch in Entwicklung begriffenen Weltstadt am ehesten materialisieren; kein Wunder, daß immer deutlicher auch Künstler und Gelehrte sich von diesem Raum angezogen fühlen. Neben einer Musiktribüne hilft ein erweiterter Restaurationsbetrieb den Aufenthalt in den meist nur unzureichend belüfteten Gebäuden aufzulockern. Ein Zeitgenosse beschreibt diese Bereicherung: Durch das neue Restaurationslokal ist die Zahl der großen Festsäle um ein Meisterwerk der Baukunst vermehrt worden. Wenn hier eine vortreffliche Militärkapelle ein Concert ausführt, dann bildet, in Folge des erhöhten Eintrittspreises, die elegante Welt die Mehrzahl der Besucher. Draußen dehnt sich eine lange Reihe Equipagen bis in die Winkel des Thiergartens; drinnen sind alle Plätze im weiten Umkreise des muschelförmig gebauten Orchesters besetzt; beim Klange der Instrumente, beim Geplätscher der Fontänen sitzt man, sich erfrischend, rauchend, plaudernd und scherzend unter den schattigen Bäumen und blickt in das abwechselnde, stets rege Thierleben hinaus, wie es sich in den benachbarten Grotten, auf Aesten und Teichen kund giebt.⁵ ‖ Die Auswahl der Tiere und der Situationen, in denen sich ihre Präsentation bewegte, erfolgt sorgfältig und bedacht, die Kuratoren entscheiden sich für besonders exotisch wirkende, kuriose, lächerliche, niedliche Tiere.⁶ Dabei ist es stets, die Konfrontation mit potentiell Abscheu oder starkes Befremden erregendem tierischem Verhalten zu verhindern. ‖ Die zunehmende Popularität der Zoos korreliert mit dem Verschwinden von Tieren aus dem Alltagsleben des städtischen Menschen. Das Tier ist entweder Haustier, also Mitbewohner der Wohnung, oder drastisch auf seine Rohstofffunktion reduziert und fristet in fabrikartigen Hallen abseits der Städte sein ökonomisch optimiertes Dasein. Mit den zoologischen Gärten beginnt ein Verdrängungsmechanismus, der sich später auch auf Naturparks und Reservate erstreckt: die Gefangenschaft erscheint angesichts der systematischen Zerstörung der Lebensräume als ein Schutz der Natur und dient dazu, das unterschwellig vorhandene schlechte Gewissen zu beruhigen.

architektur Franz Hessel
erinnert sich
in seinen Beobachtungen berlinischen Le-
bens an die merkwürdigen Behausungen
der Tiere: Liebt das Zebra sein afrikani-
sches Gehöft, der Büffel sein Borkenpa-
lais? Die Steine von Bärenzwinger, Vogel-
haus und Löwenheim deutet Hessel als
Baukastensteine, der Zoo wird in seiner Interpretation zur natürlichen Fortsetzung
einer Kinderstube und einem Ort, wo die
vorzeitlichen Tierkulte Gelegenheit haben,
wiederaufzuleben. F. Lichterfeld bezieht
sich in einem Artikel der ILLUSTRIRTEN ZEI-
TUNG von 1873 auf die anfänglich vorhandene
Verwunderung der Stadtbewohner ob der
neuen, ungewohnten Bauwerke: Was sollen
diese Thürme mit der flammenden Sonne
und den phantastischen Drachen- und Ele-
fantenbildern in einer christlichen Stadt
wie Berlin? Diese Frage wurde früher häufig aufgeworfen, zumal von Landleuten,
welche ihr Weg nach der Stadt an dem
fremden Heidentempel vorüber-
führte. Jetzt weiß jedermann in und um Berlin, daß der
fremde Heidentempel das neue Elefantenhaus ist. [...]
Nicht diesen, sondern dem Publikum zulieb wurde der
Neubau so reich ausgestattet, denn selbst dem Ele-
fanten ist eine Portion Moorrüben oder ein Bund Heu
lieber als der ganze architektonische und musivische
Schmuck seines neuen Hauses, und nun gar erst dem
Rhinoceros! Die stilistische Gestaltung der Bauten
steht offensichtlich auch in Zusammenhang mit der
Einbindung der zoologischen Gärten in kolonialistische
Zusammenhänge. Die Repräsentation fremdkulturel-
ler Elemente erlaubt Rückschlüsse auf die Konturen
eines rudimentär entwickelten Kosmopolitismus. Das
Einbringen von Elementen aus anderen Kulturzusam-
menhängen markiert den Wandel vom systematischen
zum geographisch orientierten Zoo. Wichtigen Einfluß
auf die Idee, Tiere in einem baulich-stilistischen Rahmen zu zeigen, der gewisse Zusammenhänge zur Eth-
nographie der Heimatlandschaften aufweist, hatte
der Zoologe Philipp Leopold Martin. In seinem 1878 in
Leipzig erschienenen Kompendium DIE PRAXIS DER NA-
TURGESCHICHTE — er maßte sich an, es als vollständiges
Lehrbuch über das Sammeln lebender und todter Na-
turkörper zu bezeichnen — rationalisiert Martin dieses Vorgehen als ethnographisch-architektonische
Belehrung: Was ist aber nun wohl natürlicher und zugleich lehrreicher, als die Natur in unseren Gärten
nach Welttheilen, Zonen und lokalen Verhältnissen
aufzustellen? [...] Der Wisent verlangt Wald und der
Buffalo die Prairie; und wenn wir dieses thun und in die
Prairie noch einen Wigwam als Stall hinsetzen, so be-
lehren wir damit zugleich das Publikum, denn es erhält
Bilder, die es niemals vergißt. Die fremdkulturelle Architektur der Stilbauten — auch wichtiger Bestandteil
der großen Weltausstellungen in dieser Phase — wird
jeglicher zeitlicher Entwicklung enthoben. Zoodirektor
Ludwig Heck schreibt rückblickend im
Jahre 1929: Man denke nur, wenn wir

*1: Franz Hessel Spazieren in Berlin Berlin 1929 , Seite 148
2: Heinz-Georg und Ursula Klös Der Berliner Zoo im Spiegel seiner Bauten
1841—1990. Eine baugeschichtliche und bauanalytische Dokumenta-
tion über den Zoologischen Garten Berlin 1990. Seite 51 Die anderen
Ausführungen über die Architektur stützen sich partiell auf diesen Band*

FORM + ZWECK 27
Journal, 1996. Designers:
Cyan, Berlin. *In the pages of
this experimental journal,
compact columns of justified
text are pushed to the outer
margins. By marking
paragraphs with symbols rather
than indents and line breaks,
the designers have maximized
the density of the text field.
Running heads, page numbers,
and images are narrow channels
cut into a solid wall of text.
Footnotes are also treated as
justified blocks, turned 90
degrees against the grain of the
page.*

Subtraction

Version 7.1
Khoi Vinh's Web Site

Search via Google

[   ] Go

| Home | Archives | About | | Previous | Next |

Fri 31 Dec 2004

Grid Computing... and Design

Posted	07:51 pm
Author	**Khoi Vinh**
Categories	**Design, Subtraction, Web Design**
Body	The layout grid I used for Subtraction Six.5 was improvised and inconsistent — I hobbled it together without much consideration or foresight, more interested in getting something finished than building something that would continue to make sense as I got more and more serious about the writing I post here. Over time, by virtue of repeated use, I became increasingly and lamentably invested in its tremendous shortcomings. When you make fairly liberal use of illustrations in your posts, you essentially wed yourself to the particulars of the CSS you've established, creating graphics of a certain width or ordering content in a particular method. It works in the short term, but it presents problems when you sit down to redesign.

Quick Access

4,791 posts since July 2000.

Dates   Select...

Categories   Select...

Email Updates

Get Subtraction.com posts sent right to your inbox.

Your Email   (Subscribe)

Powered by Mailchimp

Recent Posts

26 Dec 2009
Basic Maths on Sale This Week
Now through the last day of the year: our WordPress theme is one-third off the regular price.

10 Dec 2009
Backing Up Over Broadband
In theory, online backup systems should work. Except for that broadband thing.

09 Dec 2009
Get Fresh with Me
Come see me Wed 16 Dec at AIGA New York's twenty-fifth Fresh Dialogue event.

30 Nov 2009
Really Basic Maths
A look at the design evolution of my WordPress theme.

24 Nov 2009
New Shell for AOL
With its new brand identity, AOL tries to do two very difficult things at once.

BOXED IN

By late this year, it pained me to know that I had written over three hundred posts that relied, in varying degrees, on that dodgy framework. So when I finally sat down down to think seriously about designing version 7.0 of this Web site, I paid serious attention to establishing a rational and sustainable layout grid that would see me through at least a few more years of doing this. Yes, I hope to keep at it that long.

The new layout uses eight columns and four 'super columns,' and it shoehorns everything into that structure, which is a kind of 'for better or worse' decision, though I think it's definitely better. Each column is 95 pixels wide and separated by a 10 pixel gutter, which means I can create graphics of logical widths in increments of roughly 95 pixels each (things get a little more complicated when accounting for in-column padding&#41 — for me, this is a big methodological improvement over the arbitrary widths imposed by the old layout.

Below: Everybody fall in line. The new grid suggests graphics of a logical width, for a change.

THE OLD WAYS ARE DEAD

I spent a tremendous amount of time fine-tuning the CSS so that it would match up very carefully with the grid, and so it would work across all modern browsers — and Internet Explorer too, though with decidedly less faithfulness. That was difficult but it least it was an intellectual challenge.

The hard part came when I had to sit down to retrofit all the posts I'd made over the past twenty-plus months which used graphics that break the grid — **like this one**. Rewriting the styles wasn't that difficult; it was making sure that the special hacks I had used in the last layout to achieve various layout effects didn't produce absolute gibberish in the redesign. Many of them did, and I had to painstaking search them out and change the flow of captions and images within the body to ensure that they'd look right. That took a long time.

95 px Wide

200 px Wide

410 px Wide

620 px Wide

To always stay on the grid, I used a background-image property on the <body> to reveal the grid throughout development for the new layout — if you're looking at this through a Web browser (versus a screen reader or a news client) you'll see the columns running under the content in this very article. While no stroke of genius, coming up with this little trick left me very pleased with myself, as it allowed me to produce easily the most precise layouts of my career. It's those little moments that are some of the reward for all of this otherwise pointless free work that I do.

+

SUBTRACTION Website, 2008. Designer: Khoi Vinh. *While countless websites are divided into three or more columns, a fully functioning grid should allow some components to "break the grid" by crossing over multiple columns within a content area. The generous swaths of white space in Vinh's webpages free the eye from relentless clutter while emphasizing the underlying grid structure. Vinh sometimes uses a grid as a background image to check alignments as he works.*

NPR.ORG Website, 2009–10. Designer: NPR staff (Darren Mauro, Jennifer Sharp, Callie Neylan, David Wright, Brian Ingles, K. Libner, Scott Stroud). *The web design process typically begins with designing a grid and wire frames that describe typical pages. The visual details, such as type choice, hierarchy, and styling of navigation elements, are added later. The site has eight page templates, each designed for a different editorial situation.*

POLITICS   BOOKS & ARTS   ECONOMY   ENERGY & ENVIRONMENT   HEALTH CARE   METRO POLICY   WORLD   LOGIN   SUBSCRIBE   Search TNR

THE NEW REPUBLIC

Place of Grace: The Uncanny Beauty of Peter Zumthor's Out-of-the-Way Buildings

Unemployment Has Crept Over Ten Percent, and I Think That's a Good Thing. What?
Noam Scheiber

INTELLECTUAL RIGOR HONEST REPORTING INFLUENTIAL ANALYSIS

THE NEW REPUBLIC

Don't miss another issue of the magazine considered "required reading" by the world's top decision-makers.
Subscribe today and get two free issues, risk free.

Did Rembrandt Reveal a Murder in One of His Paintings? An Intriguing Whodunnit Film. PLUS: 'The Maid.'
Stanley Kauffmann

The UN Report on Gaza Is Biased, Shoddy, and Unrealistic. But Israel Must Deal Honestly With Its Own Failures.
Moshe Halbertal

THE **PLANK**
By the TNR STAFF and GUESTS

What Warren Buffett's Investment Says About the Global Economy
November 7, 2009 | 10:47 am - Simon Johnson

Phony Conservative Anti-Elitism, Revealed!
November 7, 2009 | 8:24 am - Isaac Chotiner

Today At TNR (November 7, 2009)
November 7, 2009 | 12:00 am - TNR Staff

Chait: Don't Blame Obama for the Bad Economic News. Blame Congress. »

From the TNR Archives: The Strange Genius of Oprah Winfrey »

Scheiber: Is David Brooks Punking Me? He's Got to Be Punking Me. »

Cohn: Is It Even Possible to Control the Cost of Heath Care? »

STAY IN TOUCH   GET THE MAGAZINE »   GET OUR E-NEWSLETTERS »   Enter Email Addre   SUBSCRIBE   RSS »

THE **Treatment**   By JONATHAN COHN
Your Must-Read Guide to Health Care Reform

The Drama Was In the History
November 8, 2009 | 12:16 am - Jonathan Cohn

SATURDAY NOVEMBER 7, 2009

WORLD
The UN Report on Gaza Is Biased, Shoddy, and Unrealistic. But Israel Must Deal Honestly With Its Own Failures.
Moshe Halbertal

FRIDAY NOVEMBER 6, 2009

POLITICS
Bush is a Genius! Health Reform is Dead! 'The Weekly Standard' and the Powerlessness of Wishful Thinking.
Jonathan Chait

THE **SPINE**   By MARTY PERETZ

A Lesson From Fort Hood: Great Moments in "Psychologically Disturbed" Gunmen Committing Mass Murder
November 8, 2009 | 12:58 am - Barry Rubin

HEALTH CARE
The House Has Seriously Weakened the Public Option—But It Still Works, and Is Still Worth Fighting For
Jacob S. Hacker and Diane Archer

THE **STA$H**   Inside the Battle to Fix Our Economy   By NOAM SCHEIBER

WPA Revisited: Should Government Create Jobs Directly?
November 6, 2009 | 6:22 pm - Zubin Jelveh

Multimedia   More Slideshows »

Slideshow: Where Have All the RINOs Gone?
▶ Videos   📷 Slideshows   🎧 Podcasts

ECONOMY
What Happens When Moderate Democrats Turn Into Pundits? Bad Things. Very Bad Things.
Noam Scheiber

THE **VINE**   The Politics of a Greener Planet   By BRADFORD PLUMER

Cap-And-Trade Politics: Carbon (Like Place) Matters!
November 6, 2009 | 4:25 pm - Mark Muro and Jonathan Rothwell

WORLD
The Losers From This Week's Protests in Iran: Khamenei, Ahmadinejad, and Obama
Abbas Milani

TNR on Latin America

The Shah of Venezuela
The ideas that keep Hugo Chavez in power.

The Case of Honduras
A fragile democracy on the edge of a whirlwind.

THE NEW REPUBLIC Online magazine, 2009. *The home page of this online magazine uses a three-column grid to provide readers with direct links to a vast quantity of editorial content. Opinion sections each have their own logotypes, designed to reflect the literary tone of the overall brand.*

WORLD
Is Barack Obama Causing a Real Estate Boom in the West Bank?
Sarah A. Topol

Confessions of a 'Contra'
How the CIA masterminded the Nicaraguan insurgency.

HEALTH CARE
Cohn: I'll Say This About the GOP Health Plan ... It's Even Worse Than I Imagined
Jonathan Cohn

The Death of Che Guevara
A firsthand account.

POLITICS
How Obama Can Help Democrats Avoid a Repeat of the Virginia Debacle in 2010
John B. Judis

Boycotting Cuba
Whose interest does it serve?

THE **AVENUE**   Rethinking Metropolitan America
In Collaboration with the Brookings Metropolitan Policy Program

Cap-And-Trade Politics: Carbon (Like Place) Matters!
November 6, 2009 | 4:25 pm - Mark Muro and Jonathan Rothwell

William Galston

Simon Johnson

Ed Kilgore

Damon Linker

John McWhorter

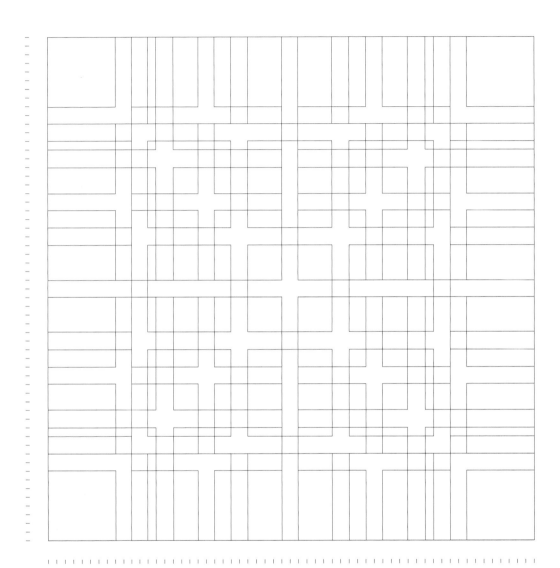

DESIGNING PROGRAMS Grid diagram, 1963 (redrawn).
Designer: Karl Gerstner. Publisher: Arthur Niggli, Zurich.
*This square grid consists of six vertical columns and six
horizontal modules, overlayed by grids of one, two, three, and
four units. Vertically, the grid is governed by a 10-pt measure,
which would determine the spacing of type from baseline to
baseline.*

Grid systems

A grid can be simple or complex, specific or generic, tightly defined or loosely interpreted. Typographic grids are all about control. They establish a system for arranging content within the space of page, screen, or built environment. Designed in response to the internal pressures of content (text, image, data) and the outer edge or frame (page, screen, window), an effective grid is not a rigid formula but a flexible and resilient structure, a skeleton that moves in concert with the muscular mass of content. Grids belong to the technological framework of typography, from the concrete modularity of letterpress to the ubiquitous rulers, guides, and coordinate systems of graphics applications. Although software generates illusions of smooth curves and continuous tones, every digital image or mark is constructed—ultimately—from a grid of neatly bounded blocks. The ubiquitous language of the gui (graphical user interface) creates a gridded space in which windows overlay windows. In addition to their place in the background of design production, grids have become explicit theoretical tools. Avant-garde designers in the 1910s and 1920s exposed the grid of letterpress, bringing it to the polemical surface of the page. In Switzerland after World War II, graphic designers built a total design methodology around the typographic grid, hoping to build from it a new and rational social order. The grid has evolved across centuries of typographic evolution. For graphic designers, grids are carefully honed intellectual devices, infused with ideology and ambition, and they are the inescapable mesh that filters, at some level of resolution, nearly every system of writing and

The typographic grid is a proportional regulator for composition, tables, pictures, etc. It is a formal programme to accommodate a unknown items.The typographic grid is a proportional regulator for composition, tables, pictures, etc. It is a formal programme to accommodate a unknown items.

The typographic grid is a proportional regulator for composition, tables, pictures, etc. It is a formal programme to accommodate a unknown items.The typographic grid is a proportional regulator for composition, tables, pictures, etc. It is a formal programme to accommodate a unknown items.

The typographic grid is a proportional regulator for composition, tables, pictures, etc. It is a formal programme to accommodate a unknown items.The typographic grid is a proportional regulator for composition, tables, pictures, etc. It is a formal programme to accommodate a unknown items.

This modular grid has four columns and four rows. An image or a text block can occupy one or more modules.

Grid systems

A grid can be simple or complex, specific or generic, tightly defined or loosely interpreted. Typographic grids are all about control. They establish a system for arranging content within the space of page, screen, or built environment. Designed in response to the internal pressures of content (text, image, data) and the outer edge or frame (page, screen, window), an effective grid is not a rigid formula but a flexible and resilient structure, a skeleton that moves in concert with the muscular mass of content. Grids belong to the technological framework of typography, from the concrete modularity of letterpress to the ubiquitous rulers, guides, and coordinate systems of graphics applications. Although software generates illusions of smooth curves and continuous tones, every digital image or mark is constructed—ultimately—from a grid of neatly bounded blocks. The ubiquitous language of the gui (graphical user interface) creates a gridded space in which windows overlay windows. In addition to their place in the background of design production, grids have

A grid can be simple or complex, specific or generic, tightly defined or loosely interpreted. Typographic grids are all about control. They establish a system for arranging content within the space of page, screen, or built environment. Designed in response to the internal pressures of content (text, image, data) and the outer edge or frame (page, screen, window), an effective grid is not a rigid formula but a flexible and resilient structure, a skeleton that moves in concert with the muscular mass of content. Grids belong to the technological framework of typography, from the concrete modularity of letterpress to the ubiquitous rulers, guides, and coordinate systems of graphics applications. Although software generates illusions of smooth curves and continuous tones, every digital image or mark is constructed—ultimately—from a grid of neatly bounded blocks. The ubiquitous language of the gui (graphical user interface) creates a gridded space in which windows overlay windows. In addition to their place in the background of design production, grids have become explicit

The typographic grid is a proportional regulator for composition, tables, pictures, etc. It is a formal programme to accommodate a unknown items.The typographic grid is a proportional regulator for composition, tables, pictures, etc. It is a formal programme to accommodate a unknown items.

The typographic grid is a proportional regulator for composition, tables, pictures, etc. It is a formal programme to accommodate a unknown items.The typographic grid is a proportional regulator for composition, tables, pictures, etc. It is a formal programme to accommodate a unknown items.

The typographic grid is a proportional regulator for composition, tables, pictures, etc. It is a formal programme to accommodate a unknown items.The typographic grid is a proportional regulator for composition, tables, pictures, etc. It is a formal programme to accommodate a unknown items.

Endless variations are possible.

A *modular grid* has consistent horizontal divisions from top to bottom in addition to vertical divisions from left to right. These modules govern the placement and cropping of pictures as well as text. In the 1950s and 1960s, Swiss graphic designers including Gerstner, Ruder, and Müller-Brockmann devised modular grid systems like the one shown here.

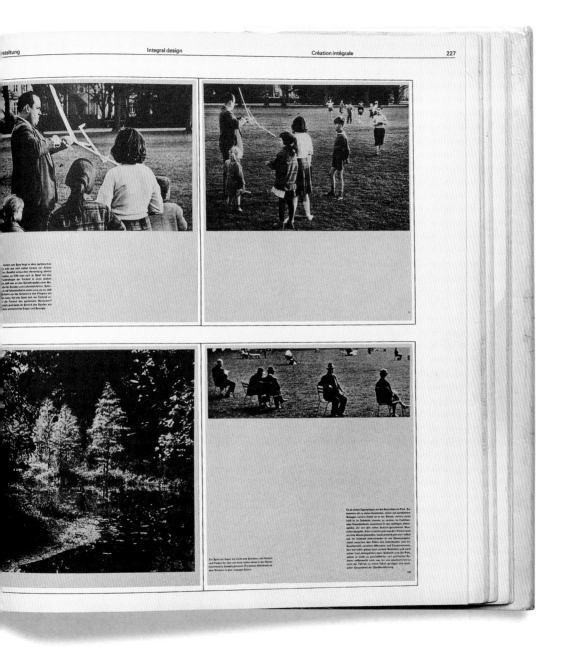

TYPOGRAPHY Book, 1967. Designer and author: Emil Ruder. Publisher: Arthur Niggli, Zurich. Photograph: Dan Meyers. *In this classic design text, Emil Ruder demonstrates the use of a modular grid.*

Modular grids are created by positioning horizontal guidelines in relation to a *baseline grid* that governs the whole document. Baseline grids serve to anchor all (or nearly all) layout elements to a common rhythm. Create a baseline grid by choosing the typesize and leading of your text, such as 10-pt Scala Pro with 12 pts leading (10/12). Avoid auto leading so that you can work with whole numbers that multiply and divide cleanly. Use this line space increment to set the baseline grid in your document preferences. Adjust the top or bottom page margin to absorb any space left over by the baseline grid.

Determine the number of horizontal page units in relation to the numer of lines in your baseline grid. Count how many lines fit in a full column of text and then choose a number that divides evenly into the line count to create horizontal page divisions. A column with forty-two lines of text divides neatly into seven horizontal modules with six lines each. If your line count is not neatly divisible, adjust the top and/or bottom page margins to absorb the leftover lines.

To style headlines, captions, and other elements, choose line spacing that works with the baseline grid, such as 18/24 for headlines, 14/18 for subheads, and 8/12 for captions. Web designers can choose similar increments (`line height` in CSS) to create style sheets with neatly coordinated baselines.

Where possible, position all page elements in relation to the baseline grid. Don't force it, though. Sometimes a layout works better when you override the grid. View the baseline grid when you want to check the position of elements; turn it off when it's distracting.

BASELINE GRID *In InDesign, set the baseline grid in the Preferences>Grids and Guides window. Create horizontal divisions in Layout>Create Guides. Make the horizontal guides correspond to the baselines of the page's primary text by choosing a number of rows that divides evenly into the number of lines in a full column of text.*

NERD ALERT: Working in InDesign, you can make your text frames automatically align with the baseline grid. Go to Object>Text Frame Options>Baseline Options and choose Leading. If your leading (line spacing) is 12 pts, the first baseline will fall 12 pts from the top of the text frame.

BETTER TEXT FRAMES *The first line of the text starts 12 pts from the top of the text frame. In the default setting, the first line is positioned according to the cap height.*

MAIN HEADLINE
32/48 pt Scala Sans Pro Bold

SUBHEAD
18/24 Scala Sans Pro Italic

baseline grids

create a common rhythm

Captions and other details are styled to coordinate with the dominant baseline grid.

Modular grids are created by positioning horizontal guidelines in relation to a *baseline grid* that governs the whole document. Baseline grids serve to anchor all (or nearly all) elements to a common rhythm. Create a baseline grid by choosing the typesize and leading of your text, such as 10-pt Scala Pro with 12 pts leading (10/12). Avoid auto leading so that you can work with whole numbers that multiply and divide cleanly. Use this line space increment to set the baseline grid in your document preferences. Adjust the top or bottom page margin to absorb any space left over by the baseline grid.

Determine the number of horizontal page units in relation to the numer of lines in the baseline grid. Count how many lines fit in a full column of text and then choose a number that divides easily into the line count to create horizontal page divisions. A column with forty-two lines of text divides neatly into seven horizontal modules with six lines each. If your line count is not neatly divisible, adjust the top and/or

bottom page margins to absorb leftover lines.

To style headlines, captions, and other elements, choose line spacing that works with the baseline grid, such as 18/24 for headlines, 14/18 for subheads, and 8/12 for captions. (Web designers can choose similar increments (line height) to create style sheets with coordinated baselines.)

Where possible, position all page elements in relation to the baseline grid. Don't force it, though. Sometimes a layout works better when you override the grid. View the baseline grid when you want to check the position of elements; turn it off when it's distracting.

InDesign, set the baseline grid in the Preferences>Grids and Guides window. Create horizontal divisions in Layout>Create Guides. Make the horizontal guides correspond to the baselines of the page's primary text by choosing a number of rows that divides evenly into the number of lines in a full column of text. Working in InDesign, you can make

CAPTION
9/12 Scala Sans Pro Italic

PRIMARY TEXT:
10/12 Scala Pro.
This measure determines the baseline grid.

DESIGN LIKE YOU GIVE A DAMN Book, 2006. Designers: Paul Carlos, Urshula Barbour, Katharina Seifert, and Farha Khan/Pure + Applied. Authors: Architecture for Humanity, Kate Stohr, and Cameron Sinclair. *This book design uses a modular grid to bring order to complex content. Some pages are dense with body text, captions, and small images, while others feature full-bleed photography layered with short statements and hard-hitting statistics.*

"Architecture is a process of giving form and pattern to the social life of the community. Architecture is not an individual act performed by an artist-architect and charged with his emotions. Building is a collective action."

Hannes Meyer, director of Bauhaus, 1928 to 1930

Walter Gropius, slab apartment blocks on the Wannsee Shore, Berlin, 1931

built two prototypes based on his ideas for exhibition: The *immeubles villas* (1922) and the Maison Citrohan (1922), a play on the automobile name Citroën. Throughout the '20s Le Corbusier expounded on his ideas for a new industrialized architecture in a series of manifestos and urban plans.

Another early pioneer of prefabrication and component building systems was the German architect Walter Gropius. Gropius, who founded the Bauhaus and served as its director from 1919 to 1928, personified the architect as public servant and teacher. Throughout the '20s and '30s Gropius experimented with prefabricated wall panels and eventually whole structures. During his tenure and that of his successors, the Bauhaus became a nexus for socially conscious design.

Gropius, along with Marcel Breuer, is also credited with designing the first slab apartment block. This new building type, which would become the model for many future affordable-housing projects, was conceived to overcome the cramped, lightless tenement housing that had resulted from rampant land speculation at the turn of the century. The basic plan consisted of parallel rows of four- to 11-story apartment blocks. Each slab was only one apartment deep with windows front and back. The slabs were sited on a "superblock" at an angle to the street with communal green spaces between them to allow maximum sunlight into each apartment.[12]

Others would also experiment with standardized building components, modular systems, and prefabrication, including the French industrial designer Jean Prouvé and Frank Lloyd Wright, but perhaps none more passionately than the American inventor R. Buckminster Fuller.

Fuller arrived on what he termed "spaceship earth" in 1895. Like Gropius and Le Corbusier, he believed that mass-manufactured dwellings represented the future of housing. His most lasting contribution, however, was his fervent belief in the power of design to improve the human condition. In a sense Fuller, who was known for his eccentric use of language and his marathon lectures (the longest lasted 42 hours and recently has been fully transcribed), was the first evangelist of humanitarian design.

In 1927, after the death of his older daughter and the collapse of his first business, he found himself at the edge of Lake Michigan contemplating suicide. He was a failure, "a throw-away." What brought him from the brink, he later recounted, was the simple idea that his experience might ultimately be somehow useful to his fellow human beings. Rather than taking his own life, he decided to embark on a lifelong experiment, using himself as his own best research subject. He became "Guinea Pig B" (for Bucky), the world's first test pilot of a "design-science revolution," the sole purpose of which was to improve "human livingry," and he started with the house.

Conventional "handcrafted" homes had undergone "no structural advances in 5,000 years," Fuller argued. They were poorly lit, required much maintenance, and did not make efficient use of raw materials. Most conventional buildings depended on gravity for their strength. But what if a building could be suspended, as a sail from a mast, allowing for greater strength and the use of fewer materials?

Fuller's thinking led to the design of the Dymaxion House, a small-scale model of which was first exhibited at a Marshall Field's department store in Chicago in 1929. His radical scheme embraced the principle of tension and aimed to do "more with less." It was spherical, to make efficient use of materials, and clad in maintenance-free aluminum. It was naturally climate controlled and could be lit by a single light source through a system of mirrors and dimmers. All the mechanicals, wiring, and appliances were built into the walls and mast to allow for easy replacement. The house was also one of the first examples of self-sufficient (or "autonomous," as Fuller put it) green design. Wind turbines produced energy. The roof collected rainwater. Water-saving "fog guns" handled washing (including people), and Fuller's "package toilet" composted waste and recovered methane gas.[13]

While the Dymaxion House was unabashedly ahead of its time (it would be two decades before Fuller could find backing to build a full-scale prototype), the concept of building with tension rather than compression would become central to Fuller's work and would eventually lead to his most lasting contribution to the field of humanitarian design: the geodesic dome. Fuller's principle of tensegrity became a staple of tent design, and by extension, emergency shelter, that endures to this day.

Like the Dymaxion House, few of these early designs for "factory-built" housing achieved widespread commercial viability. For example, Le Corbusier's low-cost housing for workers in Pessac, near Bordeaux, France, went unoccupied for eight years after it was built. However, this concept of mass-produced housing would have a number of lasting implications for low-cost shelter. It prefigured a move away from the craft of building toward the technology of building. It took design out of the realm of the many and put it in the hands of an educated few. Perhaps more important, it negated the need for a dialogue between the architect and the occupant.

1929	1930	1930	1931	1934
Dymaxion House Chicago, Ill., USA R. Buckminster Fuller		**Housing Act of 1930** England	**Prefabricated houses built for the Hirsch Copper and Brass Works** Finow, Germany Walter Gropius	**Flood** China The Yellow River, the second largest river in China, floods. Death toll estimates range from 850,000 to four million. The flooding is followed by famine and outbreaks of disease.	***Modern Housing*** Catherine Bauer
		1930–39 Drought and Dust Storms Midwestern and southern plains, USA	**1931 Slab apartment blocks on the Wannsee shore** Berlin, Germany Walter Gropius		**1934 National Housing Act of 1934** USA

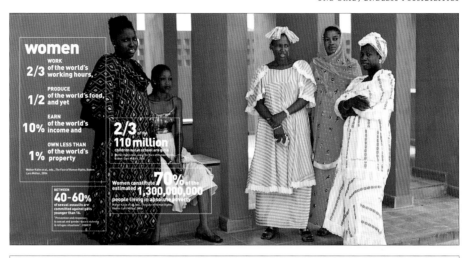

women

2/3 WORK of the world's working hours,

1/2 PRODUCE of the world's food, and yet

10% EARN of the world's income and

1% OWN LESS THAN of the world's property

Walter Kälin et al., eds., *The Face of Human Rights*, Baden: Lars Müller, 2004.

2/3 of the 110 million children not in school are girls

Walter Kälin et al., eds., *The Face of Human Rights*, Baden: Lars Müller, 2004.

Women constitute **70%** of the estimated 1,300,000,000 people living in absolute poverty

Walter Kälin et al., eds., *The Face of Human Rights*, Baden: Lars Müller, 2004.

BETWEEN **40-60%** of sexual assaults are committed against girls younger than 16.

"Prevention and response to sexual and gender-based violence in refugee situations", UNHCR

Lightweight Emergency Tent

Location Various
Date 2002–present
Organization Office of the United Nations High Commissioner for Refugees (UNHCR)
End client Refugees, internally displaced populations
Design consultant Ghassem Fardanesh
Manufacturer H. Sheikh Noor-ud-Din & Sons (Pvt.) Limited, Lahore, Pakistan
Cost per unit Approx. $100
Area 178 sq. ft./14.5 sq. m
Occupancy 4–5 people
Dimensions 18 x 9.8 x 6.9 ft./5.5 x 3 x 2.1 m
Weight 97 lb./41.5 kg

In war-torn countries and areas devastated by disaster, the presence of UNHCR tents is one of the first signs of aid.

Designers have tried to rethink this basic tent for decades. Everything from prefabricated structures to shipping containers to polyurethane yurts has been suggested or attempted. But as the agency politely points out in its guide to emergency materials, to date none of these systems has proven effective in refugee situations. Most fail simply because other emergency shelter arrangements will have been made before these systems even arrive. Some tent alternatives are perceived as too permanent, making them difficult to site in host communities and creating less incentive for a refugee to return home. Others are difficult or costly to replicate.

But in recent years there has been a growing sense within the agency that the design of the standard family tent could and should be radically overhauled. In most emergencies the agency sends out plastic sheeting first. Depending on the size and complexity of the crisis, this sheeting may be the response of first and last resort. However, in cases where local materials are not available to build more permanent structures, where families cannot find shelter within the community or are displaced for longer periods of time, the UNHCR provides more durable alternatives — typically a ridge-style or center-pole double-fly tent made from canvas. Yet these canvas tents are not only heavy, cumbersome to carry, and costly to ship, but because canvas rots they deteriorate quickly and cannot be stockpiled for long periods. Wear and tear on the weakened material in the field significantly shortens the useful lifespan of the shelter.

In 2002 the UNHCR began testing a new design for the basic family tent it regularly dispatched to areas of crisis. The agency's

The UNHCR's new Lightweight Emergency Tent is in use in Meulaboh, West Sumatra, following the Indian Ocean tsunami of 2004.

GripClips

Location Various
Date 1975–present
Designer Robert Gillis
Manufacturer Shelter Systems
Cost $8–10 (set of 6)

It would be safe to say that few people know the ins and outs of tents better than Robert Gillis.

Not only did he design the first geodesic backpacking tent, based on Buckminster Fuller's ideas, for The North Face in the 1970s, but he also lived in a collection of tents (with his wife and three children) for more than 20 years—all of which he designed himself, including the tent that housed the family washing machine.

Although many of Gillis's tent innovations have stemmed from efforts to improve his own living conditions, from the beginning he saw the potential for translating his ideas to emergency shelter—in particular using the plastic sheeting that has become a standard

component of relief projects. However, working with plastic sheeting meant finding a way to "hold on to it". Gillis explains: "It was difficult to join the material without puncturing it. But puncturing it is a bad idea because it weakens it. The material deteriorates less if you don't injure it." The designer went through more than 10 different iterations before arriving at the GripClip, a small plastic fastener that clips into any type of sheeting and ties it to a frame.

Reducing the shelter to its most fundamental element, the connection between the sheeting and the support, enabled Gillis to design a number of tents, from a basic shelter frame kit to more elaborate dome structures.

The clips also offered another advantage. They allowed for a range of shapes. Whereas most relief agencies distribute tunnel-shaped tents because the structure can be covered

with one large sheet of material, these tents are less stable in the wind than dome-shaped tents. Using GripClips, Gillis found he was able to layer multiple shingles to create a more stable structure that would also shed rain. "And I didn't have to sew it or heat-weld it or anything," he recalls. "Here was the perfect thing. It was totally wonderful."

More recently Gillis has focused on creating clips and fasteners to attach plastic sheeting to roofs, frameworks, piping, or plywood, allowing families to turn damaged structures into transitional homes while they rebuild.

opposite
A GripClip, secured to a cross-piece of frame, shown from inside a shelter. The frame pieces are secured with plastic wrap.

above
GripClip's two plastic parts are designed to be twisted together with a piece of sheeting between them. The clip itself can be fastened to a frame structure with plastic ties, rope, or pipe clamps.

right
Robert Gillis inside a tent built with GripClips.

Use a modular grid to arrange a text in as many ways as you can. By employing just one size of type and flush left alignment only, you will construct a typographic hierarchy exclusively by means of spatial arrangement. To make the project more complex, begin adding variables such as weight, size, and alignment.

Common typographic disorders

Various forms of dysfunction appear among populations exposed to typography for long periods of time. Listed here are a number of frequently observed afflictions.

typophilia
An excessive attachment to and fascination with the shape of letters, often to the exclusion of other interests and object choices. Typophiliacs usually die penniless and alone.

typophobia
The irrational dislike of letterforms, often marked by a preference for icons, dingbats, and—in fatal cases—bullets and daggers. The fears of the typophobe can often be quieted (but not cured) by steady doses of Helvetica and Times Roman.

typochondria
A persistent anxiety that one has selected the wrong typeface. This condition is often paired with okd (optical kerning disorder), the need to constantly adjust and readjust the spaces between letters.

Common typographic disorders

Various forms of dysfunction appear among populations exposed to typography for long periods of time. Listed here are a number of frequently observed afflictions.

typophilia
An excessive attachment to and fascination with the shape of letters, often to the exclusion of other interests and object choices. Typophiliacs usually die penniless and alone.

typophobia
The irrational dislike of letterforms, often marked by a preference for icons, dingbats, and—in fatal cases—bullets and daggers. The fears of the typophobe can often be quieted (but not cured) by steady doses of Helvetica and Times Roman.

typochondria
A persistent anxiety that one has selected the wrong typeface. This condition is often paired with OKD (optical kerning disorder), the need to constantly adjust and readjust the spaces between letters.

Common typographic disorders

Various forms of dysfunction appear among populations exposed to typography for long periods of time. Listed here are a number of frequently observed afflictions.

typophilia
An excessive attachment to and fascination with the shape of letters, often to the exclusion of other interests and object choices. Typophiliacs usually die penniless and alone.

typophobia
The irrational dislike of letterforms, often marked by a preference for icons, dingbats, and—in fatal cases—bullets and daggers. The fears of the typophobe can often be quieted (but not cured) by steady doses of Helvetica and Times Roman.

typochondria
A persistent anxiety that one has selected the wrong typeface. This condition is often paired with OKD (optical kerning disorder), the need to constantly adjust and readjust the spaces between letters.

Panel 1 (top left)

Common typographic disorders		Various forms of dysfunction appear among populations exposed to typography for long periods of time. Listed here are a number of frequently observed afflictions.
	typophilia	An excessive attachment to and fascination with the shape of letters, often to the exclusion of other interests and object choices. Typophiliacs usually die penniless and alone.
	typophobia	The irrational dislike of letterforms, often marked by a preference for icons, dingbats, and—in fatal cases—bullets and daggers. The fears of the typophobe can often be quieted (but not cured) by steady doses of Helvetica and Times Roman.
	typochondria	A persistent anxiety that one has selected the wrong typeface. This condition is often paired with OKD (optical kerning disorder), the need to constantly adjust and readjust the spaces between letters.

Panel 2 (top right)

Common typographic disorders	typophilia	typophobia	typochondria
Various forms of dysfunction appear among populations exposed to typography for long periods of time. Listed here are a number of frequently observed afflictions.	An excessive attachment to and fascination with the shape of letters, often to the exclusion of other interests and object choices. Typophiliacs usually die penniless and alone.	The irrational dislike of letterforms, often marked by a preference for icons, dingbats, and—in fatal cases—bullets and daggers. The fears of the typophobe can often be quieted (but not cured) by steady doses of Helvetica and Times Roman.	A persistent anxiety that one has selected the wrong typeface. This condition is often paired with OKD (optical kerning disorder), the need to constantly adjust and readjust the spaces between letters.

Panel 3 (bottom left)

An excessive attachment to and fascination with the shape of letters, often to the exclusion of other interests and object choices. Typophiliacs usually die penniless and alone.	typophilia		Various forms of dysfunction appear among populations exposed to typography for long periods of time. Listed here are a number of frequently observed afflictions.
	The irrational dislike of letterforms, often marked by a preference for icons, dingbats, and—in fatal cases—bullets and daggers. The fears of the typophobe can often be quieted (but not cured) by steady doses of Helvetica and Times Roman.	typophobia	
		A persistent anxiety that one has selected the wrong typeface. This condition is often paired with okd (optical kerning disorder), the need to constantly adjust and readjust the spaces between letters.	typochondria
Common typographic disorders			

Panel 4 (bottom right)

		Common typographic disorders	Various forms of dysfunction appear among populations exposed to typography for long periods of time. Listed here are a number of frequently observed afflifictions.
typophilia		An excessive attachment to and fascination with the shape of letters, often to the exclusion of other interests and object choices. Typophiliacs usually die penniless and alone.	
	typochondria	typophobia	The irrational dislike of letterforms, often marked by a preference for icons, dingbats, and—in fatal cases—bullets and daggers. The fears of the typophobe can often be quieted (but not cured) by steady doses of Helvetica and Times Roman.
		A persistent anxiety that one has selected the wrong typeface. This condition is often paired with okd (optical kerning disorder), the need to constantly adjust and readjust the spaces between letters.	

The design of charts and graphs is a rich area of typographic practice. In a data table, the grid acquires semantic significance. Columns and rows contain different types of content that readers can scan and quickly compare. Designers (and software defaults) often over-emphasize the linear grid of a table rather than allowing the typography to command the page and stake out its own territory. As columns of text align visually, they create implied grid lines on the page or screen.

ACCOUNT	ACCOUNT NAME	TOTAL FOR ACCC
101001	Instructional Supplies	$3,65
101002	Office Supplies	$46
102004	Equipment - Non-Capital	$1,28
105009	Travel-Conference Fees	$56
110004	Miscellaneous Entertainment	$8
114006	Postage/Shipping-Local Courier	$21
151108	Temp Staff-Contractual	$7
151181	Honoraria-Critics/Vis Artist	$1,00
	DEPARTMENTAL EXPENDITURES	$7,35

TYPE CRIME: DATA PRISON *The rules and boxes used in data tables should illuminate the relationships among data, not trap each entry inside a heavily guarded cell.*

Train No.	XM 3301	3801	A 67	3 3803	3 3201	A3 51	3 3703	3 3807	3 3203	A3 61	3 3809	A3 47	3 3901	3 3811	3 3903	3 3813	3205	3815	3817	3819	3207	3821	3823	3825	3209	3827	3829	3831
	A.M.	A.M.	A.M.	A.M.	A.M.	A.M.	A.M.	A.M.	A.M.	A.M.	A.M.	A.M.	A.M.	A.M.	A.M.	A.M.	A.M.	A.M.	A.M.	A.M.	A.M.	A.M.	A.M.	A.M.	A.M.	P.M.	P.M.	P.M.
New York, N.Y.	12.10	12.40	1.30	3.52	4.50	6.10	6.25	6.35	6.50	7.10	7.30	7.33	7.45	7.50	8.05	8.25	8.40	8.50	9.10	9.40	10.10	10.25	10.40	11.10	11.40	11.50	12.10	12.40	1.10
Newark, N.J. P	12.24	12.55	1.44	4.07	5.04	6.24	6.38	6.49	7.04	7.24	7.45	7.47	7.59	8.04	8.19	8.39	8.54	9.04	9.24	9.54	10.24	10.39	10.54	11.24	11.54	12.04	12.24	12.54	1.24
North Elizabeth								7.30						8.10															
Elizabeth	12.31	1.03	1.51		5.11	6.31		6.56	7.11	7.32		7.54		8.13	8.26	8.46	9.01	9.11	9.31	10.01	10.31	10.46	11.01	11.31	12.01	12.11	12.31	1.01	1.31
Linden	12.36		1.56		5.16	6.36		7.01	7.15	7.37		7.59		8.18	8.31	8.51	9.06		9.36	10.06	10.36		11.06	11.36	12.06		12.36	1.06	1.36
North Rahway								7.03		7.39				8.20	8.33	8.54													
Rahway	12.40	1.11	2.00		5.20	6.40		7.06	7.20	7.42		8.03		8.24	8.36	8.57	9.10	9.18	9.40	10.10	10.40	10.53	11.10	11.40	12.10	12.18	12.40	1.10	1.40
Metro Park (Iselin)	12.44		2.04	4.26	5.24		6.56	7.10	7.25		8.04	8.07	8.15		8.40		9.14		9.44	10.14	10.44		11.14	11.44	12.14		12.44	1.14	1.44
Metuchen	12.48		2.08		5.28			7.14	7.29			8.11			8.44		9.18		9.48	10.18	10.48		11.18	11.48	12.18		12.48	1.18	1.48
Edison	12.51		2.11				7.17	7.32				8.14			8.47		9.21			10.21			11.21		12.21			1.21	
New Brunswick	12.55		2.15		5.35		7.05	7.21	7.35			8.18	8.25		8.50		9.25		9.54	10.25	10.54		11.25	11.54	12.25		12.54	1.25	1.54
Jersey Avenue	1.02		2.18					7.28				8.21					9.28			10.28			11.28		12.28			1.28	
Princeton Jct. S			2.31		5.50		7.19		7.50			8.34	8.41		9.05		9.41		10.09	10.41	11.09		11.41	12.09	12.41		1.09	1.41	2.09
Trenton, N.J.			2.42	4.58	6.03		7.28		8.01		8.31	8.44	8.52		9.16		9.52		10.19	10.52	11.19		11.52	12.19	12.52		1.22	1.52	2.20

	am ●																							
New York, NY	12.10	12.40	1.30	3.52	4.50	6.10	6.25	6.35	6.50	7.10	7.30	7.33	7.45	7.50	8.05	8.25	8.40	8.50	9.10	9.40	10.10	10.25	10.40	11.10	11.40
Newark, NJ P	12.24	12.55	1.44	4.07	5.04	6.24	6.38	6.49	7.04	7.24	7.45	7.47	7.59	8.04	8.19	8.39	8.54	9.04	9.24	9.54	10.24	10.39	10.54	11.24	11.54
North Elizabeth									7.30					8.10											
Elizabeth	12.31	1.03	1.51		5.11	6.31		6.56	7.11	7.32		7.54		8.13	8.26	8.46	9.01	9.11	9.31	10.01	10.31	10.46	11.01	11.31	12.01
Linden	12.36		1.56		5.16	6.36		7.01	7.15	7.37		7.59		8.18	8.31	8.51	9.06		9.36	10.06	10.36		11.06	11.36	12.06
North Rahway								7.03		7.39				8.20	8.33	8.54									
Rahway	12.40	1.11	2.00		5.20	6.40		7.06	7.20	7.42		8.03		8.24	8.36	8.57	9.10	9.18	9.40	10.10	10.40	10.53	11.10	11.40	12.10
Metro Park (Iselin)	12.44		2.04	4.26	5.24		6.56	7.10	7.25		8.04	8.07	8.15		8.40		9.14		9.44	10.14	10.44		11.14	11.44	12.14
Metuchen	12.48		2.08		5.28			7.14	7.29			8.11			8.44		9.18		9.48	10.18	10.48		11.18	11.48	12.18
Edison	12.51		2.11					7.17	7.32			8.14			8.47		9.21			10.21			11.21		12.21
New Brunswick	12.55		2.15		5.35		7.05	7.21	7.35			8.18	8.25		8.50		9.25		9.54	10.25	10.54		11.25	11.54	12.25
Jersey Avenue	1.02		2.18					7.28				8.21					9.28			10.28			11.28		12.28
Princeton Junction S			2.31		5.50		7.19		7.50			8.34	8.41		9.05		9.41		10.09	10.41	11.09		11.41	12.09	12.41
Trenton, NJ			2.42	4.58	6.03		7.28		8.01		8.31	8.44	8.52		9.16		9.52		10.19	10.52	11.19		11.52	12.19	12.52
TRAIN NUMBER	3701	3301	3801	67	3803	3201	51	3703	3807	3203	61	3809	47	3901	3811	3903	3813	3205	3815	3817	3819	3207	3821	3823	3825
NOTES		XM		▶━	3	3	▶3	3	3	3	▶3	3	▶3	3	3	3	3								

NEW JERSEY TRANSIT, NORTHEASTERN CORRIDOR TIMETABLE Original schedule with redesign by Edward Tufte. From Edward Tufte, *Envisioning Information* (Cheshire, Conn.: Graphics Press, 1990). *The original design (top) is organized with heavy horizontal and vertical divisions. Tufte calls this a "data prison." His redesign uses the alignment of the typographic elements themselves to express the table's underlying structure.*

ORTHOGONAL

| 94 SHREDDED WHEAT | 41 RICE CHEX | 55 FR. SHREDDED WHEAT | 57 FROSTED MINI-WHEAT | 62 LIFE | 75 CRUNCHY CORN BRAN | 83 CRISPIX | 92 CRACKLIN' OAT BRAN |

FLAKE

| 02 CORN FLAKE | 24 WHEATIE | 28 RAISIN BRAN | 52 FROSTED FLAKE | 55 SPECIAL K | 61 TOTAL | 73 100% NATURAL | 96 OATMEAL CRISP |

GRAIN

| 02 PUFFED RICE | 04 PUFFED WHEAT | 28 RICE KRISPIE | 50 CORN POP | 54 SUGAR SMACKS | 58 COCOA KRISPIES | 69 FRUITY PEBBLES | 76 SUGAR CRISP |

ROUND

| 37 KIX | 41 CHEERIO | 58 COCOA PUFF | 63 FROOT LOOP | 64 APPLE JACK | 79 HONEY NUT CHEERIO | 84 HONEY GRAHAM OH'S | 96 FROSTED CHEERIO |

FAKE

| 54 TRIX | 57 ALPHABITS | 61 FRANKENBERRY | 64 LUCKY CHARMS | 68 CRUNCHBERRIES | 69 KABOOM | 76 HONEYCOMB | 96 FRENCH TOAST CR |

33

	YEAR INTRODUCED	MARKET SHARE	PRICE PER LB	MAKER
	00	15	3.01	P

G GENERAL MILLS
K KELLOGG'S
P POST
Q QUAKER OATS

SUGAR 1
FIBER 4
PROTEIN 4
SODIUM 0

PERIODIC BREAKFAST TABLE Magazine page (detail), 1998. Designer: Catherine Weese. Photography: John Halpern. Publisher: Patsy Tarr, 2wice Magazine. *This chart organizes breakfast cereals by shape and annotates them according to a dozen characteristics, from fiber content to price per pound. Visual displays of data allow readers to quickly compare items. One might observe, for example, that in breakfast cereals, intensity of sugar is usually accompanied by intensity of color.*

Find a chart from an old science book or other source and redesign it. Shown at right is a nineteenth-century table documenting an experiment about ants. The old design emphasizes vertical divisions at the expense of horizontal ones, and it jumbles together text and numbers within the table cells.

The redesign below eliminates many of the ruled lines, replacing them, where needed, with a pale tone that unifies the long horizontal rows of data. The redesigned chart also replaces most of the numerals with dots, a technique that lets the eye visually compare the results without having to read each numeral separately.

CHLOROFORMED ANTS

	LEFT ALONE	TAKEN TO NEST	THROWN IN WATER	BOTH NEST AND WATER	LEFT ALONE	TAKEN TO NEST	THROWN IN WATER	BOTH NEST AND WATER
PT 10	••••						••••	
14			••••				••	••
15			•	•	••		••	
29			•••••				••••	
CT 02			•••••				••••	•
06			•••••				••••	
AL	04		20	01	02		20	03

INTOXICATED ANTS

	LEFT ALONE	TAKEN TO NEST	THROWN IN WATER	BOTH NEST AND WATER	LEFT ALONE	TAKEN TO NEST	THROWN IN WATER	BOTH NEST AND WATER
OV 20		•••	••		•		•••••	
22	••	••					•••••••••	
EC 01		•••••••	••				••••••	•••
05		••••••••••••••	•••••				••••••••••••••••••	•••
AN 15	••••				•		•••	
17		••••				••	••••••	•
AL	06	32	09		02	02	43	07

INTOXICATED FRIENDS Data table from Sir John Lubbock, *Ants, Bees, and Wasps* (New York: D. Appleton and Company, 1893). *The author of this experiment studied how ants responded upon meeting either "friends" (members of their own colony) or "strangers." In the first experiment, the friends and strangers were rendered unconscious with chloroform. In the second experiment, the ants were merely intoxicated. The chloroformed ants—whether friends or strangers—were usually taken for dead and pitched into a moat of water surrounding the colony. The intoxicated ants were treated with more discrimination. Many of the drunken friends were taken back to the nest for rehabilitation, whereas drunken strangers were generally tossed in the moat. Ants, one might conclude, should not rely on the kindness of strangers.*

118   BEHAVIOUR TO INTOXICATED FRIENDS.

Tabular View.—Experiments on Ants under Chloroform and Intoxicated.

	FRIENDS			STRANGERS		
	To Nest	To Water	Unre-moved	To Nest	To Water	Unre-moved
CHLOROFORMED ANTS.						
Sept. 10	...	...	4	...	4	...
14	...	4	...	2 and brought out again	2	...
15	1 and brought out again	1	...	...	2	2
29	...	5	...	...	4	...
Oct. 2	...	5	...	1 and brought out again	4	...
6	...	5	...	...	4	...
	1	20	4	3	20	2
INTOXICATED ANTS.						
Nov. 20	3	2	...	...	5	1
22	2	...	2	...	8	...
In these cases some of the Ants had partly recovered; in the following they were quite insensible.						
Dec. 1	7 none brought out again	2	...	3 all these brought out again	6	...
8	16 none brought out again	5	...	3 all these brought out again	15	...
Jan. 15	...	...	4	...	3	1
17	4 none brought out again	...	...	3 one brought out again	6	...
	27	7	4	2	30	1

{APPENDIX}

SPACES AND PUNCTUATION

Writers or clients often supply manuscripts that employ incorrect dashes or faulty word spacing. Consult a definitive work such as *The Chicago Manual of Style* for a complete guide to punctuation. The following rules are especially pertinent for designers.

WORD SPACES are created by the space bar. Use just one space between sentences or after a comma, colon, or semicolon. One of the first steps in typesetting a manuscript is to purge it of all double spaces. Thus the space bar should not be used to create indents or otherwise position text on a line. Use tabs instead. HTML refuses to recognize double spaces altogether.

EN SPACES are wider than word spaces. An en space can be used to render a more emphatic distance between elements on a line: for example, to separate a subhead from the text that immediately follows, or to separate elements gathered along a single line in a letterhead.

EM DASHES express strong grammatical breaks. An em dash is one em wide—the width of the point size of the typeface. In manuscripts, dashes are often represented with a double hyphen (--); these must be replaced.

EN DASHES serve primarily to connect numbers (1–10). An en is half the width of an em. Manuscripts rarely employ en dashes, so the designer needs to supply them.

HYPHENS connect linked words and phrases, and they break words at the ends of lines. Typesetting programs break words automatically. Disable auto hyphenation when working with ragged or centered text; use discretionary hyphens instead, and only when unavoidable.

DISCRETIONARY HYPHENS, which are inserted manually to break lines, only appear in the document if they are needed. (If a text is reflowed in subsequent editing, a discretionary hyphen will disappear.) Wayward hyphens often occur in the mid-dle of a line when the typesetter has inserted a "hard" hyphen instead of a discretionary one.

QUOTATION MARKS have distinct "open" and "closed" forms, unlike hatch marks, which are straight up and down. A single close quote also serves as an apostrophe ("It's Bob's font."). Prime or hatch marks should only be used to indicate inches and feet (5'2"). Used incorrectly, hatches are known as "dumb quotes." Although computer operating systems and typesetting programs often include automatic "smart quote" features, e-mailed, word-processed, and/or client-supplied text can be riddled with dumb quotes. Auto smart quote programs often render apostrophes upside down ('tis instead of 'tis), so designers must be vigilant and learn the necessary keystrokes.

ELLIPSES consist of three periods, which can be rendered with no spaces between them, or with open tracking (letterspacing), or with word spaces. An ellipsis indicates an omitted section in a quoted text or...a temporal break. Most typefaces include an ellipsis character, which presents closely spaced points.

MAC OS KEYSTROKES *These keystrokes listed below are commonly used in word processing, page layout, and illustration software. Some fonts do not include a full range of special characters.*

DASHES		KEYSTROKES
—	em dash	shift-option-hyphen
–	en dash	option-hyphen
-	standard hyphen	(hyphen key)
-	discretionary hyphen	command-hyphen

PUNCTUATION		
'	single open quote	option-]
'	single close quote	shift-option-]
"	double open quote	option-[
"	double close quote	shift-option-[
...	ellipsis	option-;

OTHER MARKS		
( )	en space	option-space bar
†	dagger	option-t
‡	double dagger	shift-option-7
©	copyright symbol	option-g
®	resister symbol	option-r
€	Euro symbol	shift-option-2
fi	fi ligature	shift-option-5
fl	fl ligature	shift-option-6
é	*accent aigu*	option-e + e
è	*accent grave*	option-` + e
à	*accent grave*	option-` + a
ù	*accent grave*	option-` + u
ç	*cédille*	option-c
ü	*umlaut*	option-u + u
ö	*umlaut*	option-u + o

These interruptions—especially the snide remarks--are killing my buzz.

CRIME: *Two hyphens in place of an em dash*

Dashes express a break in the flow of a sentence. In a word-processed document, dashes can be indicated with two hyphens. Em dashes are required, however, in typesetting. No spaces are used around dashes.

El Lissitzky lived 1890–1941. Rodchenko lived longer (1891-1956).

CRIME: *Hyphen between numbers*

An en dash connects two numbers. It means "up to and including," not "between." No spaces are used around en dashes.

It's okay to be second-best, but never, ever second–best.

CRIME: *En dash in hyphenated word*

Do not use en dashes where the humble hyphen is required.

In the beginning was…the word….Typography came later.

An ellipsis character is used here in place of separate points.

The periods in an ellipsis can be separated with word spaces, or, as we prefer, they can be tracked open (letterspaced). Most typefaces include an ellipsis character, whose points are more tightly spaced. After a sentence, use a period plus an ellipsis (four dots).

She was 5'2" with eyes of blue. "I'm not dumb," she said. "I'm prime."

CRIME: *Prime marks (a.k.a. dumb quotes) used in place of quotation marks*

The purpose of prime marks, or hatch marks, is to indicate inches and feet. Their use to mark quotations is a common blight across the typographic landscape.

"I'm not smart," he replied. "I'm a quotation mark."

Unlike prime marks, quotation marks include an opening and closing character. Single close quotes also serve as apostrophes. Incorrectly used prime marks must be routed out and destroyed.

Don't put two spaces between sentences. They leave an ugly gap.

CRIME: *Two spaces between sentences*

Although writers persist in putting double spaces between sentences (a habit often learned in high school), all such spaces must be purged from a manuscript when it is set in type.

EDITING

Since the onslaught of desktop publishing back in the dark days of the mid-1980s, graphic designers have taken on roles formerly occupied by distinct trades, such as typesetting and mechanical pasteup. Designers are often expected to be editors as well. Every project should have a true editor, a person with the training and disposition to judge the correctness, accuracy, and consistency of written content. Neither a project's author nor its designer should be its editor, who is rightly a neutral party between them. If a project team includes no properly trained editor, try to find one. If that fails, make sure that *someone* is responsible for this crucial role, for the failure to edit carefully is the source of costly and embarrassing errors.

Editing a text for publication has three basic phases. *Developmental editing* addresses broad issues of the content and the structure of a work; indeed, it can include judging a work's fitness for publication in the first place. *Copy editing* (also called line editing or manuscript editing) seeks to root out redundancies, inconsistencies, grammatical errors, and other flaws appearing across the body of the work. The copy editor—who must study every word and sentence—is not expected to question the overall meaning or structure of a work, nor to alter an author's style, but rather to refine and correct. *Proofreading*, which checks the correctness, consistency, and flow of designed, typset pages, is the final stage. Depending on the nature of the project and its team, each of these phases may go through several rounds.

ANATOMY OF AN ERROR After a document has been written, edited, designed, and proofread, a printer's proof is created by the printer from the digital files supplied by the designer. Many clients (or authors) fail to recognize errors (or make decisions) until the printer's proofs are issued. This luxury has its costs, and someone will have to pay.

PE'S (PRINTER'S ERRORS) These are errors that can be assigned to the printer, and they must be corrected at no expense to the designer or client. A printer's error is an obvious and blatant divergence from the digital files and other instructions provided by the designer and agreed to by the printer. Printer's errors are surprisingly rare in the digital age.

AA'S (AUTHOR'S ALTERATIONS) These are not so rare. Author's alterations are changes to the approved text or layout of the work. If the change originates with the designer, the designer is responsible. If it originates with the client or author, she or he is responsible. Keeping records of each phase of a project's development is helpful in assigning blame later. Designers can charge the client a fee for the AA on top of the printer's fee, as the designer must correct the file, print out new hard copy, get the client's approval (again), communicate with the printer (again), and so on. If agreed to in advance, designers can charge AA fees for *any* change to an approved document, even before the printer's proof is issued.

EA'S (EDITOR'S ALTERATIONS) Errors made by the editor are the responsibility of the editor's employer, typically the client or publisher of the work. Good editors help prevent everyone's errors from occurring in the first place.

For more detailed information about the editorial process, see *The Chicago Manual of Style, 15th Edition* (Chicago: University of Chicago Press, 2003).

Manuscript editing, also called copyediting or line editing, requires attention to every word in a manuscript, a thorough knowledge of the style to be followed, and the ability to make quick, logical, and defensible decisions. —*THE CHICAGO MANUAL OF STYLE*, 2003

Only an editor can see beyond a writer's navel.

No matter how brilliant your prose, an editor will discover errors in spelling, grammar, consistency, redundancy, and construction.

Writers should not over-format their texts.

The time you spend fiddling with formatting will be spent again by the editor and/or designer, removing extra keystrokes. Provide flush left copy, in one font, double-spaced.

Some lessons learned in high school are best forgotten.

One of them is dotting your i's with hearts and smiley faces. The other is leaving two spaces between sentences. In typesetting, one space only must be left between sentences.

The space bar is not a design tool.

Don't use the space bar to create indents (just key in a single tab), and don't use extra spaces to create centered effects or layouts (unless you really are E. E. Cummings).

Every change threatens to introduce new errors.

Each time a file is "corrected," new errors can appear, from problems with rags, justification, and page breaks to spelling mistakes, missing words, and botched or incomplete corrections.

Don't wait for the proofs to seriously examine the typeset text.

Changes made after a printer's proof has been made (blue line, press proof, or other) are expensive. They also will slow down your project, which, of course, is already late.

Famous last words: "We'll catch it in the blue lines."

delete
delete

pose trans
transpose

let it stand
stet ("let it stand")

add space
separate; add space

second rate
add hyphen

left-over
remove hyphen

Dashing-no?
em dash (—)

1914-1918
en dash (–)

italic
italic

boldface
boldface

remove underline
remove underline

CASE
lowercase

case
uppercase

case
small caps

Writers, editors, and designers use special symbols to mark changes such as deleting, posing trans, or correcting words or phrases. If you change your mind about a deletion, place dots beneath it. Remove a comma by circling it. Add a period with a circled dot. If two words run together, insert a straight line and a space mark.

To combine two paragraphs, connect them with a line and note the comment "run-in" in the margin. (Circling notes prevents the typesetter from confusing comments with content.)

Insert two short lines to hyphenate a word such as secondrate. When removing a hyphen, close up the leftover space. To replace a hyphen with an em dash-a symbol that expresses a grammatical break-write a tiny m above the hyphen. If a manuscript indicates dashes with double hyphens--like this-- the typesetter or designer is expected to convert them without being told. Use an en dash, not a hyphen, to connect two numbers, such as 1914-1918.

In addition to correcting grammar, spelling, punctuation, and clarity of prose, editors indicate typographic styles such as italic (with an underscore) and boldface (with a wavy line). Underlining, which is rarely used in formal typography, is removed like this. Draw A Line Through A Capital Letter to change it to lowercase. underline a letter with three strokes to capitalize it. Use two underlines to indicate small capitals.

Double-space the manuscript and leave a generous margin to provide room for comments and corrections. Align the text flush left, ragged right, and disable automatic hyphenation.

Don't mark manuscripts or proofs with Post-It notes. They can fall off, block the text, and make the document hard to photocopy.

Editing an electronic file and allowing the author to see the changes is called *redlining* (also referred to as "editing online"). Basic housekeeping includes removing all double spaces and converting hatches (a.k.a. "dumb quotes") to quotation marks and apostrophes (a.k.a. "smart quotes"). The editor need not point out these changes to the author.

Changes to the structure and wording of the text must be communicated to the author. A visual convention is needed for showing ~~deleted~~ and added material. ~~Words to be removed~~ are typically struck out, and words added or substituted can be <u>underlined</u>, highlighted, or rendered in color. A line in the margin indicates that a change has been recommended. [Queries to the author are set off with brackets.][A]

Underlining or striking out~~,~~ punctuation is visually confusing, so the editor often strikes out an entire word~~, or phrase,~~ —or phrase—and types in the freshly punctuated passage as an addition. To hyphenate a word such as ~~secondrate~~ *second-rate*, strike it out and add the hyphenated form. When converting hyphens to en dashes (1914–18)—or changing double hyphens to em dashes—the editor simply keys them in. Typographic styles such as *italic*, **boldface**, and small capitals can also be changed directly.

Although redlining is wonderfully fluid and direct, it can be dangerous. The editor must scrupulously remove all traces of the editing process before releasing the file for design and typesetting. Potential disasters include words that are stucktogether, a missing , or a forgotten comment to the author [Are you out of your mother-loving mind?].

A. Queries to the author can also take the form of footnotes. Identify these notes with letters, so they are not confused with footnotes that belong to the text.

PROOFREADING

PROOFREADING takes place *after* an edited manuscript has been designed and typeset. New errrors can appear at any time during the handling of a document, and old errors previously unrecognized— can leap to the eye once the text has been set in type. The proofreader corrects gross errors in spelling, grammar, and fact, but avoid changes in style and content. Changes at this stage are not only expensive but they can affect the page design and introduce new problems.

Proofreading is different task from editing, although the editor may play a role in it, along with or in addition to the author or client. Although the *designer or typesetter*[1] should not be given the role of proof reader, designers must nonetheless inspect their work carefully for errors before sending it back to the editor, author, or client.

Mark all corrections in the margin of the proof, and indicate the position of changes within the text. Don't write between the lines. Many of the same interline symbols are used in proofreading and in copy editing, but proofreaders use an additional set of flags for marginal notes.

Don't obliterate what is being crossed out and deleted so the typesetter can read it.

Mark all changes on one master proof. If several copies of the proof are circulated for approval, one person (usually the editor) is responsible for transferring corrections to a master copy.

Don't give the designer a proof with conflicting or indecisive comments.

TYPES OF *proofs* Depending on how a project is organized and produced, some or all of the following proofs may be involved.

Galley proofs are typically supplied in a book-length project. They consist of text that has been typeset but not paginated and do not yet include illustrations.

Page proofs are broken into pages and include illustrations, page numbers, running heads, and other details.

Revised proofs include changes that have been recommended by the proofreader and input by the designer or typesetter.

Printer's proofs are generated by the printer. At this phase, changes become increasingly costly, complex, and ill-advised. In theory, one is only looking for printers' errors—not errors in design or verbal style—at this stage. Printer's proofs might include blue lines (one color only) and/or color proofs.

---

1. The designer and typesetter may be the same person. In a design studio, as opposed to a publishing house, designers are generally responsible for typesetting.

EDITORIAL CHANGE	MARK IN TEXT	MARK IN MARGIN
delete	~~delete~~	℘
delete and close up	delete and cl/ose up	℘
let it stand (stet)	let it stand	(stet)
insert text or character	insert ∧	text
run in paragraph	run in / paragraph	(run in)
start new paragraph	start new paragraph	¶
insert punctuation	insert∧ punctuation	∧
change punctuation	change/ punctuation	? /
insert hyphen	insert∧ hyphen	=
insert parentheses	insert∧ parentheses∧	(/)
insert en or em dash	insert∧ en dash	N̲ M̲
insert quotes	insert∧ quotes∧	⸀⸀ ⸃⸃
capitalize	capitalize	(cap)
change to lowercase	LOWERCASE	(lc)
change to small caps	small caps	(sc)
change to bold	bold	(bf)
change to roman	(roman)	(rom)
wrong font	wrong (font)	(wf)

EDITORIAL CHANGE	MARK IN TEXT	MARK IN MARGIN
letterspace	(letterspace)	(ls)
close up	clo se up	⌒⌣
insert space	insert#space	#
reduce space	reduce /space	less #
transpose	pose⌐trans⌐	(tr)
flush right	⌐flush right	(fr)
flush left	⌐flush left	(fl)
indent 1 em	☐ indent 1 em	☐
move to next line	move to next⌐line	(T.O.)
superscript	superscript⌄	⌄1
align vertically	‖ align vertically	‖
align horizontally	align horizontally	=
spell out abbreviation	spell out(abbrev.)	(SP)
use ligature	use ligature (flour)	(fl)
query that cannot be resolved by proofreader	(query)	(?)

Proofreader's marks derived from The Chicago Manual of Style and David Jury, About Face: Reviving the Rules of Typography (East Sussex: Rotovision, 2001). Marking conventions do vary slightly from source to source.

FREE ADVICE

Think more, design less.

Many desperate acts of design (including gradients, drop shadows, and the gratuitous use of transparency) are perpetrated in the absence of a strong concept. A good idea provides a framework for design decisions, guiding the work.

Say more, write less.

Just as designers should avoid filling up space with arbitrary visual effects, writers should remember that no one loves their words as much as they do.

Spend more, buy less.

Cheap stuff is usually cheap because of how it's made, what it's made of, and who made it. Buy better quality goods, less often.

May your thoughts be deep and your wounds be shallow.

Always work with a sharp blade. Although graphic design is not a terribly dangerous occupation, many late-night accidents occur involving dull X-Acto blades. Protect your printouts from senseless bloodshed.

Density is the new white space.

In an era of exurban sprawl, closely knit neighborhoods have renewed appeal. So, too, on page and screen, where a rich texture of information can function better than sparseness and isolation.

Make the shoe fit, not the foot.

Rather than force content into rigid containers, create systems that are flexible and responsive to the material they are intended to accommodate.

Make it bigger. *(Courtesy of Paula Scher)*

Amateur typographers make their type too big. The 12-pt default—which looks okay on the screen—often looks horsey on the page. Experienced designers, however, make their type too tiny: shown here, 7.5-pt Scala Pro.

It is easier to talk than to listen.

Pay attention to your clients, your users, your readers, and your friends. Your design will get better as you listen to other people.

Design is an art of situations.

Designers respond to a need, a problem, a circumstance, that arises in the world. The best work is produced in relation to interesting situations—an open-minded client, a good cause, or great content.

No job is too small.

A graphic designer can set out to change the world one business card at a time— as long as it is the business card of a really interesting person.

An interface calls attention to itself at its point of failure.

Design helps the systems of daily life run smoothly, letting users and readers ignore how things are put together. Design should sometimes announce itself in order to shed light on the system, exposing its construction, identity, personality, and politics.

The idea is the machine that makes the art. *(Courtesy of Sol Lewitt)*

A powerful concept can drive decisions about color, layout, type choice, format, and so on, preventing senseless acts of whimsy. (On the other hand, senseless acts of whimsy sometimes lead to powerful concepts.)

The early bird gets to work before everyone else.

Your best time for thinking could be early in the morning, late at night, or even, in rare circumstances, during class or between nine and five. Whether your best time is in the shower, at the gym, or on the train, use it for your hardest thinking.

Build the discourse.

Design is social. It lives in society, it creates society, and it needs a society of its own— a community of designers committed to advancing and debating our shared hopes and desires. Read, write, and talk about design whenever you can.

Go forth and reproduce.

LETTER

Bartram, Alan. *Five Hundred Years of Book Design.* London: British Library, 2001.

Benjamin, Walter. *One Way Street and Other Writings.* London: Verso, 1978.

Blackwell, Lewis. *Twentieth-Century Type.* New Haven: Yale University Press, 2004.

Boyarski, Dan, Christine Neuwirth, Jodi Forlizzi, and Susan Harkness Regli. "A Study of Fonts Designed for Screen Display." *CHI* 98 (April 1998): 18–23.

Broos, Kees, and Paul Hefting. *Dutch Graphic Design: A Century.* Cambridge: MIT Press, 1993.

Burke, Christopher. *Paul Renner: The Art of Typography.* New York: Princeton Architectural Press, 1998.

Clouse, Doug and Angela Voulangas. *The Handy Book of Artistic Printing.* New York: Princeton Architectural Press, 2009.

Christin, Anne-Marie. *A History of Writing, from Hieroglyph to Multimedia.* Paris: Flammarion, 2002.

Crouwel, Wim. *New Alphabet: An Introduction for a Programmed Typography.* Amsterdam: Wim Crouwel/Total Design, 1967.

―――, Kees Broos, and David Quay. *Wim Crouwel: Alphabets.* Amsterdam: BIS Publishers, 2003.

Cruz, Andy, Ken Barber, and Rich Roat. *House Industries.* Berlin: Die Gestalten Verlag, 2004.

De Jong, Cees, Alston W. Purvis, and Jan Tholenaar, eds. *Type: A Visual History of Typefaces, Volume I, 1628–1900.* Cologne: Taschen, 2009.

Eason, Ron, and Sarah Rookledge. *Rookledge's International Directory of Type Designers: A Biographical Handbook.* New York: Sarabande Press, 1994.

Gray, Nicolete. *A History of Lettering.* Oxford: Phaidon Press, 1986.

Heller, Steven, and Philip B. Meggs, eds. *Texts on Type: Critical Writings on Typography.* New York: Allworth Press, 2001.

Johnston, Edward. *Writing & Illuminating & Lettering.* London: Sir Isaac Pitman & Sons, 1932.

Kelly, Rob Roy. *American Wood Type: 1828–1900.* New York: Da Capo Press, 1969.

Kinross, Robin. *Unjustified Texts: Perspectives on Typography.* London: Hyphen Press, 2002.

Lawson, Alexander. *Anatomy of a Typeface.* Boston: David R. Godine, 1990.

Lewis, John. *Anatomy of Printing: The Influences of Art and History on its Design.* New York: Watson-Guptill Publications, 1970.

―――. *Typography: Basic Principles, Influences and Trends Since the Nineteenth Century.* New York: Reinhold Publishing, 1963.

McMurtrie, Douglas. *The Book: The Story of Printing and Bookmaking.* New York: Dorset Press, 1943.

Morison, Stanley. *Letter Forms.* London: Nattali & Maurice, 1968.

Noordzij, Gerrit. *Letterletter: An Inconsistent Collection of Tentative Theories That Do Not Claim Any Authority Other Than That of Common Sense.* Vancouver: Hartley and Marks, 2000.

Pardoe, F. E. *John Baskerville of Birmingham: Letter-Founder and Printer.* London: Frederick Muller Limited, 1975.

Perry, Michael. *Hand Job: A Catalog of Type.* New York: Princeton Architectural Press, 2007.

Shelley, Mary. *Frankenstein.* New York: The Modern Library, 1999. First published 1831.

Re, Margaret. *Typographically Speaking: The Art of Matthew Carter.* New York: Princeton Architectural Press, 2002.

Triggs, Teal. *The Typographic Experiment: Radical Innovation in Contemporary Type Design.* London: Thames & Hudson, 2003.

Updike, Daniel. *Printing Types: Their History, Forms, and Use, Volumes I and II.* New York: Dover Publications, 1980.

VanderLans, Rudy, and Zuzana Licko. *Emigre: Graphic Design into the Digital Realm.* New York: Van Nostrand Reinhold, 1993.

Vanderlans, Rudy. *Emigre No. 70: The Look Back Issue, Selections from Emigre Magazine, 1984–2009.* Berkeley, CA: Gingko Press, 2009.

Willen, Bruce and Nolen Strals. *Lettering & Type: Creating Letters and Designing Typefaces.* New York: Princeton Architectural Press, 2009.

TEXT

Armstrong, Helen. *Graphic Design Theory: Readings from the Field.* New York: Princeton Architectural Press, 2009.

Barthes, Roland. *Image/Music/Text.* Trans. Stephen Heath. New York: Hill and Wang, 1977.

―――. *Mythologies.* Trans. Annette Lavers. New York: Hill and Wang, 1977.

Baudrillard, Jean. *For a Critique of the Political Economy of the Sign.* St. Louis, MO: Telos Press, 1981.

Benjamin, Walter. *Reflections.* Ed. Peter Demetz. New York: Schocken Books, 1978.

Bierut, Michael. *Forty Posters for the Yale School of Architecture.* Cohoes, NY: Mohawk Fine Papers, 2007.

Bolter, Jay David. *Writing Space: Computers, Hypertext, and the Remediation of Print.* Mahwah, NJ: Lawrence Erlbaum Associates, 2001.

Derrida, Jacques. *Of Grammatology.* Trans. Gayatri Chakravorty Spivak. Baltimore: Johns Hopkins University Press, 1976.

Diamond, Jared. *Guns, Germs, and Steel: The Fates of Human Societies.* New York: W. W. Norton, 1997.

Kaplan, Nancy. "Blake's Problem and Ours: Some Reflections on the Image and the Word." *Readerly/Writerly Texts,* 3.2 (Spring/Summer 1996): 115–33.

Gould, John D. et al. "Reading from CRT Displays Can Be as Fast as Reading from Paper." *Human Factors* 29, 5 (1987): 497–517.

Helfand, Jessica. *Screen: Essays on Graphic Design, New Media, and Visual Culture.* New York: Princeton Architectural Press, 2001.

Lessig, Lawrence. *Free Culture: How Big Media Uses Technology and the Law to Lock Down Culture and Control Creativity.* New York: Penguin, 2004.

Laurel, Brenda. *Utopian Entrepreneur.* Cambridge: MIT Press, 2001.

Lunenfeld, Peter. *Snap to Grid: A User's Guide to Digital Arts, Media, and Cultures.* Cambridge: MIT Press, 2001.

Manovich, Lev. *The Language of New Media.* Cambridge: MIT Press, 2002.

McCoy, Katherine and Michael McCoy. *Cranbrook Design: The New Discourse.* New York: Rizzoli, 1990.

―――. "American Graphic Design Expression." *Design Quarterly* 148 (1990): 4–22.

McLuhan, Marshall. *The Gutenberg Galaxy*. Toronto: University of Toronto Press, 1962.

Millman, Debbie. *The Essential Principles of Graphic Design*. Cincinnati: How, 2008.

Moulthrop, Stuart. "You Say You Want a Revolution? Hypertext and the Laws of Media" in *The New Media Reader*. Noah Wardrip-Fruin and Nick Monfort, eds. Cambridge: MIT Press, 2003. 691–703.

Nielsen, Jakob. *Designing Web Usability*. Indianapolis: New Riders, 2000.

Ong, Walter. *Orality and Literacy: The Technologizing of the Word*. New York: Methuen, 1982.

Raskin, Jef. *The Human Interface: New Directions for Designing Interactive Systems*. Reading, MA: Addison-Wesley, 2000.

Ronell, Avital. *The Telephone Book: Technology, Schizophrenia, Electric Speech*. Lincoln, NE: University of Nebraska Press, 1989.

GRID

Berners-Lee, Tim. *Weaving the Web: The Original Design and Ultimate Destiny of the World Wide Web*. New York: HarperCollins, 1999.

Bosshard, Hans Rudolf. *Der Typografische Raster/The Typographic Grid*. Sulgen, Switzerland: Verlag Niggli, 2000.

Cantz, Hatje. *Karl Gerstner: Review of 5 x 10 Years of Graphic Design etc.* Ostfildern-Ruit, Germany: Hatje Cantz Verlag, 2001.

Elam, Kimberly. *Geometry of Design*. New York: Princeton Architectural Press, 2001.

Gerstner, Karl. *Designing Programmes*. Sulgen, Switzerland: Arthur Niggli Ltd., 1964.

Gibson, William. *Neuromancer*. New York: Ace Books, 1984.

Higgins, Hannah P. *The Grid Book*. Cambridge: MIT Press, 2009.

Hochuli, Jost, and Robin Kinross. *Designing Books: Practice and Theory*. London: Hyphen Press, 1996.

Krauss, Rosalind. "Grids" in *The Originality of the Avant-Garde and Other Modernist Myths*. Cambridge: MIT Press, 1985. 9–22.

Küsters, Christian and Emily King. *Restart: New Systems in Graphic Design*. London: Thames and Hudson, 2002.

Lidwell, William, Kritina Holden, and Jill Butler. *Universal Principles of Design*. Gloucester, MA: Rockport Publishers, 2003.

Müller-Brockmann, Josef. *The Graphic Artist and his Design Problems*. Sulgen, Switzerland: Arthur Niggli Ltd., 1961.

____. *Grid Systems in Graphic Design*. Santa Monica: Ram Publications, 1996. First published in 1961.

____. *A History of Graphic Communication*. Sulgen, Switzerland: Arthur Niggli Ltd., 1971.

Nicolai, Carsten. *Grid Index*. Berlin: Die Gestalten, 2009.

Roberts, Lucienne, and Julia Shrift. *The Designer and the Grid*. East Sussex, UK: RotoVision, 2002.

Rothschild, Deborah, Ellen Lupton, and Darra Goldstein. *Graphic Design in the Mechanical Age: Selections from the Merrill C. Berman Collection*. New Haven: Yale University Press, 1999.

Ruder, Emil. *Typography*. Sulgen, Switzerland: Arthur Niggli Ltd., New York: Hastings House, 1981. First published in 1967.

Rüegg, Ruedi. *Basic Typography: Design with Letters*. New York: Van Nostrand Reinhold, 1989.

Samara, Timothy. *Making and Breaking the Grid: A Graphic Design Layout Workshop*. Gloucester, MA: Rockport Publishers, 2002.

Tufte, Edward R. *Envisioning Information*. Cheshire, CT: Graphics Press, 1990.

———. *The Cognitive Style of PowerPoint*. Cheshire, CT: Graphics Press, 2003.

Zeldman, Jeffrey with Ethan Marcotte. *Designing with Web Standards*, Third Edition. Berkeley, CA: New Riders, 2009.

MANUALS AND MONOGRAPHS

Baines, Phil, and Andrew Haslam. *Type and Typography*. New York: Watson-Guptill Publications, 2002.

Bringhurst, Robert. *The Elements of Typographic Style*. Vancouver: Hartley and Marks, 1992, 1997.

The Chicago Manual of Style, 15th Edition. Chicago: University of Chicago Press, 2003.

Dwiggins, W. A. *Layout in Advertising*. New York: Harper and Brothers Publishers, 1928.

Eckersley, Richard *et al. Glossary of Typesetting Terms*. Chicago: University of Chicago Press, 1994.

Felton, Paul. *Type Heresy: Breaking the Ten Commandments of Typography*. London: Merrell, 2006.

French, Nigel. *InDesign Type: Professional Typography with Adobe InDesign CS2*. Berkeley, CA: Peachpit Press, 2006.

Jardi, Enric. *Twenty-Two Tips on Typography (That Some Designers Will Never Reveal)*. Barcelona: Actar, 2007.

Jury, David. *About Face: Reviving the Rules of Typography*. East Sussex, UK: RotoVision, 2001.

Kane, John. *A Type Primer*. London: Laurence King, 2002.

Kunz, Willi. *Typography: Macro- and Micro-Aesthetics*. Sulgen, Switzerland: Verlag Arthur Niggli, 1998.

Lupton, Ellen and J. Abbott Miller. *Design Writing Research: Writing on Graphic Design*. London: Phaidon, 1999.

Lupton, Ellen and Jennifer Cole Phillips. *Graphic Design: The New Basics*. New York: Princeton Architectural Press, 2008.

Lynch, Patrick, and Sarah Horton. *Web Style Guide: Basic Design Principles for Creating Web Sites*. New Haven: Yale University Press, 2001.

Millman, Debbie. *The Essential Principles of Graphic Design*. Cincinnati: How, 2008.

Rosendorf, Theodore. *The Typographic Desk Reference*. New Castle: Oak Knoll, 2008.

Samara, Timothy. *Typography Workbook: A Real-World Guide to Using Type in Graphic Design*. Beverly, MA: Rockport, 2004.

Scher, Paula. *Make It Bigger*. New York: Princeton Architectural Press, 2002.

Spiekermann, Erik, and E. M. Ginger. *Stop Stealing Sheep and Find Out How Type Works*. Mountain View, CA: Adobe Press, 1993.

Strizver, Ilene. *Type Rules: The Designer's Guide to Professional Typography*. Cincinnati: North Light Books, 2001.

Strunk, William Jr. and E. B. White. *The Elements of Style*. Illustrated by Maira Kalman. New York: Penguin Press, 2005.

Tschichold, Jan. *The Form of the Book: Essays on the Morality of Good Design*. Point Roberts, WA: Hartley & Marks, 1991.

INDEX